Conqueror's Son

Conqueror's Son

Duke Robert Curthose, Thwarted King

Katherine Lack

The History Press

For Paul and Chris

First published 2007 by Sutton Publishing

This edition published 2018 by
The History Press
The Mill, Brimscombe Port
Stroud, Gloucestershire, GL5 2QG
www.thehistorypress.co.uk

British Library Cataloguing in Publication Data.
A catalogue record for this book is available from the British Library.

ISBN 978-0 7509 8682 3

Typesetting and origination by The History Press
Printed and bound by CPI Group (UK) Ltd

CONTENTS

LIST OF ILLUSTRATIONS

LIST OF MAPS

ACKNOWLEDGEMENTS

This book arose from an M.Phil. thesis on the *de obitu Willelmi* and the 1087 Anglo-Norman succession. I must therefore begin by paying especial tribute to my supervisor for that degree, Nicholas Brooks, who led me gently along the sometimes convoluted paths of medieval scholarship until a presentable end product emerged. Without his help and support, the thesis, never mind this book, would not have been completed. I would also like to thank Steve Bassett and Elisabeth van Houts for their generous encouragement, and all those members of the Department of Medieval History at Birmingham University, sadly too numerous to mention, who have listened patiently to me over the last three years and have made many valuable suggestions and observations.

The town of Tinchebray held a splendid conference in September 2006, on the 900th anniversary of the battle at which Duke Robert Curthose was taken prisoner. Among the many people who attended, I would particularly like to record the assistance of Richard Barton, Matthew Bennett, Peter Damian-Grint, Hugh Doherty, Judith Green, Ann Nissen-Jaubert, Ian Peirce and Thomas Roche.

I am most grateful to the following for help with supplying illustrations: Ann Nissen-Jaubert, Ian Peirce, The Bridgeman Art Library, Mme Christèle Potvin at the Seine-Maritime Archives, The British Library, Sonia Halliday Photographs, Mrs P. Hatfield and the Provost and Fellows of Eton College. Quotations from *The Anglo-Saxon Chronicle*, ed. D. Whitelock, D.C. Douglas and S.I. Tucker (Eyre and Spottiswoode, 1961), are reproduced by permission of Cambridge University Press; those from *The Deeds of the Franks and the other*

Pilgrims to Jerusalem, ed. R. Hill (Nelson, 1962), are reproduced by permission of Oxford University Press. Quotations from *Eadmer's History of Recent Events in England: Historia Novorum in Anglia*, trans. G. Bosanquet (Cresset Press, 1964), are reprinted by permission of the Random House Group Ltd. Quotations from C. Cahen, *Orient et occident au temps des Croisades* (Aubier Montaigne, 1983), are reproduced by kind permission of Flammarion, Paris. Quotations from William of Malmesbury's *The Gesta Regum Anglorum*; *The Charters and Custumals of Holy Trinity Caen*; *The Chronicle of John of Worcester*; *Henry, Archdeacon of Huntingdon: Historia Anglorum*; *The Gesta Normannorum Ducum*; *The Ecclesiastical History of Orderic Vitalis* and *The Letters of Lanfranc* are all reproduced by permission of Oxford University Press.

Many people have helped with reading individual chapters, or with particular areas of expertise, most notably Deryn Chatwin, Peter Damian-Grint, Iestyn Daniel (who alerted me to the fact that a Welsh poem Curthose is reputed to have written at Cardiff is almost certainly an eighteenth-century forgery), Howard Edwards, Hugh Houghton, Graham Loud, Janet Maxwell-Stewart, Philippa Semper, Richard Sharpe, Chris Wickham and above all Matt Edwards, who read the entire typescript at very short notice, made pertinent comments throughout and yet remains on friendly terms with me. Inevitably, however, it is the home team who suffer the most, and it is to them that this book is dedicated – to a husband who does not really like history that much, and a son who now knows far more about the *de obitu* than any 17-year-old should.

ABBREVIATIONS

AA	*Historia Hierosolymitana . . . Albert of Aachen* (RHC Oc. 4)
Anna Comnena	*The Alexiad of Anna Comnena*, trans. E.R.A. Sewter (1969)
Annales Monastici	*Annales Monastici*, ed. H. Luard (5 vols; RS 36; 1864–9)
Anselm's Letters	*The Letters of Saint Anselm of Canterbury*, trans. W. Fröhlich (3 vols; 1990–4)
ASC	*The Anglo-Saxon Chronicle*, ed. D. Whitelock, D.C. Douglas and S.I. Tucker (1961)
B	*Regesta Regum Anglo-Normannorum: The Acta of William I (1066–1087)*, ed. D. Bates (1998)
BD	Baldric of Dol: *Historia Jerusalem . . . Domini Baldrici Archiepiscopi* (RHC Oc. 4)
DB	*Domesday Book: History from the Sources*, ed. J. Morris (1975–86)
F	*Receuil des actes des ducs de Normandie de 911 à 1066*, ed. M. Fauroux (1961)
FC	Fulcher of Chartres: *Fulcherii Carnotensis Historia Hierosolymitana* (PL 155; 1880)
GF	*Gesta Francorum . . . The Deeds of the Franks and the other Pilgrims to Jerusalem*, ed. R. Hill (1962)
GND	*The Gesta Normannorum Ducum . . .*, ed. E. van Houts (2 vols; 1992)
GR	*The Gesta Regum Anglorum. The History of the English Kings of William of Malmesbury*, ed. R.A.B. Mynors, R.M. Thomson and M. Winterbottom (2 vols; 1998)

HA	*Henry, Archdeacon of Huntingdon: The Historia Anglorum. The History of the English People*, ed. D. Greenway (1996)
HC	The Hyde Chronicle: *Liber monasterii de Hyda*, ed. E. Edwards (RS 45; 1886)
HN	*Eadmer's History of Recent Events in England: Historia Novorum in Anglia*, trans. G. Bosanquet (1964)
HR	*Symeonis Monachi . . . Historia Regem*, ed. T. Arnold (RS 75 ii; 1885)
JW	*The Chronicle of John of Worcester . . .*, ed. P. McGurk (1998)
MGH	Monumenta Germaniae Historica
OV	*The Ecclesiastical History of Orderic Vitalis*, ed. M. Chibnall (6 vols; 1969–80)
PL	Patrologia Latina, ed. J.-P. Migne
PR 31 HI	*The Pipe Roll for 31 Henry I* (1929)
Prou	*Receuil des actes de Philippe I . . .*, ed. M. Prou (1908)
PT	*Petri Tudebodi . . . de Hierosolymitana itinere* (PL 155; 1880)
RA	*Raimundi de Agiles . . . Historia Francorum . . .* (RHC Oc. 3.i)
RC	*Gesta Tancredi in Expeditione Hierosolymitana. Ralph of Caen* (RHC Oc. 3.ii)
Regesta, i	*Regesta Regum Anglo-Normannorum 1066–1100*, ed. H. Davis (1913)
Regesta, ii	*Regesta Regum Anglo-Normannorum 1100–1135*, ed. C. Johnson, H.A. Cronne and H.W.C. Davis (1956)
RHC Oc.	Receuil des historiens des Croisades, Occidentaux
RHC Or.	Receuil des historiens des Croisades, Orientaux
RHGF	Receuil des historiens des Gaules et de France
RS	Rolls Series
Suger	*The Deeds of Louis the Fat: Suger*, trans. R. Cusimano and J. Moorhead (1992)
VCH	Victoria County History
Wace	*The History of the Norman People: Wace's Roman de Rou*, ed. G. Burgess (2004)

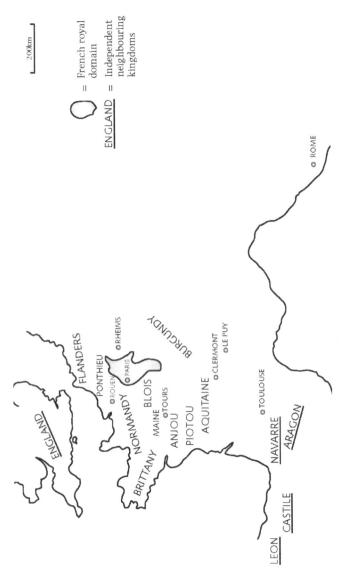

France, c. AD 1100, with some of its constituent principalities

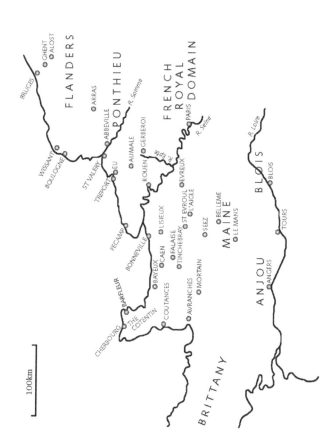

100km

CHERBOURG
BARFLEUR
THE COTENTIN
COUTANCES
AVRANCHES
MORTAIN
BAYEUX
CAEN
FALAISE
TINCHEBRAY
LISIEUX
ST EVROUL
L'AIGLE
SEEZ
BELLÊME
LE MANS
FÉCAMP
BONNEVILLE
TRÉPORT
EU
ST VALERY
BOULOGNE
WISSANT
BRUGES
GHENT
ALOST
ARRAS
ABBEVILLE
R. Somme
AUMALE
GERBEROI
ROUEN
R. Epte
R. Eure
ÉVREUX
PARIS
R. Seine
BLOIS
TOURS
ANGERS
R. Loire

BRITTANY
ANJOU
MAINE
BLOIS
FRENCH ROYAL DOMAIN
PONTHIEU
FLANDERS

Normandy and its neighbours

Norman England

Lower Normandy and Maine

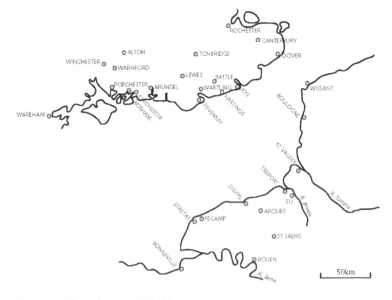

The eastern Channel coasts, *c.* AD 1100

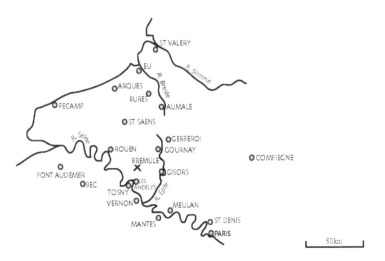

The Vexin

FAMILY TREES

The following family trees are intended as a guide through the maze of relationships surrounding Robert Curthose's life. It should be noted, however, that they can be regarded only as approximate, owing to the paucity of evidence, the extreme complexity of some family alliances and the desperate parsimony of name choice at this period.

1. The Dukes of Normandy
2. The French Royal Dynasty
3. The English Royal Dynasty
4. The Counts of Flanders
5. The Counts of Maine
6. The Montgomery–Bellême family
7. The Counts of Evreux and the Tosny family
8. The Family of Robert Guiscard
9. The Clare and Giffard Families

KEY

Italics	indicates a crusader
Bold	indicates a ruler in the dynasty concerned, with dates of rule where known
=	indicates a marriage
= = =	indicates a betrothal that did not result in a marriage
- - - - -	indicates illegitimate offspring
1, 2, 3	indicate sequential marriages, referring to the person named adjacent to the numbers

1. The Dukes of Normandy

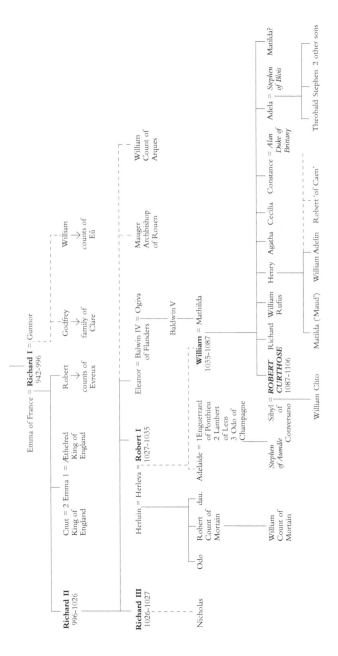

2. The French Royal Dynasty

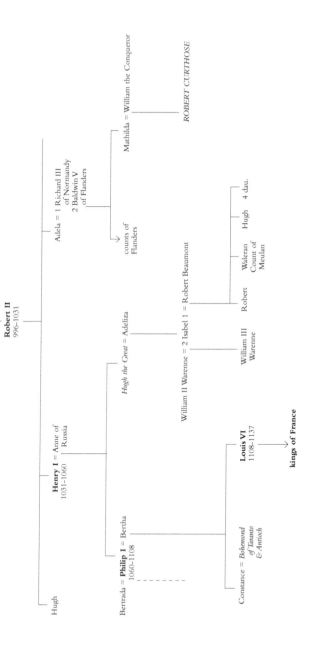

3. The English Royal Dynasty

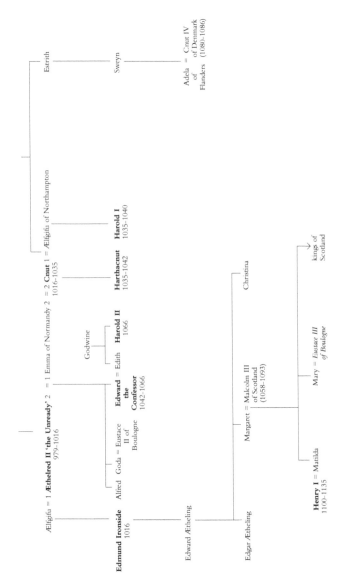

4. The Counts of Flanders

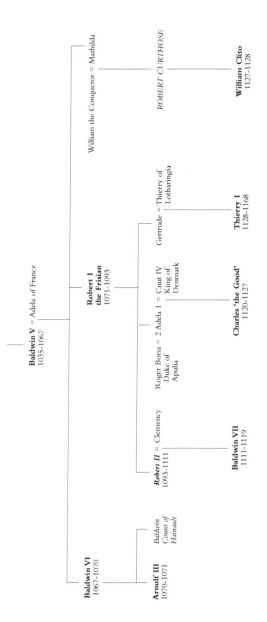

Baldwin V = Adela of France
1035–1067

Baldwin VI
1067–1070

*Baldwin
Count of
Hainault*

Arnulf III
1070–1071

Robert II = Clemency
1093–1111

Baldwin VII
1111–1119

**Robert I
the Frisian**
1071–1093

Roger Borsa = 2 Adela 1 = Cnut IV
Duke of   King of
Apulia   Denmark

Charles 'the Good'
1120–1127

Gertrude = Thierry of
Lotharingia

Thierry I
1128–1168

William the Conqueror = Mathilda

ROBERT CURTHOSE

William Clito
1127–1128

5. The Counts of Maine

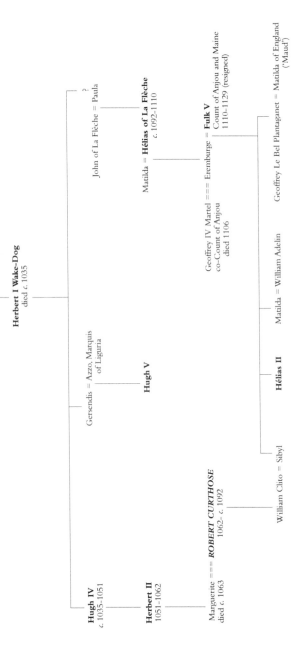

Herbert I Wake-Dog
died c. 1035

Gersendis = Azzo, Marquis of Liguria

John of La Flèche = Paula
?

Hugh IV
c. 1035–1051

Herbert II
1051–1062

Hugh V

Matilda = **Hélias of La Flèche**
c. 1092–1110

Marguerite === ***ROBERT CURTHOSE***
died c. 1063   1062– c. 1092

Geoffrey IV Martel === Eremburge = **Fulk V**
co-Count of Anjou   Count of Anjou and Maine
died 1106   1110–1129 (resigned)

Hélias II

Matilda = William Adelin

William Clito = Sibyl

Geoffrey Le Bel Plantaganet = Matilda of England ('Maud')

6. The Montgomery-Bellême Family and the Earldom of Shrewsbury

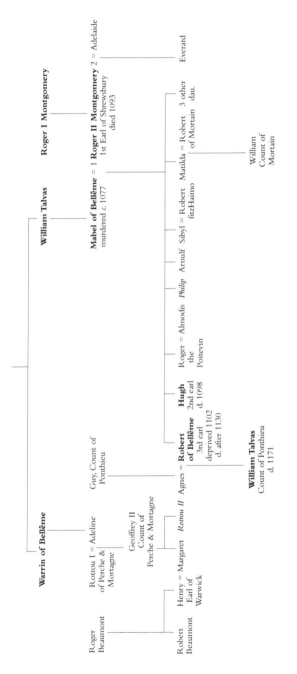

7. The Counts of Evreux and the Tosny Family

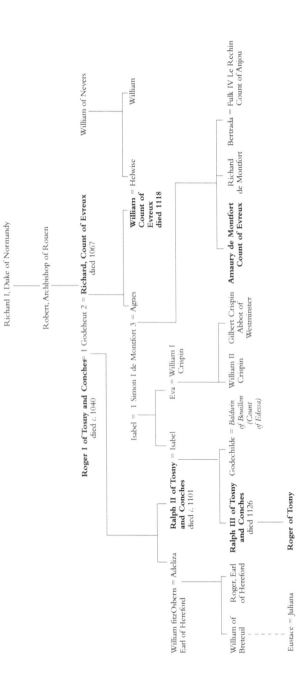

8. The Family of Robert Guiscard

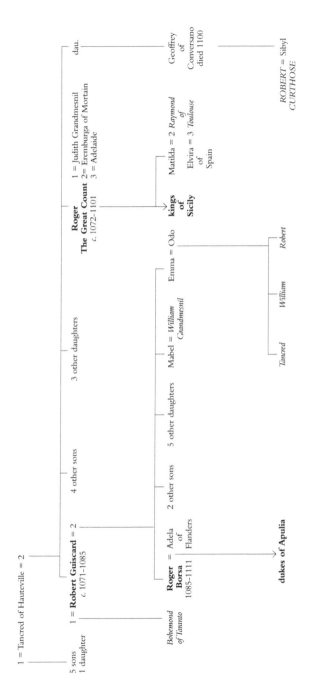

Tancred of Hauteville = 2

1 = Robert Guiscard = 2
c. 1071–1085

5 sons
1 daughter

Bohemond
of Taranto

4 other sons

3 other daughters

dau.

Roger
The Great Count
c. 1072–1101

1 = Judith Grandmesnil
2 = Eremburga of Mortain
3 = Adelaide

Roger = Adela
Borsa of
1085–1111 Flanders

2 other sons

5 other daughters

Mabel = William
Grandmesnil

Emma = Odo

kings
of
Sicily

Matilda = 2 Raymond
of
Elvira = 3 Toulouse
of
Spain

Geoffrey
of
Conversano
died 1100

dukes of Apulia

Tancred

William

Robert

ROBERT = Sibyl
CURTHOSE

9. The Clare and Giffard Families

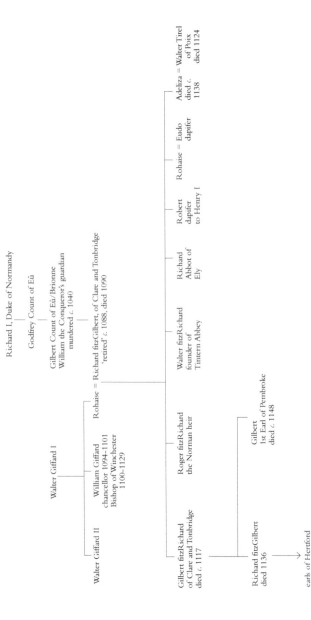

Chapter 1

OF PATRONS AND PROPAGANDA

Duke Robert Curthose was a man destined for greatness. The eldest son of William the Conqueror, he was by all accounts generous to his supporters, quick-witted and brave. Indeed, in the words of a contemporary, apart from 'his small size . . . in other respects there was nothing to criticize, for he was neither unattractive in feature nor unready in speech, nor feeble in courage nor weak in counsel'.[1] But when the Conqueror died, the Anglo-Norman 'empire' was divided, and William Rufus, a much less appealing younger son, was crowned King of England. Robert succeeded only to the Duchy of Normandy, and began a long descent into obscurity and opprobrium.

Despite all the promise of his youth, and an exalted career as a crusader, few people have heard of Curthose now. To those who have, he is usually known as 'the lazy duke', 'the weak duke', 'an administrative incompetent'. This is largely because he spent the last twenty-eight years of his life in prison, while his youngest brother, Henry, sat on the English throne and ruled Normandy in his place. During Henry's reign, there was an unprecedented flowering of historical writing, and since history is generally written by the victors, the story that is told is not kind to the defeated duke.

THE MEN WHO MADE CURTHOSE'S HISTORY

Foremost among the sources used to tell the conventional story of Curthose is the 'history' written by Orderic Vitalis, who lived at the Norman abbey of Saint-Evroul from 1085.

Orderic's descriptions of Curthose's active life were written in the closing years of the reign of Henry I, and probably relied heavily on oral sources, including his personal memories for the later years, and on his own classically influenced imagination. For example, of his list of people at the Conqueror's deathbed, there is nobody whose presence is unexpected; the entire scene could as well have been composed from imagination and common sense as from factual information, even though it has the aura of verisimilitude. When Orderic's facts can be checked against independent sources, he is often found to err.

There are two over-riding characteristics of Orderic's work. Where he differs from other twelfth-century sources, he is almost invariably the more hostile to Curthose. Conversely, he seldom misses an opportunity to extol the virtues of Henry I, whom he fervently admired. 'In reading Orderic's repeated assertions of the justice of Henry's cause when he took Normandy from his incompetent brother Robert and disinherited Robert's son, one seems at times to catch the tones of Henry's own voice.'[2] It has been Curthose's misfortune that Orderic's thirteen volumes comprise much the largest and by far the most widely quoted source for the period.

Among the other important 'histories', William of Malmesbury's *Deeds of the English Kings* has until recently been supposed to support Orderic's character studies of Curthose, Rufus and Henry. It is conspicuous, however, that, although William's patrons were Henry I's wife Queen Matilda and the king's favourite bastard son, Robert, he was not afraid to criticise Henry, even if he was forced to do so by stealth. He did not dedicate any of his work to the king, and sometimes he reveals considerable support for Curthose. Recently, scholars have begun to look more carefully at William of Malmesbury's text, and are discovering that it carries many undercurrents of hostility to Henry.[3]

Another Norman source for Curthose's life is the *Deeds of the Norman Dukes*, usually known by its Latin title the *Gesta Normannorum Ducum*. This is a complex group of histories with many strands, rather than a single work, although few authors have been positively identified. William of Jumièges worked on his version or 'redaction' of the text between the 1050s and about 1070. It was probably written before the Conquest, with only small changes afterwards. Four copies of William's text survive, but even the oldest, which is incomplete, is not an 'autograph' version. His work is characteristically slanted to the Norman ducal viewpoint, and is a good source for information about Curthose's youth.

Between about 1109 and 1113, possibly after preliminary work as early as 1095, Orderic Vitalis rewrote William of Jumièges's *Gesta Normannorum Ducum*, adding additional information about William the Conqueror and bringing it up to date. Most of his autograph copy survives. Its modern editor comments: 'It is curious that Orderic is the only redactor . . . who does not refer to Robert Curthose.'[4]

A CURIOUS DOCUMENT

The one thing above all others that has doomed Curthose in the judgement of history is the fact that he did not succeed his father on the throne of England. Here, it seems, is a man who was not deemed worthy to inherit the throne, who was passed over in favour of a younger son.

Yet surprisingly, there is very little evidence for what William the Conqueror's dying wishes actually were. How confident can we be, therefore, that William Rufus was his father's preferred heir? Only two manuscripts describe the deathbed in anything like authentic detail, and one of these was written by Orderic Vitalis (who, as we have already seen, is very hostile to Robert) some forty-five years after the event. The other, on which all our evidence for the Conqueror's intentions about the succession ultimately rest, is a very curious document indeed.

This Latin text opens with the words 'concerning the death of William' (*de obitu Willelmi*), and it is by this title that it has become known. It survives in full in only one copy, added on to the end of one manuscript of the *Gesta Normannorum Ducum*.[5] This is a Durham manuscript, which was almost certainly written by the northern historian Symeon of Durham, who died just before 1130.[6] But the *de obitu* is quite different in style from the rest of the *Gesta Normannorum Ducum*, and may not originally have been a part of it. If it was written and circulated independently before being copied in at the end of the Durham manuscript, then it could have been composed at any time between the Conqueror's death in 1087 and about 1130.[7] It is almost certainly the earliest detailed account of the 1087 succession, and may have been written very soon afterwards.

The *de obitu* itself is very short, only 654 words. It describes how the Conqueror wished to disinherit Curthose completely, but was eventually persuaded to let him succeed to the duchy because it had already been publicly promised to him. For many years this text was accepted uncritically as a valuable factual account of the Conqueror's deathbed, until in 1965 two scholars independently noted that certain passages describing William had been lifted from a ninth-century *Life* of Charlemagne.[8]

A major study then revealed that the *de obitu* is in fact a pastiche of not one but two ninth-century sources, *The Life of Charlemagne* and a *Life* of his son Louis the Pious.[9] The first part of the *de obitu* is presented as a description of the Conqueror's deathbed and arrangements for the succession, in a block of text lifted almost unchanged from *The Life of Louis the Pious*, while the latter part is a series of disconnected extracts from *The Life of Charlemagne*, purporting to describe William the Conqueror's habits and physical appearance.

This extraordinary revelation should have destroyed the credibility of the *de obitu*, but, remarkably, the story it tells is still believed: Curthose was only grudgingly allowed to become duke on his father's death, and William Rufus was the preferred heir. Perhaps even more surprisingly, no one has considered why or by whom the *de obitu* was compiled. Was it just that the lives of these two ninth-century monarchs had widely understood symbolic value at the turn of the twelfth century? Or was there a particular need for a written account of the last days of the Conqueror and his choice of successors (hallowed perhaps by the antiquity of the original texts), which met the required formulae without adhering too closely to the facts? Did these models supply a plausible short cut?

Charlemagne's legendary status was widely known in both lay and ecclesiastical milieu, and his *Life* was readily available for copying: the most recent study reveals 134 surviving manuscripts, of which 24 are eleventh century or earlier. Any ruler might be flatteringly compared with Charlemagne, and especially one such as William the Conqueror, for whom at least some of the parallels were accurate.[10] He endowed monasteries generously and reformed the church in Normandy and England, and had undoubtedly built up a greatly increased 'empire'.

The Life of Louis the Pious, on the other hand, is an unlikely model to use for the life of a great ruler. Louis faced three major rebellions by his sons, failed to live up to his great father's standards and was once forced to abdicate for a year. If the source for these extracts was understood, it was very unflattering.

If, as is more likely, it was relatively unknown in Anglo-Norman society, how readily available was it for copying and what prompted the choice?

Twenty-two manuscripts of *The Life of Louis the Pious* survive, and only five are eleventh century or earlier.[11] There may, of course, have been many more in the medieval period, but nevertheless it is relatively scarce. Of these five manuscripts, four now have the two *Lives* we have been considering bound adjacent to each other, so one problem is perhaps resolved: even if the *Life* of Louis was not as widely available, it may have travelled with *The Life of Charlemagne*. Moreover, the manuscript that is closest to the text used for the *de obitu* is one of these four.[12] Here, then, is a partial explanation for the choice of *The Life of Louis the Pious* as a model: it may have been to hand when the copyist was making his extracts from *The Life of Charlemagne* and composing the *de obitu*.

But this alone does not explain the choice of text nor the extracts taken from it. Unlike *The Life of Charlemagne*, it has been used (with one exception) as a block of text, selected from three consecutive chapters. The one place where the text has been rearranged has a very important effect. Here, the phrase 'which with God and the leading men of the palace as witnesses he had already granted to him a long time previously' is carried forward to make it refer directly to the prodigal son (Curthose), and not to the favoured heir as in the original. Stress is thus laid on the Conqueror's initial desire to disinherit Curthose completely, and the constraints that forced him to yield.

The resulting emphasis in this first part of the *de obitu* is very distinctive. There is no mention at all of the youngest brother, Henry, despite there being a place for him in the model. In other words, Henry seems to have been deliberately omitted, as if he was of no importance at the time of composition. There is a brief mention of the promise of the regalia to Rufus, who by implication is to succeed to the throne, while almost half of it describes the rift with Curthose, his unsuitability for rule and his father's reluctant agreement to confirm him as duke. Here, then, is a possible explanation for the choice of *The Life of Louis the Pious*. It is a text that includes the settlement of a disputed succession between brothers, which could be readily adapted to describe the situation at the death of William the Conqueror.

Thus we seem to have a very precisely constructed document, which goes out of its way to disparage Curthose. A major aim of the author seems to have been to stress the Conqueror's disillusionment with his eldest son. This effect is further emphasised by placing these extracts at the beginning, instead of after the description of the Conqueror in life, which would be a more conventional order to adopt. William the Conqueror himself is only described in formulaic terms, and the whole might better be entitled 'The Fall of Robert Curthose' than 'The Death of William'. Henry is of no interest in the *de obitu*, which reads distinctly like propaganda for Rufus, accounting for his claim to the throne.

Whether we look at the succession to England and Normandy in 1087 as described in the *de obitu*, or at Curthose's later encounters with his youngest brother as portrayed during Henry's reign, it soon becomes apparent that the surface 'facts' are not necessarily reliable. To uncover a clearer picture of Robert Curthose's life, it is necessary to dig below the propaganda and try to use alternative sources, less tarnished by vested interests and misinformation.

Chapter 2

REBELLIOUS SON, JEALOUS FATHER

Robert Curthose has had nine hundred years of bad publicity. It began with the propaganda and spin of his brothers' reigns, and it is exaggerated by the selective use of these same sources today: a 'pick-and-mix' approach in which already hostile chronicles are used to perpetuate the story of his failings. In particular, the abiding image of him as 'an undutiful, graceless son, often harassing his father with wild acts of insubordination'[1] is hard to dislodge.

Robert first makes his appearance in the pages of history in 1051, witnessing two charters for his father, Duke William II of Normandy. His parents were married in late 1049 or 1050, and since among all the accusations flung at him in the course of his long life illegitimacy was never one, he can only have been an infant at this time. There is no need, however, to imagine the child tracing his own cross beside his name 'Robert the young count'. There would have been enough dramatic symbolism in him being brought into the room and shown to the assembled magnates as his father's heir. In a generation where few laymen were confident handling pens, even adult witnesses did not always make autograph crosses on documents, but literally 'witnessed' the writing of them.[2]

It is scarcely possible to overstate the importance of the young Robert for his father. Following in a long tradition going back to the first Norman leader Rollo, William's father Duke Robert had not been married to his mother, but had lived with her *more Danico* – according to the Scandinavian custom. But even Rollo was believed to have married in a Christian ceremony after he had been baptised, and by the mid-eleventh century ecclesiastical attitudes were hardening. There is little firm evidence that William felt the stigma of his illegitimacy too keenly, and he was to be known more often as The Conqueror than as The Bastard. Nevertheless, the moral climate had changed to such an extent that it was unlikely that a bastard would be able to succeed to Normandy again. A legitimate heir was vital for the survival of the duchy.

After inheriting Normandy at the age of 8, and a long struggle to retain control of it, William had married Mathilda of Flanders, granddaughter of King Robert of France. At the age of 24, he was now related closely by marriage to his overlord, the French king, and also to the powerful counts of Flanders. In a complex and constantly changing political situation, such alliances counted for a great deal. Often, however, they also involved marrying within the officially prohibited 'degrees of relationship'. The law governing marriages was still evolving, and, despite two connections between their families that might have rendered their union invalid, and its prohibition in a letter from the pope and at the Council of Rheims in October 1049, William and Mathilda's wedding went ahead. (The story that they were ordered to found an abbey each as penance may be a later accretion, as there is no suggestion of this in the foundation charters.[3])

In this situation, a male heir was doubly important. Above all, Robert represented the future of Normandy. Also, his birth would have helped to silence any voices of protest at his parents' marriage. In an age when evidence for God's divinely ordained plan was eagerly sought and found, children were seen as a blessing while a barren marriage was often taken as a sign of unforgiven sin.

Over the years that followed, many more children were born: in all, nine survived infancy, four boys and five girls. The middle two boys, Richard and William, were probably born about 1055 and 1060 respectively, and the youngest, Henry, was born in 1068 or possibly early 1069.[4]

The royal charters from this period, and in particular their witness lists, can be used to build up a picture of the activities of Duke William's family. Histories intended for wider circulation, in a later reign, are bound to have been influenced by their anticipated audience and to have been written with the perspective of hindsight. But, because there was as yet no centralised system for keeping copies of all the charters that a ruler and his family witnessed, these were preserved in small private collections, usually in religious houses. When an original document has survived down to the present day, it can provide a tiny but precise glimpse back through the keyhole of time.

Using these early charters is not without difficulty, however. It is impossible to know what proportion of them have survived, but after nearly a thousand years of accident, neglect and deliberate destruction, only a minority will have done so. The surviving material will also be biased towards those families and religious houses that were more interested in obtaining and preserving written records. The situation is further compromised because many existing charters are either badly damaged or later copies. When a charter has been copied into the cartulary of the monastery for which it was written, it is always possible that the witness list, as well as the detail in the text, has been altered. Where multiple copies exist, it is sometimes possible to see how these changes have been made.

Despite these difficulties, it seems clear from the charter evidence that Robert was in an entirely different category from his younger brothers. He frequently witnessed legal documents with his parents: twenty-three times in the years before 1066, compared to five for Richard and four for William. It is also apparent that there was no comparable distinction made between the younger boys. Neither Richard nor William witnessed charters in his infancy, and they may have begun doing so only on the eve of the Conquest.[5] Until then, Robert was also the only one who ever witnessed without any of his brothers. After 1066, Richard went to England with his parents, and witnessed three extant charters there before his death in about 1070. But this seems to have been the exception not the rule. In the whole of their father's reign as king, William witnessed alone only six times, and Henry five times, while Robert did so on fifteen occasions.

The same impression is gained by looking at the order in which the brothers witnessed charters when several of them were present. All the extant original charters place Robert's name before those of his brothers. Only in two eighteenth-century copies does his name come after William Rufus's.[6] Out of a total of seventy-five documents witnessed by Robert, and forty-nine by William, this clearly demonstrates that Robert took precedence over his younger brothers during their father's lifetime.

Robert is also set apart from his brothers in this charter material by the titles he is given. As we have seen, from the moment when he first witnessed a charter as a toddler, he was known as 'the young count'. The titles 'count' and 'duke' were not fixed in the eleventh century, but there was already a tendency for the greatest of the rulers of what is now France to aspire to call themselves 'duke', no longer content with the designation 'count', with its old associations of service to the French Crown. Foremost among these men were the rulers of Normandy, who began using the title in the reign of Duke Richard II (996–1026).[7] The older title lingered, however, and even William the Conqueror continued to be styled 'count' on occasion, although mainly in English documents.[8]

From infancy to adult life, Robert was referred to as 'count'. An original document dated 1063 goes further, and specifically describes him as 'elected by his parents to govern the *regnum* after them'. Describing Normandy as a *regnum* was rather presumptuous, as it was a term normally reserved for kingdoms, but it is found occasionally in early Norman documents, including an original charter of Robert I (1027–35).[9]

This arrogation of a royal style highlights the finely nuanced political situation at the time. Normandy, like many other territories, was notionally part of 'France' and under the rule of the French king. But, even though the king was anointed, and in principle set apart by that divine blessing from mere counts, in practice the royal domain (the land over which a monarch had direct control) was quite small, and the king was obliged to deal with his magnates more or less as equals. This meant that individual personalities were of greater importance, and the whole system was more fluid than the theory might suggest, and open to challenge when opportunities arose. Rulers who failed to take offensive action were liable to become targets for the aggression of others.

The 1060s were pivotal in the development of the relationship between Robert and his father. In these years when Robert was growing up, Normandy's situation also underwent significant changes, as its two main continental adversaries, Anjou and royal France, both lost their powerful rulers. Their resulting weakness in turn facilitated the invasion of England.

Duke William's first opportunity presented itself when Count Geoffrey Martel of Anjou died in 1060. Lacking a son, the old count left the heartlands of Anjou to his nephew Geoffrey the Bearded, but gave the rich Saintogne region to Geoffrey's younger brother Fulk Le Rechin ('The Snarler').[10] Geoffrey was unable to govern effectively in this difficult situation. A civil war broke out between the brothers, and by late 1063 things were beginning to go Fulk's way, with the rulers of Brittany and Poitou helping to exert a pincer movement on Geoffrey. In 1067 Fulk obtained a decree from the papal legate declaring that Geoffrey was unfit to rule, and, aided by the uncle of the King of France, had him deposed and incarcerated in Chinon castle for three decades. In these unsettled conditions, the great abbey of Marmoutiers at Tours, which had for many years been a political ally of the Counts of Anjou, loosened its ties there and transferred its attention more to its Norman neighbours to the north.

William, always aware of the danger posed by the Angevins along his southern border, took advantage of this situation. In 1063 he invaded and subdued Maine, a small semi-independent 'county' wedged uncomfortably between its aggressive neighbours. Normandy thereby acquired a buffer state, and, as an insurance for the future, William brought the heiress of Maine, Marguerite, back to Normandy and betrothed her to his son Robert. Orderic Vitalis says (although there is no proof) that at this time Robert paid homage to Count Geoffrey for Maine, acknowledging him as his overlord.[11] A charter from soon after this event refers to Robert as 'Count of Maine' in honour of the victory.[12] Because Robert was only 12, the wedding was delayed, and in the interval Marguerite unfortunately died, leaving Robert in the anomalous position of being regarded as count by those among the population of Maine who had taken the Norman side in the war, and perhaps having paid homage to the Angevin ruler who was now losing his own civil war. Duke William certainly persisted as long as he lived in the belief, or the legal fiction, that Maine belonged to Normandy, even though his grip on it was seldom secure.[13]

By the 1060s William was in control of his own duchy. He was fortunate that, instead of brothers to threaten his position, he had two loyal half-brothers, the sons of his mother and the husband who had been found for her, Herluin of Conteville. William seems to have treated his mother with great consideration, and for most of his life he got on well with both her other sons. Odo, the older, he made Bishop of Bayeux at a relatively young age and later used him as one of his principal ministers in England. His other uterine brother, Robert, was only a few years older than Robert Curthose, and was given the strategic border domain of Mortain, guarding the Breton and Angevin marches.

King Henry of France, who had for many years been hostile to William, had also died in 1060. His heir, Philip I, was a boy of 8 who was to remain under the care of his guardian (Count Baldwin of Flanders) until 1067. With

Anjou distracted by its protracted civil war, Normandy was relatively secure both at home and beyond its borders.

Meanwhile, in England, the long reign of Edward the Confessor was drawing to a close. Harold Godwineson was restored to favour and acting as the king's right-hand man, and in 1064, for reasons that are now a mystery, he made a journey to Normandy. There was a belief in some Norman circles, perhaps based on fact or perhaps originating with the Norman prelate Robert of Jumièges (who had been appointed and then deposed as Archbishop of Canterbury during the upheavals earlier in the reign), that Edward had wished Duke William to succeed him on the English throne. The Norman sources are unanimous that King Edward had sent Harold to William to confirm him as his heir, although it is not even clear that Harold intended to go to Normandy, since he landed first in Ponthieu, where he was captured and taken to Normandy. Indeed, Edward already had a potential heir, a grandson of King Edmund Ironside called Edgar, who was known as the *Ætheling* ('prince'). Edgar's claim was much better than William's tenuous link through his great-aunt Emma.

An alternative explanation for Harold's visit, favoured by some historians, is that he was sent to negotiate a marriage alliance. The Bayeux Tapestry does suggest that a marriage may have been contemplated, but its evidence is tantalisingly unclear, just naming a lady 'Aelfgyva', which could either refer to Harold's sister, or could mean that Harold was promised the hand of William's daughter Agatha (or Adeliza). The most precise explanation, but not the most reliable since it was written fifty years later, is that William 'promised him [Harold] that he would give him his daughter Adeliza with half the kingdom of England'.[14] Whatever the cause of his stay in Normandy, the sources both sides of the Channel agree that Harold swore an oath (the English version of events was that it was extracted under duress and was not therefore binding) promising to support William's claim to the throne. He was then allowed to return to England.

When Edward the Confessor sickened suddenly and died in January 1066, Edgar Ætheling was still an inexperienced youth in his early teens. He had been in England since his family's return from exile in 1057, but, because his father had left in 1016, the boy was not well known, and may not even have been a fluent English speaker. Harold, by contrast, was an experienced war leader, with considerable estates and a broad following. The Norman and

English sources agree that Harold was nominated as the next king by Edward on his deathbed, even though he had no blood ties to the ruling dynasty. But, while the Norman sources claim that the earlier promise to Duke William could not be overturned by a subsequent gift to Harold, the election seems to have been uncontested in England, and he was crowned on the same day as King Edward's burial.[15]

William's reaction to these events is now part of the fabric of our history. While he prepared his invasion fleet, he made arrangements for the government of Normandy in his absence, and also against the possibility that he might not return. His eldest son, Robert, was by now about 15 years old, the age at which rulers 'came of age' and could take their place, under guidance, in the adult world. This is spelled out in a charter of 1066, which says it was made 'as Count William was preparing to cross the sea to wage war against the English'; it is authorised by Robert 'his son, who is now of a sufficient age to do so', at Rouen, the ducal capital.[16] Here we have a glimpse of Robert entrusted, as soon as he had come of age, with the administration of the duchy, assisted by men such as his tutor Ilger, who is present as another witness, leaving his father free to attend to supplying and equipping ships and men for the expedition to England.

There is evidence, although from later sources, that before he left William formally appointed Robert as his heir to Normandy. Orderic Vitalis, writing in the mid-1130s, makes William say 'I invested my son Robert with the duchy of Normandy before I fought against Harold on the heath of Senlac; because he is my first-born son and has received the homage of almost all the barons of the country the honour then granted cannot be taken from him'.[17] This would have been a reasonable precaution. A Channel crossing, the invasion of a country on war alert and all the usual risks of battle made the whole enterprise extremely dangerous. With hindsight, it is easy to assume that William would succeed, but in fact the odds were stacked heavily against him. It may well be that, but for one stray arrow, the outcome would have been quite the reverse. Certainly, without the sudden invasion on the east coast that sent Harold marching post-haste to Stamford Bridge, William could not have landed and established his bridgehead unopposed. It was a hazardous gamble, but for one convinced of the justice of his cause it was one worth taking. God would display His judgement, and so in the event the Normans believed He had.

Two parallels exist for making arrangements for the succession at such times. When William's own father, Robert I, was preparing for his pilgrimage to Jerusalem in 1035, he summoned his magnates and asked them to swear homage to the 8-year-old boy as their next duke. Because he was a minor, tutors and guardians were appointed for him, who ruled on his behalf. Like Robert Curthose, William seems to have been designated as heir from a very young age, being named in this way in a charter when he was about 3. Five years later, 'in that year when Count Robert left for Jerusalem', he is styled 'the boy William, son of the said Count Robert, who will be ruling after him'.[18] In the same year, Geoffrey Martel was left in charge of neighbouring Anjou, while his father, Count Fulk III Nerra, also went on pilgrimage. Geoffrey, however, was 29, and had already been used to some independent authority. William of Malmesbury says that Fulk resigned his position, enabling Geoffrey to take up the 'emblems of power', but on his return he criticised his son for his policies, humiliated him and took up the reins again himself. Father and son were eventually reconciled, and four years later Anjou was entrusted to Geoffrey once more, when Fulk left on his fourth and final pilgrimage, from which he did not return alive.[19] In both these examples there was an expectation that the father might not return, and in William's case this proved to be true, Duke Robert I dying in Asia Minor. The son was presumably therefore invested with full plenipotentiary powers; what we cannot know of course are the expectations for his status in the event of his father's return.

Nor do we know what practical arrangements were made for the government of Normandy in 1066. Ilger the tutor almost certainly remained with Robert, as did his mother, the Duchess Mathilda, who had already witnessed many charters for her husband. Another person who was probably available to advise and support him was Roger of Beaumont, who was often present at court and did not take part in the Conquest in person, although his elder son certainly did so.

As it turned out, William was away from Normandy for only about six months, defeating Harold at Senlac, or Hastings, on 14 October and being crowned at Westminster on Christmas Day. He returned in February 1067, and made a triumphal tour of the duchy. Mathilda, Robert and Richard were all with him in April, when they witnessed a charter together. In it William is described as King of England and Duke of Normandy, while Robert is called

Count of Normandy.[20] Orderic Vitalis says that William brought several key hostages, including Edgar Ætheling, 'in honourable captivity . . . by this friendly stratagem he ensured that they would cause no disturbances during his absence'.[21] Edgar seems to have been well treated, and this may have been the beginning of his close friendship with Robert, which was to last for many decades.

In early December 1067, William the Conqueror returned to England and spent most of the next five years there, crossing over to Normandy for brief periods. Robert meanwhile almost certainly remained in Normandy. What role would he have now, having been granted the duchy and having received oaths of allegiance from the magnates? Was his father still duke, and he merely his heir, or had power been transferred irrevocably, leaving his father free to attend to the pacification and reorganisation of England? Or was there some intermediate position, with Robert sometimes acting as regent in Normandy on his father's behalf?

As far as can be discovered, William was rather like old Fulk Nerra of Anjou: more inclined to shout than smile, unwilling to relinquish power, more eager to retain control than to delegate to his son. Despite this, William of Jumièges, who completed his narrative in about 1070, stated clearly that the duchy had been made over to Robert:

> after the king had settled to his satisfaction all affairs for which he had come, he entrusted the lordship of the Norman duchy to his son Robert, who was blossoming in the flower of his youth. He himself returned to the kingdom of the English . . . But since we have decided to write down the history of the peace and wars of the dukes of the Normans we shall now direct our pen to Robert, son of the king, [in] whom at present we rejoice as duke and advocate.[22]

For William of Jumièges, then, a man with no obvious axe to grind on the question, there was no doubt that between 1066 and about 1070 William was concentrating his efforts on England, while Robert, in his late teens, was ruling as *de facto* duke. But this is not the conventional version of things. Those who take the opposite view, wishing to suggest, perhaps, that Robert was already revealing defects of character that made him unfit to hold office, either base their arguments on Orderic Vitalis, who says very little about the legal situation but consistently denigrates him, or cite William of Poitiers, whose eulogistic *Deeds of William* as duke and king omits all mention of Robert. Instead, it says that the Conqueror entrusted Normandy to Mathilda, assisted by leading men including Roger of Beaumont.[23] But, although William of Poitiers may have written his account as late as the mid-1070s, the single known manuscript (from which a copy was made in 1619 before it was lost) was incomplete, lacking a beginning and ending abruptly in 1067. It is impossible, therefore, to know what he might have gone on to say about Robert or the later government of Normandy, if indeed it came within the scope of his work.[24]

This is clearly an important question, especially in view of what was to be written later about Robert being incapable of governing. It would be helpful if we could clarify whether at the time of his father's death he was inexperienced and unreliable, or had many years of useful service behind him.

Orderic Vitalis is ambiguous on this point. He says 'the king entrusted the duchy of Normandy to his wife Mathilda and his young son Robert, leaving God-fearing bishops and war-like lords to help them . . .',[25] although by December 1067 Robert was at least 16, the age at which William had himself taken up the reins of power.[26] Elsewhere, Orderic says something rather different: 'Duke William, both before the battle of Senlac and afterwards when he was sick, had named his first-born son Robert as his heir, and ordered all the nobles to do homage and swear fealty to him. They were ready enough for their part to accept his rule.'[27] If any reliance can be placed on the detail of this passage, and Orderic is admittedly often unreliable, he must be describing two quite separate events here. First, Robert was appointed heir before the Conquest, which could have been merely conditional on his father dying during the invasion of England. Secondly, we have an unknown date at which this appointment was confirmed. In between the two, then, Robert does not seem to have been a disappointment to his father, nor to the magnates who were ready to restate their acceptance of him.

In a later passage, Orderic says that there was a third ceremony, but this time he says it was only ever a promise for the future, not an immediate transfer of power: 'he again granted Robert the duchy of Normandy after his death, as he had once before granted it to him when he lay sick at Bonneville.'[28] As we shall see, this third ceremony almost certainly took place in or after 1079, placing the second investiture, associated with the king's illness, some time between 1066 and 1079.

William of Jumièges's implication that Robert was already in some sense duke in the 1070s is supported by the only other narrative source that has come down to us from this time. The last entry in the Anglo-Saxon Chronicle D manuscript, which was written almost contemporaneously, says that in 1079 the king 'would not let him rule his county in Normandy which he himself and also King Philip with his consent had given him; and the chief men in that county had sworn oaths to him and accepted him as liege lord'. Here we have a valuable insight into how the situation was understood in England.

There are other hints that William the Conqueror was reluctant to delegate power. A later editor of William of Jumièges repeatedly refers to him as 'duke' in his father's lifetime, but in one place he indicates that it was not always easy, since 'he had not been allowed to rule either Normandy or Maine as he would. He had been designated heir to the former a long time previously . . .'. John of Worcester's chronicle says Robert 'had not been able to take possession of Normandy, which William had given him, in the presence of the French king, Philip, before his coming to England', while another narrative may imply existing tenure when it says he 'was hard put to it to retain the duchy of Normandy' when his father eventually died.[29] Taken together, these references suggest that William of Jumièges could be correct in saying Robert was already duke. If so, the silence in William of Poitiers might simply demonstrate a lack of interest in the matter, whether because it was irrelevant to his eulogy of the Conqueror or because in 1067 Robert was not yet making a mark on Norman society.

In early 1068, Mathilda crossed over to England for her coronation, leaving Robert in Normandy. He seems to have remained there for the next decade, as his parents and younger brothers came and went across the Channel. Roger of Beaumont, Count Alan of Richmond and Robert's uncle Robert of Mortain may all have been available as counsellors from time to time, until he had gained experience. Throughout this period, Robert continued to be set apart from his younger brothers. William Rufus and Henry are only styled 'count' after they reach the age of 15 or 16, and then only occasionally. Richard, who died in his teens, never has the title.[30] Robert had not only been given this title from birth, but in many post-Conquest charters he also has an additional title: Count of Maine, or Count of Normandy (this occurs in five examples), consul or 'first-born'. There are also three explicit designations of him as heir to Normandy. Two charters, both of which must date to before 1083, call him 'the Second Robert'. (This anticipatory title has a Norman precedent in a charter of 1025 or 1026, where father and son are called 'Richard the Second and Richard the Third'.) The third designation is not in an original document but in a late eleventh-century copy, and describes Robert as 'my son who is succeeding me in the duchy'.[31]

There are six further charters that shed some light on Robert's status in Normandy after 1066. One of these survives only in post-medieval copies, but was originally produced between 1073 and 1077. It refers to Robert's recapture of Maine after a rebellion there, and is witnessed by him at Le Mans and by his father separately at the ducal residence of Bonneville-sur-Touques. It may well be coincidence, but it is interesting that in this, the earliest extant example of Robert acting alone in an official capacity, his father was at his residence at Bonneville. Could this be the time when William feared for his life and formally invested his heir? Another, probably dated to 1075 and surviving as an original, specifies that a gift to Rouen Cathedral was made in the presence of Queen Mathilda and other magnates, and is witnessed by Robert, presumably in the absence of his father, who was almost certainly in England at this time. Two further very closely related charters, which were destroyed in the devastating bombing of Saint-Lô in the Second World War but are fortunately known from copies that had been made, also seem to have been witnessed on separate occasions by father and son; this time William was at Bonneville on 14 July 1080 and four days later Robert made the confirmation at Caen.[32]

The last two charters in this group are not from William the Conqueror's reign, but from after his death. They are both originals dated May 1096, and give the year as 'the 19th year of the reign of Robert son of William . . .'. This would mean that Robert's independent rule had began in 1076 or 1077.[33] Is this possible, or must it be a scribal error, or a conceit on the part of Robert himself? Scribal error can probably be ruled out on something as important as a charter heading. Supposing William of Jumièges and all the other sources were right, and Robert was invested with Normandy in 1066, when he was too young to rule unaided, and supposing moreover that Orderic Vitalis was right when he said that the investiture or transfer of power was somehow formalised later, when William the Conqueror was sick, it is not difficult to see how the rest of the picture could fit into place. We have evidence in original charters that Robert was active in the government of Normandy from the mid-1070s, we have original charters from twenty years later that assert that Robert's reign began in the mid-1070s, and we have the evidence of the Anglo-Saxon Chronicle that it was in 1079 that Robert was struggling with his father because, having granted him Normandy, the older man was incapable of relinquishing his grasp on power.

William the Conqueror certainly did not stop using the title Duke of Normandy. There are eight extant charters that he witnessed in the last decade of his reign together with one or more of his sons, in which this title is reserved for him alone. Also, and perhaps crucially for his relationship with his heir, between summer 1076 and mid-1080 the Conqueror spent much more time than normal in Normandy, paying at most only fleeting visits to England. For Robert, now approaching 30 and presumably eager to be given more responsibility, this must have been a trying time. One can imagine that Orderic Vitalis might not be too far from the truth when he describes an imaginary argument between father and son, with Robert crying out in frustration 'give me Normandy, which you recently granted me . . .', and William replying: ' . . . as long as I live I will not relax my grip on it.'[34]

As if this were not enough, Robert's position was further undermined by his mother's unusually active role in politics. From soon after her marriage, she witnessed charters for her husband, and she was sometimes authorised to do so in his absence. From 1066 onwards, she was available to act as a regent in Normandy. In all, she witnessed a quarter of William's surviving ducal and royal documents, and in almost all of them her name comes immediately after his, before any of the archbishops, or Robert, or the chief magnates.

Mathilda brought many things to William. Her coronation in 1068 was an opportunity to make up for his own difficult and rather ill-omened crowning in 1066. A new setting of the *Laudes regiae* anthem for the rulers of the realm was almost certainly written for the occasion. It was unusual enough for a queen to be crowned, but if the late-eleventh-century copy of the *Laudes* that is now preserved in the British Library is part of the liturgy used in 1068, Mathilda was elevated to a position close to her husband. King William is associated in the text with two archangels and the Blessed Virgin Mary, and, whereas queens were normally linked with relatively minor female saints, Queen Mathilda is named in the company of four male apostles. One recent writer has described her as 'partially masculinised', an honorary man in a man's world. Mathilda was also dignified with her own crown, sceptre and coronation ring, which she gave to her foundation at Caen when she died. Her status was further apparent in the great estates William gave her to hold in England in her own right.[35]

Mathilda brought royal blood to the Norman line, and she thereby enhanced William's claim to rule England as a king. In particular, as a granddaughter of a French king, she gave his line a vital infusion of the blood of Charlemagne, that semi-mystical link to the golden age of European Christendom, and, as a daughter of the Count of Flanders, she associated him with a family who were conspicuously proud of their Carolingian ancestry. The troubadour traditions were already stirring, although they did not find a written form for some time to come, and notions of knightly prowess and heroism in the mould of Charlemagne were in the air. For a man such as William, a direct bond to these values could only increase his legitimacy.

There is no evidence anywhere that the relationship between Robert and his mother was strained; indeed, Orderic lays especial emphasis on her deep affection for him. But, no matter how close they were, how devoted he was, his mother's availability as an experienced, able and trusted regent must have seriously compromised Robert's own position as his father's deputy and his chances of being given genuinely independent power.

THE REBELLIOUS SON

The picture that is emerging is of Robert Curthose being created *de facto* Duke of Normandy in his father's lifetime, perhaps in about 1075 when he was 25 years old. This could coincide with the occasion when we are told the Conqueror repeated his grant of the duchy to his son, when he was sick at Bonneville. But William did not relinquish control. The usual reason given is that Robert proved himself to be a poor ruler, but two other possibilities present themselves: either it suited William to rely on his wife to act as regent for him when he was in England, or he was constitutionally incapable of handing over power. What is clear is that for most if not all of the four years from summer 1076, after some experience of sole rule, Robert was again forced to see his father take charge in Normandy. Eventually, this became too much to bear, and Robert rebelled.

The rebellions are what Robert is chiefly remembered for. Indeed, they were linked in his own lifetime to his pejorative nickname 'short-boots' or 'stubby-legs'. For, when his father refused to yield power, 'driving the young man away with jeers in that terrific voice of his, Robert went off in a passion, and harried his own country . . . At first his father merely laughed. "By God's resurrection!", he used to say, "He'll be a hero, will our [little] Robin Curt-hose!" This was his nickname because of his small size.'[36] The modern perception of this period is summarised as follows: Curthose rose against his father soon after September 1077, and was reconciled to him at Easter 1080; then, after 18 July 1083, 'Robert disappears entirely from view for over four years'.[37]

As before, this reading of events depends on a highly selective use of the chronicles, and can also now be challenged using materials that have only recently become available.

The picture of Robert in rebellion against his father for almost eight years relies on the narrative of Orderic Vitalis, which we now know is strongly biased against him. Moreover, Orderic's chronology is confused, or possibly even disingenuous. In book V, Orderic suggests that Robert's demand for independent rule in Normandy was made soon after 1066, and describes him as a young man. But he then moves straight on to a description of what is known as the 'first revolt' of the late 1070s, by which time Robert was over 25. Book IV further confuses things by linking this revolt to the death of Marguerite of Maine in 1063, but implies that Robert and his younger brothers were on equal terms, which is manifest nonsense, since Henry was barely 10. In these passages, Orderic writes condescendingly of Robert, calling him 'youth', *tiro* (a technical term for a new recruit) and 'boy'.[38]

The Anglo-Saxon Chronicle D manuscript gives 1079 as the year when 'Robert, son of King William, deserted from his father to his uncle Robert, in Flanders'. This manuscript was completed soon after the events described and is likely to be a reliable source. Unfortunately, John of Worcester, who is often trustworthy and who based much of his chronicle on the Anglo-Saxon Chronicle, gives the year as 1077. A possible explanation is that neither the D nor the E Chronicle has an entry for 1078, and 1079 is the last entry in the D manuscript. Thereafter the E Chronicle continues alone. Perhaps as a result, there is some confusion in the text of John of Worcester, which seems to have conflated the entries for 1077 and 1079, as he transferred from D to E as his source. What is much harder to explain is why, almost without exception, modern commentators adopt John's date in preference to that in the Anglo-Saxon Chronicle.

Curthose was certainly present at Caen in September 1077, for the consecration of his father's abbey of St Stephen. The next definite date is that he was with his father on 12 April 1080.[39] But this apparent gap in the charter evidence is because few of the documents from this period have precise dates, and some have been assigned dates on the basis that, if Curthose witnessed them, they must have been presented when he was not in rebellion. Thus, for example, the modern commentary on one charter dates it to between 1077 and 1081 on the basis of the names of the other witnesses, but then goes on to say 'the attestation of William's son Robert Curthose narrows the limits still further, since he was in rebellion against his father from 1077/8 to 1080. The charter therefore dates from 1077 x 1078 or 1080 x 1081.'[40] Such circular arguments are a common feature of discussions of the length and severity of Curthose's rebellions.

What is clear is that the climax of this rebellion was an armed encounter between Robert and his father. King Philip had given him the castle of Gerberoi, well into French territory but next to the disputed eastern border region of the Vexin. It is not clear how long Robert had been in possession of the castle, but he now used it as a base for raids into Normandy. Early in 1079, and so perhaps after only a few weeks of this provocation, William the Conqueror brought up his army, including the youthful William Rufus, and confronted Robert, who was supported by his overlord King Philip. Philip was now in his mid-twenties, and no doubt concerned to assert his authority and repel this Norman incursion. It may also have suited him that Robert and his father were at odds, since it restricted William's freedom of action.

In the ensuing skirmish, William was knocked from his horse by Robert, and for a moment his life was in danger. There is an interesting variation in the way the different chroniclers describe the scene, which hints at their underlying attitudes. John of Worcester, for example, finds much to praise and excuse in Robert's conduct:

> King William whilst he was campaigning against his son Robert before the
> castle of Gerberoi (which King Philip had given Robert) was wounded in the
> arm by him, and forced off his horse. As soon as Robert recognised William's

voice, he quickly dismounted, and ordered his father to mount his horse, and in this way allowed him to leave. William then retreated, after many of his men had been slain, and some had been taken prisoner, and his son William and many others wounded.[41]

In particular the image of Robert *ordering* his father to escape on his own mount is intriguing. Quite apart from the idea of William the Conqueror taking orders from his own son, the monastic audience for which John was writing will have been aware of the parallel with the story of David in the cave, sparing the life of King Saul, who was seeking to harm him, and thereby risking his own. Robert is portrayed here as a good vassal and an exemplary warrior, but also as a dutiful son.

In complete contrast, Henry of Huntingdon omits the explanation of how the battle originated, and says: 'King William also, fighting against his son Robert in a military uprising at Gerberoi, which is a castle in France, was thrown from his horse, and William his son was wounded and many of his men killed. The king cursed his son Robert.'[42] Here, the emphasis is on Robert rebelling and in so doing endangering his father's life, while the conflicting claims of his duty to his father and to King Philip are ignored.

The Anglo-Saxon Chronicle D manuscript gives an account that lacks the detailed setting, but contains interesting circumstantial evidence in this, the last and tantalisingly incomplete passage in the manuscript: 'Robert fought against his father and wounded him in the hand; and his horse was shot under him; and the man who brought him another horse was at once shot from a cross-bow; his name was Toki, son of Wigod; and many were killed there and captured; and Robert came back to Flanders; nor will we write more of the harm he inflicted on his father . . .'.[43] Soon after this, William concluded a new treaty with King Philip, perhaps associated with a French royal diploma they attested together at Gerberoi in early 1079.[44]

The reconciliation between William and Robert took rather longer, but, once accomplished, it seems to have been full and complete. As before, the evidence from conventional dating of charters is confusing, because it is assumed that Robert was still in rebellion until 1080. He must, however, have been restored to his father's confidence early that year, because he attested two clearly dated charters in April and July. The former was delivered at the Easter court, one of the greatest ceremonial occasions of the year, where his appearance with his father would be richly symbolic. He then attested the July one independently at Caen, an important ducal centre; this too indicates his full rehabilitation. There are also three letters from Pope Gregory VII, part of a correspondence with William's family, all dated 8 May 1080. To Mathilda the pope wrote in gratitude for her piety and charity; to William he sent an admonishing letter, urging greater attention to his duties to the church. The one addressed to Robert, commending him because he had heeded his father's advice, and urging him to be a patient model of filial duty until such time as William passed on his lands to his heir, makes it clear that the pope (who was then in Rome) had already heard of the reconciliation, which must therefore have occurred some weeks before.[45]

There are other charters that also suggest a relatively early healing of the breach. Two relate to a dispute over land tenure, heard in two separate locations on 7 and 31 January 1080 respectively. Although Robert and his brothers are not named, prayers for all the royal children are requested, and the royal couple and their sons (plural) were present for its final resolution and confirmation. This suggests that Robert was there, although it could possibly just refer to William and Henry. But, since Henry was then only 11 and seldom appears in documents this early, this seems unlikely without some specific reference.[46] Apart from this pair of documents, there are also ten undated ones witnessed by Robert, which on internal evidence could be allocated to 1079 or 1080.[47]

It is clear then that Robert and his father were reconciled and a new understanding had been reached by Easter 1080 at the very latest. There are no surviving documents that prove William's whereabouts for Christmas the previous winter, but the case he presided over at Caen, immediately after the festival, may indicate that he had held the court there. The mention of at least two of his sons in the manuscripts relating to that case suggests that Robert may have returned to his father's household before Christmas 1079.

According to Orderic, the reconciliation was accomplished by a group of the leading magnates, many of whose sons had joined Robert in his rebellion.[48] There are also indications that an aristocratic monk called Simon de Crépy was involved in the negotiations. He had grown up at the ducal court, fostered by William and Mathilda, of whom he had fond memories. He was by birth the Count of Amiens and the French Vexin, a key border territory between Rouen and Paris. But Simon was a religious young man, and, when his father died (while Simon himself was away on pilgrimage), he decided to abandon his wealth and become a monk. He was so revered for his sanctity that his achievements were recorded in *The Life of The Blessed Simon, Count of Crépy*, which is a source of valuable incidental information. In particular, the *Life* records that he was present at the translation of a relic of the Holy Shroud at Compiègne into its new golden reliquary, which had been given by Queen Mathilda. A later charter of King Philip I refers to this event as having taken place on the fourth Sunday in Lent, but does not specify the year.[49] The *Life* goes on to say that Simon set off in haste the day after the translation and became involved in the attempts to settle the trouble between Robert and William. The translation at Compiègne can, therefore, have taken place only in Lent 1079 or 1080. Charles David, who wrote a biography of Robert Curthose in 1920, commented that it was 'probably the latter', but this is in fact far from certain, as a consideration of the text, the distances travelled and the time available reveals.

Easter in 1079 was 24 March, so, if Simon's journey took place that year, it would have begun on 11 March; if in 1080, with Easter falling on 12 April, it would have begun only on the 30th. The text of the *Life* of Simon specifies that he set off with haste to Normandy, as far as the place where the battle between the king and his son had taken place. This sounds much more like a visit to the district near Gerberoi (which was close to Simon's former estates) within about two months of the battle than a journey made a year later.

Assuming he travelled on foot, Simon could have reached the Gerberoi area in about two days; if he went on to Rouen, the whole journey would have taken five days; riding, he would have been rather quicker. So, if this was in 1080, as David proposed, the earliest that Simon could have met William (who by then would have been en route for Rouen or already there, for the Easter court) would have been on 2 or 3 April, leaving a maximum of nine days to contact Robert, to recall him to court and for the reconciliation to take place. This all supposes that Robert's whereabouts were known, and that he returned at once, in which case the negotiations must already have been well advanced. Simon's presence would just have been a catalyst for the peace-making, and perhaps a face-saving device for both Robert and his father.

If, on the other hand, Simon's intervention occurred in 1079, he could have heard about the Battle of Gerberoi soon after it took place, and travelled there 'in haste' as soon as his commitments at Compiègne were over. Despite having renounced the world three years before, he would still feel concern for his foster parents and their son with whom he had grown up. There is a possibility that Mathilda herself or a representative for her was also present at the translation, since it was she who had donated the reliquary. Who more likely to beg Simon, who was a relation of hers, to come and help arbitrate in the war between her husband and her favourite son? There are hints in both the *Life of Simon* and in Orderic Vitalis that the quarrel was not settled at once, which is plausible in view of the recent near-fatal encounter between two vigorous men, and also fits better with the idea of Simon coming to court in 1079. There would then be plenty of time for father and son to make their peace, for Robert to be invested with the duchy again and for him to witness several charters with his father, all before Christmas 1079.[50]

The evidence assembled so far suggests that Curthose's first rebellion began, not in autumn 1077, but in the winter of 1078–9, and that it was over by Christmas 1079, perhaps earlier. Thus we are looking at a maximum period of about a year, and a minimum of only a few months, certainly not the prolonged exile envisaged by Orderic Vitalis, as with 'unprofitable companions-at arms . . . the young knight Robert wandered through foreign lands for about five years'.[51]

Once restored to his father's favour, Robert seems to have been trusted completely. Father and son now crossed to England together for the first time, perhaps to introduce him to the kingdom. Towards the end of 1080, Curthose was given command of a major military and diplomatic mission to the Scottish borders. The region had never been fully subdued, and the north of England was still feeling the consequences of the brutal 'Harrying of the North' a decade earlier. According to the monk Symeon of Durham, little grew between York and Durham except wolves and outlaws. Wide tracts of Yorkshire and Lancashire were so dangerous that, when the Domesday survey was carried out, they were ignored, and large areas of the land that could be surveyed were recorded as 'waste'. The need now was to renegotiate a peace with the Scottish king Malcolm, and stabilise the borders. This Robert achieved, with the help of his other foster-brother, Edgar Ætheling, whose sister was Margaret, Malcolm's queen. On his return journey, he founded a castle, as his father had done ten years before, but this one extended the garrisoned zone much closer to Scotland. Curthose's New Castle on the Tyne demonstrated to the local population, and to the Scots, that the Norman writ ran far into the north.[52]

After his return south Robert remained a visible figure in England. In February 1081 he was with his parents at Salisbury for the Feast of the Purification,[53] and soon after he was named, as 'Count Robert', with his parents in a confraternity foundation for Ramsey Abbey.[54] In May he and his brothers were at Winchester, and in late 1082 he was in England again, having spent several months in Normandy in between. Easter 1083 was spent with his father at Fécamp Abbey, one of William's favourite residences.[55]

At some point, however, Robert again became disenchanted with life under his father's tutelage. This is perhaps understandable, since he was now over 30, still kept single and without an independent household. But the idea, which is sometimes quoted, that this 'second rebellion' lasted for four years has no sound basis and stems, unsurprisingly, from an enigmatic phrase in Orderic Vitalis.

One event that some have seen as the trigger for Robert's second rebellion is that Queen Mathilda fell ill in 1083 and died on 2 November. In her last bequest she donated her regalia, a set of vestments and altar furnishings and three properties in England and Normandy to her foundation of Holy Trinity Caen. She was buried there beneath a black marble slab that survives to this day, although there is now no trace of the ornate, jewel-encrusted gilt monument that adorned it. Her epitaph is still legible, and, even allowing for its conventional eulogising, it is a fitting tribute to a remarkable woman:

> The lofty structure of this splendid tomb
> Hides great Mathilda, sprung from royal stem;
> Child of a Flemish duke; her mother was
> Adela, daughter of a king of France,
> Sister of Henry, Robert's royal son.
> Married to William, most illustrious king,
> She gave this site and raised this noble house,
> With many lands and many goods endowed,
> Given by her, or by her toil procured;
> Comforter of the needy, duty's friend;
> Her wealth enriched the poor, left her in need.
> At daybreak on November's second day
> She won her share of everlasting joy.[56]

Mathilda's death must certainly have altered the family dynamics. William seems to have been faithful to her for all the thirty-three years of their married life, an extraordinary record for the times. She had, moreover, been his political support as well as his domestic consolation. For Robert, she had been a devoted mother and probably a confidante. But it is not true that, with Mathilda gone, there was an immediate breakdown of Curthose's relationship with his father. There is, for example, a firmly dated charter that they witnessed together on 9 January 1084 in Normandy, just after the Christmas court following her death. There is also a notice in the Abingdon Abbey chronicle that says that the teenaged Henry spent Easter 1084 with the community at Abingdon, while his father and brothers (plural) were in Normandy. The reference is also notable because it specifically omits Mathilda in this, the first year after her death.[57]

There is a much-quoted passage in Orderic Vitalis about the start of Curthose's second rebellion, which states that the peace concluded after Gerberoi 'was soon clouded. The stubborn young man contemptuously refused to follow or obey his father; the quick-tempered king continually poured abuse and reproach on him in public for his failings. So, shortly afterwards, he once more left his father's court, taking only a few companions with him, and never returned until his father, on his deathbed, sent Earl Aubrey to him in France to invite him to take possession of the duchy . . .'. There is, however, another passage that gives a rather different impression, one that is much more in line with the charter evidence. In it Orderic remarks, in passing, that in 1087 'his son Robert, who was the eldest, had often quarrelled with his father and again *quite recently* taking offence for some trivial cause, had gone off to the King of France'.[58]

Another way of approaching the question of when the relationship between father and son was severed is to consider how William dealt with external politics in the last years of his reign. In 1084 there was trouble in Maine, and the king spent some time there conducting operations, although he seems to have been content to let others take a lead. In 1085, according to the Anglo-Saxon Chronicle, rumours reached him that Cnut, the King of Denmark, was planning an invasion of England, supported by his father-in-law, Robert of Flanders. In response, William gathered together a great army and crossed to England. This he surely would not have been able to do if Curthose was at the same time threatening Norman security. Indeed, no chronicler other than Orderic refers to any such prolonged rebellion at all.

There is a charter from the Christmas court of 1085–6 at Gloucester, which indicates that father and son were still working together then. This charter has been the focus of some debate. David Bates, who has edited all the extant copies of William the Conqueror's charters, challenges its authenticity because it is witnessed by Curthose 'in a year when he was undoubtedly in exile'.[59] But, as we have seen, there is a substantial body of evidence against Orderic's widely believed version of events. Far from being in rebellion against his father for two periods of about four years, Robert Curthose was loyal to him for the great majority of his reign, while some heirs were driven to much more extreme measures.[60]

There are four particular reasons for believing that the Gloucester charter is an authentic witness to Robert's presence with his father at his last Christmas court in England. First, one of the gifts to Gloucester that the charter records is also mentioned in Domesday, in an unusual wording, which Bates considers is likely to have been copied from the charter. If this is so, the charter must have been written before Domesday was compiled. Secondly, the charter specifically states that it was drawn up in the presence of the king's sons and magnates. Thirdly, the attestations are in the order 'King William of England, Robert the king's son, William the king's son, bishop Lanfranc [the Archbishop of Canterbury] . . .'. This is the order one would expect, and casts doubt on Bates's explanation that the fourteenth-century copyist who produced the extant version of it somehow mistook an H for an R. In all the documents that they witness, Henry never takes precedence over Rufus in the way this explanation would imply. Fourthly, an apparently minor point, but one that is worth noting for its practical implications, is that Roger Montgomery is absent from the witness list of this charter. If both William and Curthose were in England, he may well have been in Normandy acting as regent.

Until at least January 1086, then, it seems that Robert Curthose remained loyal to his father. He did not witness the last charter that can be confidently assigned to England, in the spring of that year, but, having been present and visible to the magnates again at the ceremonies of the Christmas court at Gloucester, he may well have been needed in Normandy. William the Conqueror spent his last summer in England travelling around the south of the country while the Domesday surveys were carried out, and then after 1 August, when he had assembled all the magnates at Salisbury and made them renew their allegiance to him, he crossed to Normandy for the last time. Sometime in the next twelve months, and only then, with the two men again together in Normandy, can we confidently assume that Robert and his father lost patience with each other, in a way that was to have dramatic results for English history and tragic consequences for Robert's future.

Chapter 3

WHEN THE CONQUEROR DIED

Hard evidence for what Robert Curthose was doing during the last year of William the Conqueror's life is almost non-existent, and into this vacuum historians have liberally poured their favourite preconceptions.

At the Christmas court of 1085–6 at Gloucester, which the previous chapter has suggested that Robert almost certainly attended, William had, in the words of the Anglo-Saxon Chronicle, 'much thought and very deep discussion' with his council. As a result, assessors were sent out far and wide across the kingdom to gather information for the great survey of the wealth of England that became known as Domesday Book. 'So very narrowly did he have it investigated, that there was no single hide nor virgate of land, nor indeed (it is a shame to relate but it seemed no shame to him to do) one ox nor one cow nor one pig which was there left out.'[1] Whether William's motivation was primarily financial or strategic (with a view perhaps to quartering or paying a future army of mercenaries), the importunate questioning of the surveyors seems to have been greeted with the sullen resentment accorded all tax collectors down the ages.

A 1086 writ in favour of Westminster Abbey 'after the survey of the whole of England' shows that the king was still in England and actively involved with the reallocation of tax liabilities after the material for Domesday had been collected.[2] The Anglo-Saxon Chronicle also relates that the Conqueror was in southern England through the first half of 1086, spending Easter at Winchester and Whitsun at Westminster, where he dubbed Henry (now 18) a knight. William Rufus and Henry were still with him after April 1086, when a plea was heard before them at Lacock in Wiltshire: they are named simply as 'the king's sons', without any titles.[3] Robert had perhaps already returned to Normandy. The king was in no hurry to go there himself, so it is unlikely that his eldest son was known to be stirring up trouble again; a more likely explanation is that, if Robert of Flanders had indeed been involved in Cnut's attempted invasion of England the previous year, Curthose had been sent back to deter further hostile activity. Cnut was murdered in July 1086, but it would have taken some time for the news to reach England.[4]

The last precise mention of William the Conqueror in England is that he summoned all the significant landholders of England to him at Salisbury for Lammas (1 August) and made them renew their oaths of allegiance to him. Again, his motives are unclear. Was he afraid of a rebellion? Did he aim to consolidate the Norman grip on England? It is probable that this Oath of Salisbury was in some way connected to the Domesday survey, clarifying the land-tenure arrangements in England and stressing the pivotal role of the king in the system. After the oath-taking, William went to the Isle of Wight, and, as we are told, after extracting more money from the kingdom (the Chronicle is distinctly hostile in its tone here), he sailed to Normandy for the last time.

There is no record of the place from which William sailed, but among the estates he held on the Isle of Wight was Freshwater, adjoining the best harbour on the island and one of the best along this part of the south coast for small shallow draught vessels.[5] It was well sheltered, with gentle currents, an ample depth of water for a good distance up the River Yare, and a mud bottom that was kind to wooden hulls. Not least, for sailors used to the dramatic tides of Normandy (Fécamp and Honfleur both have neap tides of about 21 feet), the modest tidal range of 6 feet at Yarmouth would have been a great boon when boats had to be manhandled up beaches until they were safe beyond the reach of the tide. It may well, therefore, have been Freshwater or Yarmouth where the Conqueror last stood on English soil.

After this, we lose sight of William for almost a year. We do know that Edgar Ætheling, who had been at the English court for some time, became tired of his circumscribed life there and went to Apulia in the heel of Italy, recently conquered by Norman adventurers. William of Malmesbury suggests that Robert Curthose also went to Italy, to Tuscany in search of an heiress, and it has been assumed that this visit also dates to 1086; but, since it is linked to Curthose rousing King Philip of France against Normandy, any such visit is more likely to have occurred in the late 1070s.[6] One surviving charter of the Conqueror, probably witnessed in Rouen in 1086, indicates that Rufus was then with his father, but Curthose was apparently not.[7] Beyond this, we have only the chroniclers to explain the background to the Conqueror's last, disastrous campaign.

At the end of July 1087, or perhaps in early August, William mounted an attack, during a heat wave, far up the Seine more than halfway to Paris, until he entered and burnt the town of Mantes, on the borders of the French Vexin. In the conflagration, among many other civilian losses and the destruction of the city's churches, two anchorites were burnt alive. The English chroniclers particularly dwell on this terrible accident, and link it to the rapid onset of William's terminal illness. The Anglo-Saxon Chronicle makes the link explicit: 'A miserable thing he did, and more miserable was his fate. How more miserable? He fell ill, and he was severely afflicted by it.'[8] Orderic Vitalis, who says that Mantes had been used as a base for raids into Normandy, omits to mention the deaths of the anchorites, but says that, as he lay dying, William made a particular gift for the rebuilding of the Mantes churches.

There is agreement in the sources that Curthose was not directly involved in the Mantes campaign. Beyond that, the picture they give is confused. It may be that William was making an attempt to regain control of the Vexin, or that the attack was in retaliation for raids from Mantes, or perhaps it was provoked by Curthose's new defection. On the other hand, Curthose may have left Normandy for France in protest at his father's plans to attack a city owing allegiance to their overlord King Philip. One version of events says that Curthose left because his father still refused to let him rule Normandy, and he based himself at Abbeville in Ponthieu, still ruled by the Count Guy who had captured Harold Godwineson all those years ago, and from there he mounted raids against his father. While Robert may indeed have spent time at Abbeville in 1087, the story of his raids may be a confusion with his earlier rebellion, since it is not clear why this should have provoked William to attack Mantes.[9] Nor is it clear why Curthose should have chosen this base for a rebellion. Ponthieu was closely allied to the Conqueror, who had recently arranged a marriage between Count Guy's daughter and heiress and one of his favourite vassals, Robert of Bellême.[10]

William returned to Rouen a sick man. At first he was cared for in the city itself, but later he was moved out to the Fécamp priory of Saint-Gervaise, which stood on a low hill to the north-west. The nature of his illness is not known, and Henry of Huntingdon aptly summed up the contemporary view: 'God submitted him to sickness and death.' It is probable that the withdrawal from Mantes was complete by mid-August, and for the next month the great king slowly faded away. Orderic Vitalis specifies that he was ill for six weeks, and, while this fits approximately with the other evidence, there are also overtones of the Lenten period of penitence and contrition in his description of the king's deathbed, so this may be a convenient literary device.

When we try to look at the actual wishes of the dying king, the so-called facts vanish like clouds of incense. No will has survived, and the two passages that purport to be descriptions of his last words and hours are of debatable value. Orderic's lengthy deathbed speech describes in detail the trials and achievements of his long reign, but it is surely no more than a rhetorical device. The other, the *de obitu Willelmi*, is an ingenious patchwork of much earlier accounts of the deaths of other kings, with almost no original material, and has no value as an eye-witness source. All that is undisputed is that William the Conqueror died on 9 September 1087, that before the king was dead Rufus set off in haste for the Channel coast, and that Curthose was not present when his father died. The king was then buried at St Stephen's Caen, as he had requested, and the only member of his immediate family who seems to have been present was Henry.

By the time that most of the chronicles were written, in the 1120s and 1130s, it was assumed that William's last wishes had been met. His great empire had been divided, with the patrimony of Normandy going to Curthose, who had after all been promised it and had probably assisted in ruling it, while the 'acquisition' of England was granted to Rufus. These writers stressed that William gave Normandy to Curthose only reluctantly, because he was persuaded that he could not reverse his earlier promises to him. Eighty years later, Wace (who wrote from the Norman viewpoint) explained the decision by saying that Robert was strong enough to rule the turbulent Normans and make them obedient to him, but that this was a full-time job for any man.[11]

Yet there is much that does not ring true in this conventional version of events. First and foremost, there is the clear agreement of all the chroniclers that Rufus set off from court before his father had died. He travelled fast, accompanied in one account only by Robert Bloet, who later became his chancellor. Having reached the coast, probably at Bonneville-sur-Touques, where he must have had a boat made ready, he waited until the news of his father's death was brought to him. This was, then, a premeditated course of action, and yet it smells of fear. Orderic suggests that the king feared lest unrest broke out in the interregnum, but if that were so, there were things he could have done sooner to avert it, for example by associating his chosen heir in his government as the Capetian rulers of France did, crowning them in their own lifetime. An ideal opportunity for this would have been at Salisbury the previous August, when his younger sons were in England, but he is clearly recorded as extracting an oath to himself alone.[12] Rufus's actions look more like a pre-emptive strike, getting as close to England as he could without crossing the Channel and thereby risking losing contact with events at Rouen, but yet giving himself as much of a head start as possible in his dash for the throne. And why the haste? There was no external threat to the realm as there had been in 1085. The only rival that could have prompted such haste was Curthose.

Another curious feature of these weeks is that Curthose did not come to his father's bedside. He was heir to Normandy and Maine, even if the succession to England remained undecided, and he was no fool: he was unlikely to imperil his inheritance by staying away. No matter how stiff-necked and irascible the Conqueror was, his eldest son had a reputation for being forgiving and generous, and the two men had been reconciled after a much more serious rift than this. If he was indeed at Abbeville, a convenient crossing point over the Somme, he could have been at his father's side in a very few days. It is possible that William died much more quickly than his doctors had led people to expect, but there also may have been forces at work that deliberately kept Curthose from knowing that his father was ill.

As to the English succession, the situation was unique and fraught with complexity. For the first time, the king was not in England when he died, and there was no one present to represent specifically English interests – neither of the archbishops, nor even any of the bishops or abbots. The old Anglo-Saxon aristocracy had been swept away in the years since the Conquest, and for most of the Norman lay magnates the position was complicated because they held land on both sides of the Channel. Moreover, there were as yet no settled rules for the succession, and since the time of Edgar Ætheling's great-grandfather there had not been a 'regular' transfer of power. Looking further back into the Anglo-Saxon past, we can see that the pattern was for a designation of the preferred heir by the king, in consultation with the royal kinsmen, followed by the assent of the witan and, at some later date, an anointing and coronation. In some cases the coronation could be several months or even years after the start of the reign.

By the eleventh century, the English succession was dominated by deathbed designation, and it was this that had enabled Harold to be crowned in 1066. Duke William, as he was then, claimed that his prior nomination should take precedence. If, then, Rufus had indeed been designated by the Conqueror on his deathbed, William would seem to have been won round to the Anglo-Saxon view of things. But election was still necessary: William had not been formally elected in 1066, but he still took the 'assent' of the defeated Anglo-Saxon nobility before his coronation. Some such agreement, however formalised, would be necessary for his successor. The third element, anointing and crowning, bestowed on the new king a God-given authority that raised him above lesser rulers but required the agreement and cooperation of an archbishop. Harold, atypically, had been crowned on the same day as Edward the Confessor's funeral, and this may have caused the Normans to believe that an English ruler was not king until he was crowned. A combination of this belief with an awareness of the sacral powers of anointing led to what has been called 'pre-emptive anointing' among all subsequent Norman rulers.[13]

There has been much debate among scholars about the methods of passing on lands among the Normans at this time, and whether there were conventions that the Conqueror would have been obliged to follow. Some have argued strongly that there was already a well-defined pattern of handing on the patrimony, or ancestral lands, to the eldest son, and the 'acquisitions' to the younger son or sons. Evidence in support of this viewpoint is found among many of the greatest Anglo-Norman families, such as the Montgomerys, who did indeed follow this practice, but others did not. There are, moreover, two major weaknesses in this argument. First, many of these partitions took place after William's death, when Normandy and England had separate rulers, and so it made more sense to divide up the family land and reduce the problems that arose from divided loyalties. Secondly, there is no reason to suppose that the practice among the Norman baronage need reflect expected practice in the new Norman royal house. Indeed, all the evidence from the history of the Norman ducal family is that their policy had been consistently towards consolidation. Younger sons might be given an apanage, but only to hold under their older brother, the new duke. From what little can be gleaned about the mentality of William the Conqueror, one might suppose that he would wish to preserve his empire intact, as a lasting memorial to his greatness, rather than to see it divided between two new sub-dynasties. But all that can safely be said is that there were no clear and undisputed rules either for the English royal succession or for the entirely novel problem of how William the Conqueror should pass on his cross-Channel domains.[14] And a lack of clarity always gives scope for opportunists.

A further question is whether Rufus was likely to have been his father's preferred choice as king. Of the three surviving sons, it was Henry who grew up to be most like his father – a clever, ruthless, determined man after his own heart. Given a few more years for him to prove himself, one could imagine Henry being a serious contender for the throne if his father did indeed wish to divide his realms. But Rufus was a rather different type. There are hints in the chronicles that Rufus made a point of behaving well in his father's company, although it is notoriously hard to get a fair view of him because of the loathing that he attracted from contemporary churchmen. But he was in his late twenties when his father died, and by that age most Norman knights had abandoned their homosexual friendships and married, or acquired mistresses and begun to produce illegitimate offspring. William the Conqueror seems never to have had any bastards of his own, but he was certainly convinced of the need to perpetuate his dynasty. Could he really have been unaware that Rufus was unlikely to marry, unlikely to produce an heir to the throne? With hindsight, we can see that his failure to marry after thirteen years as king suggests a combination of selfishness and a clear homosexual orientation that, however acceptable among his peer group, fitted ill with the expectations placed on a king. The question needs to be asked, therefore. Is it likely that William was blind to Rufus's character to this extent? Or, if he was aware of it, would he have chosen him as his heir to England?

The choice of an heir to a kingdom is not made lightly. One might expect that there would be some hint in the sources that William was considering Rufus for the role. There are certainly suggestions that Rufus was ambitious; for example, William of Malmesbury says 'his hopes gradually rose and he began to covet the succession'.[15] But the charters from the last years of the reign give no indication that Rufus might have been in any way supplanting

Robert: the order of attestations remains according to age, and Rufus is never given any title other than 'count'. Indeed, he is styled count in only three extant charters that could date from the last years of the reign, and in the last two he has no title at all.[16] For the writers of these documents, then, Rufus was not a man who was accorded particular respect beyond that due to a son of the king. Nor does William appear to have given him a prominent role during his last year in England. There are only four surviving English charters that definitely date from this time, so the evidence is extremely sparse, but Rufus witnesses only one of them.

The Canterbury monk Eadmer, who was secretary to the Archbishop of Canterbury, gives the clearest indication of just how unexpected was the choice of Rufus as heir to the throne. Eadmer kept a journal of his life at Canterbury, which sheds much light on the lives of the first two Norman archbishops, Lanfranc and Anselm. His 'History of Recent Events' is a personal view of current affairs from the perspective of the archbishop's household.

Lanfranc was more than an archbishop. He was a close personal friend, adviser and supporter of William the Conqueror. He often acted as one of a small group of men in England to whom the king addressed letters and requests for action when he himself was in Normandy. Yet Eadmer stresses that Lanfranc had no idea that the king had been ill, nor apparently did he have any inkling that Rufus might be his chosen heir. It seems that no message had been sent to Canterbury, and Lanfranc had not been prepared for the division of the empire. Eadmer's comments are all the more interesting since Rufus had been brought up in Lanfranc's household.

> But how distressed Lanfranc was at his death, who could describe, when so great was the shock that we who were with him when the news of the King's death came, were afraid that he would die on the spot from anguish of heart.
>
> So King William died and was succeeded on the throne by William his son. He, when he was intent on seizing the prize of the kingdom before his brother Robert, found Lanfranc, without whose support he could not possibly attain the throne, not altogether favourable to the fulfilment of this his desire. Accordingly, fearing that any delay in his consecration might result in the loss of the dignity which he coveted, he began, both personally and indirectly by all whom he could get to support him, to make promises to Lanfranc with plighted word and

oath, to the effect that if he were King, he would in all his dealings throughout the whole kingdom maintain justice, mercy and equity; that he would defend the peace, liberty and security of the Churches against all adversaries; and that through all and in all he would follow Lanfranc's bidding and counsel. But when he was once firmly established on the throne he turned his back on his promise . . .[17]

Rufus had the great advantage of having secured access to the royal treasury before he approached Lanfranc. The Bishop of Winchester, the guardian of the treasury, was by chance the uncle of a royal clerk named Gerard who was already known to Rufus and who became increasingly close to him later.[18] This personal link was a stroke of fortune for Rufus, and made his path to the throne smoother. Although Archbishop Lanfranc himself was immune to bribery, there were plenty of others in England whose support could be bought, and the treasury was well stocked; one chronicler, who probably obtained his information from sources at court, says there was £60,000 in silver alone.[19] (This corresponds to about twenty years' income from the greatest of the lay Anglo-Norman estates.) After two weeks, Lanfranc gave way and agreed to crown Rufus. One consideration that may have weighed with him was that the previous two coronations had been conducted by the Archbishop of York; Lanfranc was engaged in a prolonged battle to assert the supremacy of Canterbury, and with this went the duty to crown monarchs. He may well have feared that if he delayed longer, Rufus might apply to York instead. So Rufus was crowned on 26 September, with only the merest token of election, but, it was believed, with the blessing of the late king.

On the Continent, meanwhile, a messenger went to find Curthose, to tell him that his father was dead, and that Rufus had gone to England before him. Orderic Vitalis alone names the bringer of the news as Aubrey de Coucy, one-time Earl of Northumbria, and says that he was sent by King William himself. Curthose was later said to have reacted with disbelief: 'By the angels of God, if I were in Alexandria, the English would have waited for me and they would never have dared to make him king before my arrival. Even my brother William, whom you say has dared to aspire to the kingship, would never risk his head without waiting for my permission.'[20] There is also a curious little passage in Orderic Vitalis, set four years later, which has no parallel elsewhere. Orderic reports King Malcolm of Scotland greeting Rufus's envoy with the words: "'I owe you nothing, King William [Rufus] . . . but if I could see King William's eldest son, Robert, I would be ready to offer him whatever I owe,"' and, to Robert himself: "'King William required my fealty to you as his first-born son. . . ." Robert replied, "what you allege is true. But conditions have changed and my father's decrees have been undermined in many ways . . ."'[21] This may be the nearest thing that survives to an admission that Curthose had been acknowledged in Britain as his father's heir.

Cheated of the throne by Rufus's swift action, Curthose returned to Normandy and entered into his patrimony without meeting any resistance. One of his first acts was to confirm a gift his father had made on his deathbed, to St Stephen's Caen. The charter was witnessed by Henry, who had decided to remain with his brother in Normandy.[22] Then Robert carried out his father's other requests, making donations to churches and to the poor, and releasing his father's political prisoners. Chief among these was Odo, Bishop of Bayeux, who had fallen foul of his brother the Conqueror in 1082 and, after being arrested on the Isle of Wight (perhaps as he prepared to sail overseas without William's permission), had been transferred to Rouen.[23] While he had been imprisoned, Odo had been deprived of the revenue of his extensive estates in England, and his episcopal lands at Bayeux, including the nearby abbey of Saint-Vigor, which he had founded and which was plundered and disbanded by the king. A series of charters from early in the reign of Curthose concern the restoration of these plundered lands, and the re-establishment of the abbey.[24]

Another of the prisoners whom Curthose released was Ulf, son of King Harold, who had been captured in the aftermath of Hastings and taken to Normandy as a teenager. Curthose knighted him and thereafter he vanishes into obscurity. The third man whom Robert is known to have set free was Duncan, eldest son of King Malcolm of Scotland by his first wife. Duncan had been given to William as a hostage, probably at the time of the Treaty of Abernethy in 1072. Like Ulf, he was knighted, and sent on his way; at first he seems to have gone to England and later he reigned briefly as King of Scotland.[25]

Rufus, too, had made the donations required by his father.[26] He also had two of his father's prisoners brought over to England, but he chose not to release them, placing them in custody at Winchester. This action, rather out of character for one who was often fair and even generous in his treatment of his prisoners, may indicate the degree of insecurity he felt.[27] One of these men, Wulfnoth, was the last surviving brother of King Harold, and had endured a particularly unfortunate life. He had been taken to Normandy as a hostage early in Edward the Confessor's reign, as a boy of 15, but had been imprisoned and kept there ever since. He lingered on in Rufus's prisons until 1094, when in his old age he probably became a monk at Winchester. Rufus's other prisoner, Earl Morkar, had once been Earl of Northumbria, and was King Harold's brother-in-law.[28] To a newly crowned Norman king, both men had the potential, no matter how slight, to be a rallying point for opposition, and Rufus seems to have felt unable to risk setting them free, despite the spiritual perils of ignoring his father's last requests.

Rufus was right to feel insecure on his throne. Within a few weeks of his coronation, a plot was taking shape to remove him and crown Robert instead. Although the reunion of the Conqueror's lands seems to have been a major motive for the plan, there is no suggestion that anyone considered deposing the elder brother and installing Rufus as duke in his place. One of the instigators was Bishop Odo of Bayeux, who presumably was grateful to Robert for his release from prison. But, like so many of the magnates, he had large estates on both sides of the Channel, and it was easy to foresee the difficulties that would arise if he owed obedience to two different lords for them. Chief among those on the Continent who were drawn into the plot were Robert of Mortain, Bishop Geoffrey of Coutances, Robert of Bellême and Eustace, Count of Boulogne.[29] All had been close to the Conqueror, they or their families held large estates in England and they had frequently witnessed charters for the late king. They were in a good position to know his wishes regarding the succession, and may have believed that the late king's wishes had been flouted. While they had a great deal to win if their coup succeeded, they were also gambling with the future of their lands in England if Rufus triumphed. Only Eustace was a relatively free agent: he held his lands in Boulogne independently of the Anglo-Norman dynasty, and had less land in England.

Odo's first move was to cross to England and attend Rufus's Christmas court, which was held at London rather than Gloucester. It is possible that the new king wished to be close to Normandy so he could monitor what his elder brother did. Odo and the king seem to have been on good terms at this stage, and although Archbishop Lanfranc may not have been pleased to see his old rival for power in Kent, Odo took part in the ceremony for the installation of the new abbot of St Augustine's Canterbury just before Christmas.[30] At the Christmas court, Odo would have had an opportunity to canvas support among the other Anglo-Norman families. He enlisted the Montgomery family – Roger, Earl of Shrewsbury, the father of Robert of Bellême and his other sons Roger 'the Poitevin', Hugh and Arnulf, and many others, including the Clare family, William of Eû, Geoffrey of Coutances's nephew Robert Mowbray, Roger Bigot, Hugh Grandmesnil and Geoffrey de Mandeville. He also, perhaps unwisely, discussed the plans with William of St Calais, Bishop of Durham.

While Odo gathered support for the rising in England, Robert was preparing an invasion fleet. A cross-Channel invasion was a major undertaking: it had taken the Conqueror five months to assemble his fleet and a further three months waiting for a favourable wind before it could sail. A story in the contemporary records of the ducal abbey of Fécamp describes Robert enlisting the help of independent ship-masters to capture boats for him to speed up the process. A Fécamp supply ship en route from England during the winter berthed in the mouth of the Seine while the crew went to warm up in the nearby town, and in their absence one of these pirates attacked and captured it for the duke. This attempt to requisition his monks' vessels was thwarted by a miracle, but indicates that Duke Robert was from an early date intent on equipping his force with all speed.[31] At the same time, the normal round of ducal duties went on – one of the surviving charters from his reign is dated 30 March 1088 and shows him 'in the year in which the revered, glorious and beloved of God, King William, died and was taken to heaven', attesting a grant of land to the abbey of Jumièges.[32]

By early 1088 Odo was probably working actively on the plans with his younger brother Robert of Mortain, who had by now crossed to England, together with Geoffrey of Coutances and Roger Montgomery, Earl of Shrewsbury. The outline plan seems to have been for a series of more or less simultaneous uprisings: Odo in Kent combining with the Clare family who held Tonbridge; Robert of Mortain focusing his efforts on his stronghold at Pevensey, assisted by William of Eû at Hastings and Roger Montgomery at Arundel; another major Montgomery rising in their lands along the Welsh marches; Geoffrey of Coutances operating from Bristol, and other key men playing their part in the north, East Anglia and the East Midlands. In Normandy, Curthose raised funds for the campaign by granting Henry the Cotentin in exchange for part of his inheritance.[33]

But things began to go wrong for the conspirators early in spring 1088, and before long their plans were unravelling in chaos.

Rufus travelled north, and was present at what was probably an impromptu turf-cutting ceremony for the new abbey of St Mary at York. With him, according to the description by Abbot Stephen, was a party that included a good number of the conspirators: Archbishop Thomas of York, Odo of Bayeux, Geoffrey of Coutances, William of Saint-Calais, Count Alan of Brittany, Odo of Champagne, William of Warenne, Henry Beaumont 'and many others too numerous to mention'.[34] Soon afterwards, on 12 March, William of Saint-Calais was abruptly arrested and charged with treason. From evidence he later gave at his trial, it seems that he was undecided what was the best course of action to take, and in the end may have tried to save both himself and the men who he knew were conspiring against Rufus. He claimed that he had warned the king of the plot, but when ordered to accompany him to meet Odo and Roger Montgomery he fled to the safety of Durham. This allowed the conspirators time to escape, but it almost certainly meant that they were then forced to begin their rising before they were ready and, more seriously, before Duke Robert was able to come to their assistance.

At first Rufus would have had only the haziest idea who was in the plot, but when men failed to attend the Easter court in mid-April he would have known what he was up against. He then began a vigorous campaign of propaganda and persuasion, using his considerable skills to charm people onto his side. One of his greatest successes was to detach Roger Montgomery from the ranks of his enemies, although most of Montgomery's sons continued to back Robert. While the duke now depended on assembling and transporting an army across the Channel as quickly as he could, and relied on the haphazard supply of information trickling back across the water from England, Rufus had at his disposal not only the Normans who remained loyal, together with their households, but also the traditional English military levy system, the *fyrd*, and the locally raised forces for which every district, abbey and manor was obliged to provide a particular number of soldiers.

Rufus may have had another weapon available, which has hitherto gone unnoticed. In the precarious atmosphere of suspicion, insecurity and autocratic power that was Norman England, one of the key tools used by the monarchy to retain control was propaganda. This took the form both of awe-inspiring events such as the crown-wearing ceremonies, accompanied by public demonstrations of the administration of justice, and also of more covert operations. An example of the latter is the systematic airbrushing of King Harold's reign from official records. Early Norman accounts of the Conquest describe him as king, as do William the Conqueror's first charters. The last time he is given the royal title is in a charter dated to May 1068, and thereafter he is 'count Harold', or simply 'Harold'. Domesday Book generally describes the handover of land from 'the time of King Edward' directly to the reign of King William, as if Harold had never existed.[35]

In rather the same way, the Normans were masters of the production of political pamphlets to present a particular version of events. Often these involved an entirely fictitious history in order to support the particular claim that was being made. Royal and papal deathbeds were a particularly rich environment for the production of what has been termed 'pious forgery': the production of written materials that give a version of events that facilitate subsequent decisions (particularly concerning the survival of the late ruler's legacy) that were considered to be desirable and divinely ordained. The easy modern distinction between truth and fabrication cannot be readily transferred to the medieval mindset, because of the powerful influence of the concept of the divine will. If a king had been anointed and crowned, then that must have been destined to happen and thus the production of written material that supported his coronation was for the good.

It is in this context that we can now look again at the mysterious document entitled *de obitu Willelmi* (concerning the death of William), which was described in Chapter 1.

It is almost certain that this document dates in its original form to before 1100, since Henry, who became king in that year, is not mentioned in it, even though there is a place for him in the model used for the writing. It is also likely to have been written before 1093, since we know from Eadmer's description of the last days of William the Conqueror that Anselm (who was made Archbishop of Canterbury in 1093) tried to spend time with the dying king but was forced to withdraw from Rouen because of an illness of his own. If the author of the *de obitu Willelmi* had known that someone as important as the Archbishop of Canterbury had been in the neighbourhood but seldom actually present, and so conveniently unable to refute the contents, it would have added greatly to the stature of the document to have included his name. The *de obitu Willelmi* reads as if it is a piece of propaganda against

Robert Curthose, taking the accession of Rufus to England almost for granted and suggesting that not only was Robert unsuited to being a king, but that he was not even worthy of being Duke of Normandy, and was allowed to succeed to that office only because he had already been promised it in a public ceremony.

The most obvious occasion on which such a piece of propaganda would have been of value to Rufus is during the critical months before the 1088 rebellion broke out, when he was aware that there was treason in the air and needed to do everything he could to swing influential men round into his camp. And there was a man to hand who could supervise its creation: Ranulf Flambard, a capable, quick-witted court clerk of humble origins who had assisted Maurice the chancellor and remained conspicuously close to Rufus once he was secure on his throne.

There is an anomalous reference in Orderic Vitalis's account of the death of William the Conqueror to a letter that William caused to be written, sealed and given to Rufus to take to Lanfranc in England. No other strand of evidence mentions this letter; there is no mention of it in Eadmer nor is the letter itself preserved at Canterbury. It may be that Orderic is referring to some sort of a 'letter' that someone told him they had seen, but a written order for the succession was otherwise unheard of, and if it had existed it would surely have attracted the notice of the other chroniclers. But the *de obitu Willelmi* is only 654 words long – just the right sort of length to be confused with a letter. Also, it survives only in England, which is where Rufus would have needed to use his propaganda in 1088.

That letters and seals were forged and used for personal advantage at this time there is no doubt. Lanfranc himself was deceived on one occasion when a monk came to him from Normandy with a letter purporting to be from the Archbishop of Rouen. After the ploy had been uncovered, he wrote in distress: 'I assure you categorically that he brought a letter sealed with your seal, which I know well; in that letter (if it was genuine) you urged me to receive him honourably . . . all this I have done out of affection for you . . . I am greatly astonished if the letter he presented was a forgery – how could he have got hold of such a great man's seal to make his tale look true?'[36]

Supposing then that the *de obitu Willelmi* is a piece of propaganda deliberately created in order to influence the magnates in England as the 1088 rising threatened. How could it have been used? It would not have been of any use to impress such an educated man as Lanfranc, who would probably have recognised some if not all the quotations in it. But skilfully used, shown to groups of illiterate magnates, with its royal seal conspicuously displayed, or read from by a royal clerk, it could have been immensely influential.

There are even two possible candidates for the forgers, namely Gerard and John, two men whose names are inserted in the *de obitu Willelmi* alongside the courtiers who have a place in the models used. Gerard was a royal clerk and the nephew of the Bishop of Winchester; he was chancellor at the end of the reign of William the Conqueror, and continued in the post briefly for Rufus before he was replaced by Robert Bloet and became instead one of Rufus's most trusted court officials. As chancellor, Gerard would have had particular responsibility for the royal seal matrix, a double-sided object of precious metal about 6cm across, with which seals were made and attached to documents with a strip of parchment. He would also have been charged with its destruction at the end of the reign or its burial with the old king, and its replacement with the new king's matrix. Who better to seal a document with the old royal seal, or to use the new one (which was very similar) in such a way that it was indistinguishable?[37]

The other man who may have been involved in the production of the *de obitu Willelmi* is someone so obscure that he occurs in no charters of William the Conqueror, nor in any from the first months of Rufus's reign, nor does he hold any land in the Domesday survey. This man was John of Tours, a doctor who, as his contemporaries never tired of reminding their hearers, practised as a *medicus* although he had never trained as one. He emerged from total obscurity to being consecrated Bishop of Wells in July 1088, before the embers of the rising were even fully extinguished. John was well educated, later doing much to establish his diocese of Bath and Wells as a centre of learning. He was just such a man as might know of the contents of the two ninth-century *Lives* of the Emperors Charlemagne and Louis and be able to supervise the composition of the *de obitu Willelmi* using them as conveniently prophetic templates. This would also explain another curious feature of the *de obitu Willelmi* – namely, that the closest text of the *Life* of Louis to that used for the *de obitu Willelmi* originated near Chartres, but yet the *de obitu* survives only in England. This fits with the *de obitu Willelmi* being composed on the Continent, perhaps in southern Normandy or northern France, and then being taken to England. Allowing for a short interval between the nomination by Rufus and the consecration, John's sudden appointment to Wells could be construed as a reward for performing some service to Rufus in the winter or spring of 1087–8. This is precisely the time when the *de obitu* would have been commissioned if Rufus was already suspicious and was gathering evidence about the plot in the weeks before the Bishop of Durham's arrest in March.

The only firm evidence that ties John to the *de obitu Willelmi* is the presence of his name in it. But there are some other pointers. There is an early history of the bishopric of Wells, known as the *Historiola*, which describes him by 1090: 'having been employed by the king in many and great affairs, and having in consequence grown into familiarity with him, he begged of the king for himself the city of Bath . . .'. This grant was confirmed by Rufus in 1091.[38] Also, there is his meteoric rise from complete obscurity to the episcopacy, only nine months after Rufus had succeeded to the throne. Rufus made only one other prompt appointment, and this was of a man who had been a royal chaplain under the Conqueror. His normal practice was to leave bishoprics vacant for two years or more – in the case of Canterbury for four years – while he creamed off their revenues to add to his own income.

By propaganda, threats, bribes and appeals to their loyalty, Rufus convinced many of the magnates based in England that it would be unwise to support the rebels. The means that he employed to detach Roger Montgomery from the rising and abandon his sons can only be guessed at, but it had important strategic as well as psychological importance, for Roger's castle at Arundel was virtually impregnable and guarded the west of Sussex. Another factor in Rufus's favour was that most of the sheriffs held firm, which meant that he was able to keep control of the administration system. This was especially crucial in Kent, where the sheriff, Haimo, kept a low profile, but did not declare for the rebels. It may be that Haimo was wavering, and it was this that persuaded Rufus to bestow his mother's lands in England (which had been promised to Henry) on his son Robert fitzHaimo. By so doing, Rufus won a loyal adherent, who remained faithful for the rest of his life.

The Anglo-Saxon Chronicle says that most of the Normans rose for Robert Curthose, but 'the Englishmen came to the help of their liege lord'. This is rather a misleading expression, and certainly need not imply that the English people had already taken Rufus to their hearts. There was a long tradition of local defence in England, and even after the Norman Conquest the English levies fought both locally and further afield: the men of Bristol organised themselves to repel Harold's sons in 1068, while English troops had fought for William the Conqueror at Exeter in 1068 and against Curthose at Gerberoi in 1079, and for Lanfranc against the rebel earls in 1075. It is not surprising, then, that in the crisis of 1088 Bishop Wulfstan of Worcester was able to raise an army to fight against Curthose's supporters who were threatening his cathedral city.

The accounts of what happened over the next few months are patchy, sometimes highly colourful, and seldom compatible with each other.[39] Written from the different perspectives of Canterbury, Durham, Peterborough, Worcester, Normandy, Shrewsbury and the West Country, they tell a tale of confusion and dislocation.

Duke Robert was able to respond to the premature start of the rising, once the news had reached him, by sending a fleet over to England, with the sons of Roger of Montgomery, Eustace of Boulogne and a large force of Flemish mercenaries, but he must have feared leaving his back exposed in Normandy and risking aggression from his continental neighbours. Instead, he concentrated on gathering further reinforcements, which he was obliged to send off in an unsatisfactory piecemeal way. His next fleet, which seems to have sailed in the early summer, perhaps late May or early June, was intercepted by a fleet operating on behalf of Rufus and was cut to pieces with heavy losses.

In England, the separate risings had failed to ignite and unite. There were outbreaks of unrest in many places, as planned, but only in the west and in Kent and Sussex were the effects sustained. In the Welsh marches, the Montgomerys and their supporters raised a large army in Herefordshire, Shropshire and their Welsh lands, took Hereford and Gloucester and marched on Worcester, where they were unexpectedly turned back by the heroic intervention of the aged Bishop Wulfstan. Further south, Geoffrey of Coutances and his nephew Robert Mowbray moved in force from Bristol, burnt Bath and Berkley and tried but failed to capture Ilchester. In the south-east, meanwhile, Odo was raiding from Rochester, Gilbert of Clare held Tonbridge and Robert of Mortain and the other rebel leaders held their castles in Sussex. Moving swiftly against this group of rebels first, Rufus forced the inexperienced young Gilbert Clare to surrender Tonbridge in just two days at the end of April, then moved on Rochester. But hearing that Odo had taken part of his army down to link up with his brother Robert of Mortain at Pevensey, Rufus turned south and invested that stronghold instead. After a siege of about six weeks, Pevensey surrendered in early June, having waited in vain for the supplies and troops that had been sent by Duke Robert on his ill-fated fleet.

Rufus now began mopping up operations, as the uncoordinated risings across the country lost touch with each other. He made a sort of peace with Robert of Mortain, and took Odo and his other prisoners back to Rochester, with the intention of forcing them to negotiate a surrender. But then the tables turned abruptly: as they approached Rochester, the garrison burst out, either as part of a premeditated plan or in a spontaneous act of foolhardy bravery, and captured the prisoners who were being led forward to begin the negotiations. Rufus now found himself forced to begin a second siege, but this time many of his enemies were bottled up in one place, the weather was getting hotter, and their supplies were running low.

For many days, the defenders of Rochester waited for a relieving fleet from Normandy, and must have expected that Duke Robert himself would come to their rescue, since they had risked so much for him. But he never came. For this he has often been blamed. It is true that, with him present in England to coordinate the campaign and act as its figurehead, the outcome might have been very different. But only one of the fleets he sent across the Channel reached its destination, and William of Malmesbury suggests that another was wrecked while on its way to relieve Rochester itself. The sources do not say how long the siege lasted, but Orderic says it was over in 'early summer' – perhaps in July.[40] If this were so, it would be a terrible irony, for a series of Norman charters make it clear that Robert was not only very serious about his plans to cross to England and fight his brother for the throne, but that, just as Rochester fell, he was on the point of departing. First, he made a grant of land to Fécamp (witnessed by Henry) on 7 July 1088 and a second one a short time later, rather as his father had made donations to Avranches, La Trinité Caen and Marmoutiers in 1066; in his father's case the last gift included the specific note that it was made 'as he prepared to cross the Channel'. The following year, long after the rising was over, Robert confirmed his grant while on a visit to Fécamp, noting that this occasion was the anniversary of the day on which he should have crossed to England. It seems, therefore, that Robert's plans to cross to England were well advanced by

7 July, and that his donations to Fécamp were closely associated in his mind with his proposed invasion, which would have taken place shortly thereafter. Far from letting his supporters down, he was still trying to come in support of them, perhaps ready for departure and waiting in vain for a favourable wind, as his father had waited so long in 1066, even as the rising drew to its inglorious end.[41]

But, whereas the wind did change in time for his father in 1066, Curthose failed to reach Rochester, and failed even to cross the Channel. At length, the city's defenders gave up hope and negotiated a surrender with Rufus. Their lives were spared, but many were forced out of England and deprived of their English lands. Bishop Odo was never allowed to return. A rising that had promised so much ended with a whimper so feeble that most of the English chroniclers fail even to describe its conclusion. Only Orderic Vitalis has a vivid story with which to end his description of the humiliation of Robert's supporters: they emerged to the sound of the royal trumpets proclaiming their defeat, and the shouts of the English soldiers in the royal army loudly demanding nooses so that Odo and his men could be hung.[42]

Chapter 4

KING RUFUS, DUKE ROBERT

The failure of the 1088 rising was a major setback for Curthose. In England, however, Rufus's stock was high. He had achieved a remarkable transformation in less than a year, from a landless younger son of a fit and healthy king, to the crowned ruler of one of the richest kingdoms of Europe. In the process he had successfully leapfrogged his elder brother's claims and put down a major rebellion. He had emerged from the shadows and taken his place on the world stage.

Rufus was a canny operator. He was intelligent, and could be charming, vivacious, gregarious and generous to his friends. He knew the value of money and land and their enormous power to sway loyalties, and he now had an abundance of both. At the same time, he was not a particularly attractive man, and his contemporaries dwell on his pot belly, his pale bright eyes and red complexion, his tendency to stammer and splutter incoherently when roused to anger, his increasing arrogance as his reign progressed, and above all his dandyism, his preference for effete, provocative clothes and pointed shoes, and his long lank yellowish hair, which he took to wearing parted in the middle, in a deliberate affront to his clergy, for whom long hair and exposed foreheads were signs of immorality.[1]

As soon as Rochester had surrendered, Rufus set about establishing himself more securely in England. He allowed the Norman vassals, such as Philip and Arnulf Montgomery, to leave unharmed; they were guilty of no crime in England, and at present they were no concern of his. Count Eustace of Boulogne, too, he permitted to depart, although he had lands in England, but the price was the forfeiture of what English estates he did possess: they

remained in the king's hands until the end of the reign.[2] Rufus's approach to
those who were guilty of treason because they were English vassals indicates
the confidence he now felt. He held a large court in the south of England
during the summer, and many of the erstwhile rebels attended it, made
their peace and witnessed some of its charters. Among these were Geoffrey
of Coutances, Robert Mowbray, Gilbert Clare and Roger Montgomery and
his son Hugh. Rufus also accepted the presence of his brother Henry at
this court: after witnessing Curthose's charter in Normandy in early July,
Henry crossed to England, perhaps as soon as he heard that Rochester had
fallen, and witnessed a charter for Rufus, in which he was styled simply 'the
king's brother'. He may have hoped to be granted his mother's extensive
English estates, as he had been promised, but if so he was disappointed,
since his inheritance had already been given to Robert fitzHaimo. Two other
charters demonstrate Rufus's skill at using his resources: St Andrew's church
at Rochester had been damaged in the siege, and the king granted it two
manors and a daughter church to pay for the repairs. But Domesday Book
reveals that these already belonged to St Andrew's, and the king was merely
confirming the status quo while making a generous public gesture. As the
editor of the charters comments: 'This grant of Rufus to Rochester was
therefore inexpensive.'[3]

The new king's treatment of his two uncles is also revealing. Robert of
Mortain, who had made a provisional surrender at Pevensey, quietly returned
to Normandy. Although notionally restored to favour in England, he took
little further part in public affairs, and died four years later. He left an only
son who was a minor, creating a power vacuum that was to have serious
consequences for Curthose. In England, meanwhile, his extensive lands and
their vast revenues, including almost the whole of Devon and Cornwall,
passed into Rufus's hands until the child came of age.[4] Bishop Odo of Bayeux,
one of the chief players in the rising, was treated much more brusquely. He
was deprived of his English estates, including the rich earldom of Kent, which
he had so recently won back, and was banished. Like his brother Robert, he
retreated to his Norman lands, but unlike him he continued to play an active
part in the duchy.

This left William of Saint-Calais, the Bishop of Durham. Rufus sent three
barons up to Durham: two whom he trusted, his uncle by marriage Count
Odo of Champagne and Count Alan of Richmond, together with one of the

Montgomery brothers, Roger 'the Poitevin', who had switched sides partway through the rising. Their orders were to capture the bishop, and bring him south to stand trial, but he managed to persuade them to arrange a safe conduct, and he was escorted to Salisbury, where he was tried by the royal court on 2 November. The charge was laid by Henry Beaumont, who claimed to have been present when Bishop William was first arrested; he was rewarded by Rufus with the earldom of Warwick. Two vivid accounts of the trial survive, both probably derived from eyewitnesses. They reveal the bishop as a skilful and persuasive debater, who had carefully prepared his case, desperately manœuvring around the minefields of secular and ecclesiastical law. In the end, after a long day haggling, everyone seemed agreed on one thing only, that the bishop should leave the kingdom as swiftly as possible. He wished to plead his case in Rome, Rufus wanted the Durham estates and to be rid of a traitor, and the barons on both sides of the rising had heard enough. Messengers were sent north, and on 14 November Durham castle was handed over to the king. Then Bishop William was put on a ship at Southampton, bound for Normandy. He was so well received by Curthose that he abandoned his appeal to Rome, and instead remained in Normandy, where his remarkable administrative and legal gifts were soon put to use in the ducal court, which thereby gained one good thing from the failures of 1088.[5]

The Montgomery family were awkwardly placed after the rising. Earl Roger and his second son, Hugh, had at some point switched their allegiance from Duke Robert to the king. Philip and Arnulf, with few if any expectations in England, had supported Curthose and had now returned to the Continent. Their middle brother, Roger (who had been granted a large holding in England by the Conqueror but had forfeited it shortly before Domesday, when he was still in his early twenties), had also been drawn into Rufus's camp and been sent on the mission to bring Bishop William south from Durham. Rufus rewarded him for his new fealty, not with a restoration of his original estates, but with lands roughly corresponding to modern Lancashire, controlling the western route to the Scottish borders.[6] Earl Roger's eldest son, Robert of Bellême, a favourite of the Conqueror, who had already inherited the great family estates straddling the south-western border of Normandy, was for the time being in England, but his loyalties had hitherto been with his duke.[7]

Late in the summer of 1088, Robert of Bellême returned to Normandy, sharing a ship with the young Prince Henry. Rufus had been very unwilling to let Bishop William travel with more than one ship, since ships were a precious commodity, and increasing their availability in the duchy was no part of his plans. This may explain why Henry and Robert travelled together, but they paid the penalty when they reached port. Curthose had been warned of their arrival, and, believing perhaps that they had made a pact with the king, and suspecting their loyalty, he had them arrested, and imprisoned Robert at Odo's castle of Neuilly-l'Evêque, Henry either at Rouen or at Bayeux.[8] Henry's actions had certainly been suspicious enough. He had remained in Normandy until it was clear that the rising had failed, and then immediately gone to England and presented himself at court, where he had been accepted, only to return some months later. While his brother was imprisoned, Curthose rescinded his grant of the Cotentin, and took direct control of it again himself, following accepted practice when dealing with unreliable relations. His father had similarly removed a cousin from Mortain before granting it to his half-brother Robert.[9] Henry's subsequent activities, even if motivated partly by a desire for revenge, suggest that Curthose's instinct was correct.

*   *   *   *   *

A cameo of Robert Curthose's reign, penned by the monk Orderic Vitalis, has become part of the established myth of his life and abilities: 'Duke Robert was weak and ineffectual. The whole province was in disorder; troops of bandits were at large in the villages and all over the countryside, and robber bands pillaged the weak mercilessly. Duke Robert made no attempt to bring the malefactors to justice, and for eight years under the weak duke scoundrels were free to treat the innocent with the utmost brutality.'[10]

There are several problems with this. While it is a fairly accurate picture of life in many places and times in the eleventh century, including Normandy during part of his father's rule, it does not fit uniquely with the evidence that can be gleaned about Robert from other sources. He was, however, faced with particularly trying challenges during his reign as duke, which restricted his capacity for proactive government.

Even Orderic admits that after the failure of the 1088 rising this 'weak and ineffectual duke' made a triumphal entry into Maine and received the homage of his subjects there. He was welcomed everywhere but the castle of

Ballon, just north of Le Mans, and this he forced to surrender. Bishop Hoel of Le Mans made him especially welcome. While Curthose was occupied in Maine, Earl Roger Montgomery crossed to Normandy, incensed that his eldest son had been imprisoned. In a demonstration of his overlordship, Duke Robert appeared before the Bellême castle of Saint-Céneri, near the Maine border, which defiantly refused to acknowledge him. When the garrison was eventually forced by hunger to surrender, Robert issued a warning to the Montgomery clan and to others who might consider opposing his authority: he personally ordered the castellan of Saint-Céneri to be blinded on the spot. The message would not have been lost on the family. Forty years earlier, Robert of Bellême's grandfather William Talvas had blinded, castrated and mutilated William fitzGiroie of Saint-Céneri, and the castle and its lands had been added to the Bellême lordship. This action was particularly memorable, since fitzGiroie was at the time William Talvas's guest at his wedding feast. After making an example of the castellan, Robert called a hearing of the ducal court, which passed sentence of mutilation on several other members of the garrison. These acts, while barbaric to modern sensibilities, reveal a duke who was by no means ineffectual, nor yet unusually brutal. He was beginning his reign as any man might – with decisive action and a show of his legitimate strength.

To limit Montgomery power still further, Curthose handed Saint-Céneri over to Robert Giroie, nephew of the mutilated William fitzGiroie, while leaving the other Bellême lands untouched.[11] Even this was a calculated risk, endangering the long-term allegiance of Robert of Bellême, who had considerable landholdings outside the borders of Normandy (and therefore other overlords) and was pivotal in the security of the Maine border. But it was a risk that Curthose had to take, if his vassal's power was to be kept in check. In the event, the fate of the castellan of Saint-Céneri had the desired effect. Earl Roger Montgomery asked for and obtained the release of his son from prison in the spring of 1089, and the Bellême seldom troubled Robert again.

Maine had for years been an unstable region. William the Conqueror had captured the county when Anjou was distracted by civil wars and when the internal politics of Maine were in confusion. The Norman Montgomerys had acquired lands there when Earl Roger married Mabel Talvas, the heiress of Bellême, and the Conqueror had depended on them to control the border region. Even so, he had to mount repeated campaigns in the area, and he had never held Maine securely. Curthose had similar problems. By the late 1080s, Maine was playing off its aggressive larger neighbours against each other. Orderic Vitalis sets out to tell a disreputable story about Curthose and Count Fulk Le Rechin, his overlord for Maine, but in the process reveals more about the fate of aristocratic women than about the character of the duke. When Robert appealed for help in quelling a Manceaux revolt in 1089, Fulk agreed on condition that Robert would procure for him Bertrada de Montfort, the ward of William of Evreux:

'My lord duke [said William], you ask something that is repugnant to me . . . you wish me to give my niece . . . a young virgin, in marriage to a man who has already been twice married . . . you wish to use my niece as a pawn . . . I will not grant your request unless you restore to me Barent and Noyon . . . [and all] our hereditary right.' . . . The outcome was that he granted the requests . . . and handed over the strongholds . . . and afterwards the count of Anjou jubilantly received the girl he desired, and married her as his third wife though the two former wives were still living.[12]

In fact, Orderic underestimates Fulk here, for, in addition to the two wives he had repudiated, he had outlived one if not two others.

In exchange for his new wife, Fulk kept the restive Manceaux in check for a year. In 1090, however, a scion of the comital house named Hélias of La Flèche claimed Maine and, realising that the popular Bishop Hoel was an important bastion of support for Curthose, had him imprisoned. The citizens of Le Mans reacted with rioting and widespread public disorder, until Hélias was forced to release the bishop. It was unfortunate that, just at this time, when a further show of strength was needed in Maine to reassert Norman power, Curthose's attention was diverted by a more immediate threat at the opposite end of his dominions.

William Rufus had not forgotten his brother's attempt to seize the English throne, and was determined to turn the tables and attack Normandy. Rufus had two great advantages over his elder brother. He had the seemingly limitless resources of English money and men at his command, being prepared to extort taxes and church revenues far beyond anything his father had attempted, and he was unscrupulous about breaking his word when the occasion demanded.

Annual English royal revenues from the crown lands at Domesday, the year before Rufus became king, were about £14,000.[13] In addition to this, the king could expect income from a range of other legitimate sources, one of the most regular of which was the *murdum*, a special fine introduced at the Conquest and imposed on local courts in whose territory unidentified corpses were found that were not demonstrably English (and might therefore be Normans killed by Englishmen). The original sum fixed for this was about £40. Another source of revenue was the *geld*. Originally a means to buy off Viking attacks, by the end of the Conqueror's reign it had become a regular tax. It was levied on a land assessment, and at the usual rate of one shilling a *hide* it yielded an income of about £2,000.[14] Then there were the sums of money known as *fines* paid to the royal treasury – for example, when land changed hands. These could be varied according to the ability of the client to pay: thus Rufus fined Robert of Bellême the enormous sum of £3,000 to succeed to the earldom of Shrewsbury on the death of his brother Hugh in 1098.[15] More usual sums are revealed in the earliest surviving royal accounts, for 1130; these show, for example, Robert de Vere being fined £350 on his marriage, and the great heiress and widow Lucy Bollingbroke paying 500 marks (£333 6s 8d) to be allowed to remain single for five years.[16] Doubtless, similar sums were frequently paid to Rufus, who had 'given' Lucy her first three husbands. Lastly, Rufus could expect a significant income from the incidental payments that kept the machinery of justice lubricated. The 1130 royal accounts show regular payments of 10 marks for almost any legal process in which people became involved, and substantially more if they wished to prove their innocence by oath rather than the still-common 'ordeal' (the accused grasped a red-hot iron, and if they survived they were innocent, but if they died of their burns then God had judged them guilty).

In addition to these established, if resented, revenues, Rufus and his financial genius Ranulf Flambard became adept at devising new ways to increase royal incomes. For this, they had the detailed information contained in Domesday Book as a guide. As sees and abbacies became vacant, beginning with Chichester and Canterbury in 1089, they delayed making appointments and channelled the revenues into the treasury, leaving a modest allowance for the upkeep of the establishment. Canterbury was the most lucrative source, remaining vacant for four and a half years and with a Domesday value of £1,500 per annum.[17] After the Abbot of Ely died in 1093, Rufus kept the vacancy until the end of his reign. It has been estimated that about half the wealthy abbeys of England were without an abbot at any one time, and Rufus's annual income was increased by £2,500 from ecclesiastical sources.[18] Another occasional windfall came from appointing bishops who were prepared to pay for their job; the otherwise worthy Herbert Losinga fell into this trap in 1091, and paid Rufus 1,000 marks for the diocese of Thetford for himself and the abbey of New Minster Winchester for his father. Last but by no means least, the new king became adroit at encouraging donations or *aids* for his ventures. Even Archbishop Anselm reluctantly offered Rufus £500 on one occasion, writing sadly to a colleague: 'our king, intending to go to Normandy, required a great deal of money . . . He rejected it as too little, so that I would give him more, but I refused . . . From that moment on he seemed to seek occasions to oppose me . . . He seemed to me to want money . . . [and] he was so angry that he said things he ought not to have said.'[19]

The Duke of Normandy, by contrast, had only a modest demesne and a relatively poorly developed fiscal system at his disposal. William the Conqueror had kept the two administrations separate, with different customs, mints and currency, but he had used England to enrich Normandy, and, when necessary, he had extracted large sums of money from the kingdom that could not be obtained in Normandy. William of Malmesbury vividly describes the two realms as conjoined twins, with the duchy supported by the taxes imposed on England.[20] Whereas the Anglo-Saxon Chronicle and Eadmer are full of complaints about unjust taxes and aids levied by Rufus, the Norman sources are strangely silent, suggesting perhaps that Normandy lacked the means to raise large additional revenues, no matter how great the need.

Rufus began his campaign against Robert by sending large quantities of treasure into the duchy. He bribed the garrison of Saint-Valery at the mouth of the River Somme, giving him a secure port, and then bought over several barons in its hinterland, including his first cousin Stephen of Aumâle and Gerard of Gournay. Most of these men, of course, also owed Rufus allegiance for their English lands. By a mixture of bribery and raiding, the forces adhering to the English king briefly held most of Normandy north and east of the Seine. Hélias of Saint-Saëns led those who held firm for Duke Robert: he had recently been married to the duke's illegitimate daughter, and Curthose had entrusted Hélias with the castles of Arques and Bures. This was to prove a wise choice; Hélias remained staunchly loyal to his duke through many twists and turns of their fortunes over the next decades.[21]

Curthose moved up to counter this new threat. He witnessed a charter for Bayeux at Vernon on the Seine on 24 April 1089, noting that he was then on his way into France. The other witnesses included several men who were normally based in the Cotentin, including the lord of Vernon himself. Three other charters relating to Cotentin lands help to confirm that Henry's temporary apanage there had been repossessed while he was imprisoned. Curthose called upon his overlord King Philip to come to his aid, and together they recaptured Eû: a charter records that it was witnessed by Duke Robert on the day of the victory.[22] After this success, they advanced against a castle of Gerard of Gournay, close to the French Vexin, but then King Philip suddenly returned to France, won over, the Anglo-Saxon chronicler believed, by English silver,[23] and perhaps also less enthusiastic about Curthose regaining control of castles so close to a disputed border with France.

For now, there was stalemate. But, in the following year, Rufus renewed his campaign by sending money to a group of Rouen merchants, who already had strong wine-trading links with London. A plot was hatched to open the city gates on 3 November to a group of Rufus's adherents. The leader of the rebel faction was a young man named Conan, the son of the richest burgher of Rouen. The loyal burghers, hearing of the plot, informed Duke Robert, who sent out urgent pleas for assistance to those barons who could muster armed contingents near Rouen most rapidly: Robert of Bellême, William of Evreux, William of Breteuil, Gilbert of L'Aigle. Even his brother Henry, who had by now been released from the ducal prisons and was already at Rouen, became involved.

According to Orderic, Rufus's troops were led by Reginald of Warenne, the younger brother of William II Warenne who had played a leading part in defeating the 1088 rising in England. As they descended on Rouen from their stronghold at Gournay and reached the west gate, Gilbert of L'Aigle arrived in the vanguard of the relieving forces, galloped over the Seine bridge and entered the city through the south gate. There he combined with Curthose and Henry, and together they attacked the armed rebels in the streets. In the confusion, someone urged Curthose to leave the fighting, lest he was injured or killed, and he is said to have taken their advice and withdrawn to a nearby church. It is not known who made this suggestion, or why, nor if the incident did indeed occur. But discretion could be a greater virtue than impetuous valour, and Curthose's response need not have been through cowardice (an accusation that has been levelled at him). He was, on the contrary, a man known for his personal bravery.

Before long, the revolt was over. Rufus's supporters fled and hid in the surrounding woods until dusk before making their way back to Gournay. Conan was captured alive, and handed over to Henry, who, according to Orderic's colourful account, was boiling with indignation. He took his prisoner up to the top of the stone tower and forced him to look at the city and its surroundings: the beautiful river, the woods, meadows and white cliffs, all that the rebels had planned to take from their duke. Then, ignoring his frantic pleas for mercy and the offer of a huge ransom, or, as a last desperate bid for time, his request to make his confession before he died, Henry seized Conan, thrust him out of the window and hurled him to his death on the pavement far below. Orderic notes with satisfaction that, even as he wrote, the spot was still called 'Conan's Leap.'

Henry's motives throughout the day were undoubtedly mixed. Anger with Rufus for denying him his mother's lands must have combined with the hope of recovering his position in the Cotentin by pleasing Curthose. Perhaps it was he who encouraged Curthose to withdraw, leaving the glory for himself alone. Above all, his reaction was perhaps about class and social stability. The 1088 rising in England had been fought between members of the aristocracy, many of them related to the ducal family, but in 1090 the Rouen riot was just that: the burghers threatening the civil order and challenging the lordship of the duke. Orderic particularly comments that Conan improperly kept household knights, and the fact that he and his fellow-conspirators were fabulously wealthy compared to some of the lesser barons would only have fuelled the sense of outrage. In acting as he did, Henry asserted the dominance of the ruling class over the increasingly influential merchants.[24]

We are told that Curthose was at first minded to be lenient with the other rebels; clemency had after all worked on the Montgomerys after the salutary treatment of the Saint-Céneri garrison. But he was won round by the demands of his vassals who had quelled the riot, and allowed them to take prisoners for ransom. Robert of Bellême and William of Breteuil are particularly named in this context, keeping their prisoners for long periods until adequate payments were made by the Rouen citizens for their release. In this way, the duke rewarded the men who had come to his rescue.

Having failed to take control of Rouen, Rufus next tried to use more financial leverage to foment trouble south of the Seine. The half-brothers Count William of Evreux and Ralph of Conches, both of whom had fought at Hastings and were now well on in years, had a disagreement: Orderic says it began with their wives quarrelling, which has always been an easy explanation for irrational behaviour among men.[25] Count William summoned his nephews William of Breteuil and Richard of Montfort, and attacked Conches. Ralph appealed to the duke for help, but Curthose was not drawn in. This even-handedness proved to be a mistake, for Ralph then contacted the northern barons who were associated with Rufus, and Stephen of Aumâle and Gerard of Gournay swiftly came to his aid. In the fighting, William of Breteuil was captured and had to pay the enormous ransom of 3,000 Norman pounds to his uncle Ralph for his liberty, and also agreed to forfeit his inheritance to Ralph's older son.

Robert of Bellême meanwhile launched a new attack on his hereditary enemies the Giroie-Grandmesnil family, and at about the same time Rufus decided to become involved in person: in late January 1091 a charter records him waiting at Dover to cross to Normandy. According to the Anglo-Saxon Chronicle, he sailed on 2 February, and set up his headquarters at Eû. When news reached Curthose that the king had landed in his territory, he again appealed to King Philip, who brought the royal army to his defence. But again Rufus's treasure was irresistible for the French king, who was now approaching 40 and already growing indolent.

With Rufus and his money proving a magnet for the Norman barons, Curthose chose to negotiate a truce. For Rufus, this must have seemed an opportune time to consolidate his gains without further expenditure of money. There is also a suggestion that the military campaign may not have gone as well as he had hoped. The brothers met somewhere near Rouen, and the conditions of a formal treaty were hammered out under the guidance of Bishop William of Saint-Calais, and witnessed solemnly by twelve magnates for the king, and twelve for the duke. The text of the treaty does not survive, but it can be reconstructed from several near-contemporary descriptions.[26] Robert agreed to cede to Rufus the castles of Aumale, Gournay and Conches, the port of Eû, Fécamp and Mont-Saint-Michel abbeys, and Cherbourg. Thus he accepted the status quo in the north, with the new border of Normandy broadly corresponding to the River Seine, and also gave Rufus a toehold in the Cotentin, in the area previously granted to Henry.

But Robert, too, made significant gains. By granting Rufus land in the Cotentin, including Mont-Saint-Michel, he had gained a potential ally against Henry. He had also been promised a cessation of hostilities and of further incursions south of the Seine. A clause of the treaty stipulated, moreover, that he was now heir to the English throne, while Rufus would inherit Normandy only if Robert died without a legitimate heir. This assumption that Rufus would not produce an heir is an interesting admission, and meant that the objective of the 1088 rising had been achieved in principal, although only in the longer term. It was also an acknowledgement that both brothers saw the reunification of the Anglo-Norman realms as a desirable goal. The drawback for Robert was that his two illegitimate sons, William and Richard, were specifically excluded from the Norman succession.

A further clause, implied in one account, may have stipulated that Curthose was to be given lands in England in compensation for the lands Rufus had acquired in Normandy, but if so he was to be disappointed. There was also a clause stating that the rebels of 1088 were to have their lands restored to them. Neither Bishop Odo nor Count Eustace benefited from this provision, but the other big loser from the 1088 rising, William of Saint-Calais, was soon afterwards restored to the bishopric of Durham. The final and in many ways the most important part of the treaty from Robert's point of view was a promise of mutual assistance in recovering the lands their father had ruled, always excepting those they had exchanged. For Rufus this might mean help against the Welsh and the Scots. For Robert it meant immediate help restoring Maine to obedience.

The brothers, acting in concert, assembled their armies and moved west. But rather than heading for Maine, they first turned their attention to the Cotentin, to which Henry had returned. The new treaty had cut Henry out of the succession, and specifically deprived him of Cherbourg and Mont-Saint-Michel, at either end of the lands he had briefly held three years before. Now his elder brothers were intent on removing him entirely, and for a time their interests coincided, for neither of them wished to partition their domains among multiple claimants. As they advanced, Henry retreated before them, and took refuge in the island abbey of Mont-Saint-Michel. During the remainder of Lent, until 13 April, the abbey was besieged. Rufus took up residence at Avranches castle, held by Hugh of Avranches, who was already well known to him as Earl of Chester, a loyalist in 1088. Until now, Hugh had also been on good terms with Henry, but his homage to Robert as his duke and William Rufus as his king far outweighed his ties to a mere dispossessed count. A company of knights were positioned at Ardevron, a small castle close to what was then the southern shore of the bay, guarding the route into Brittany, while Curthose took charge at Genêts, an important priory of Mont-Saint-Michel at the end of the shortest route across the treacherous sands of the Bay.

Mont-Saint-Michel may be impregnable, but it also suffers from a poor water supply, and before the fifteenth-century water tanks were built this problem was acute. Before long, the defenders were becoming desperate, surrounded by water yet suffering increasingly from thirst. Meanwhile the besieging armies patrolled the sands, even organising impromptu jousts in full view of Henry and his men. Three vignettes are recorded from this time, which, whether grounded in fact or not, illustrate the different attributes of the brothers. Rufus, taking part anonymously in a skirmish on the beach, was knocked from his horse and almost killed; bellowing that he was the king, he leapt onto a fresh horse, demanded to know who had attacked him and, impressed by the knight's honesty and courage (the man was a Breton, an enemy, in one account), impetuously enlisted him in the royal household. Henry, when finally forced to withdraw from the abbey, managed to negotiate until he was allowed to take his baggage-train and remaining treasure with him into exile in Brittany. But Robert, when he heard that the defenders of the abbey were perilously short of water, allowed them ashore for supplies; in a later version of the story, he sent a barrel of wine for Henry's personal use. When Rufus protested, he is said to have retorted: 'Good heavens, should I leave our brother to die of thirst? And where shall we look for another if we lose this one?'[27] It is tempting to wonder if Robert was thinking of his brother Richard, only a few years his junior and whom Rufus would scarcely have known, who had died in his teens.

With Henry exiled to Brittany and removed from the Anglo-Norman succession, Curthose and Rufus held a joint court at Caen. They witnessed charters together, and held a formal inquest to record the rights and customs of the duchy as they had been accepted in the time of their father. The result, committed to writing on 18 July 1091 in the presence of the magnates, emphasises that it is not a complete list of the laws and customs of Normandy, but addresses some key issues for the future government of the realm. It also gives the modern reader a rare glimpse into eleventh-century life and some of the challenges facing the ruling classes, and some basis for assessing the expected levels of violence in Norman society.[28]

The inquest required that two tiers of justice were to remain in operation, namely the ducal and baronial courts, and much of the document is devoted to a description of their respective powers. The ducal court had power over those guilty of assaulting several categories of people, including those on their way to or from its meetings, pilgrims, those participating in the ducal levies, and all those abusing the coinage either by tampering with legal coin or setting up false mints in addition to those at Rouen and Bayeux. Baronial courts were free to deal with cases of rape, arson, damage to houses and seizure of distrained goods. The ducal court reserved the right to sentence captives of war to the loss of a limb, but baronial courts could mutilate felons. Violation of the duke's peace attracted forfeiture of property, land or life, and the duke's forests were not to be used as places for private warfare and assaults, nor for jousts, since these were often indistinguishable in intent or in outcome from an affray. Private feuds between the magnates were to be conducted in a controlled way: burning, plunder, capture of weapons and horses, and the erection of castles and fortifications without the duke's consent were all forbidden. Baronial castles were to have ducal garrisons installed in them, and, as a further guarantee, hostages were to be granted to the duke for their safety. These clauses on independent castle-building returned to an issue that had troubled the Conqueror throughout his reign, and that he had legislated against unsuccessfully at the Council of Lillebonne in 1080.[29]

With these customs agreed and committed to writing, the next step was to move south and subdue Maine. With Rufus's treasure available for purchasing mercenaries, and their success in driving Henry out of the Cotentin to boost their confidence further, it would have been an ideal opportunity to move there in force and settle that problem thoroughly. Hélias of La Flèche was still a contender for the county, while Geoffrey of Mayenne, a border baron of uncertain loyalty and independent ambitions, was trying to persuade the barons to unite behind Hélias's cousin Hugh, a claimant in the female line whose father was from the prosperous colony of Normans in Italy. But at the news that duke and king had large forces at their disposal, and were considering a campaign against him, 'Count Hugh V' sold his interest in Maine back to Hélias for 10,000 Manceaux shillings, and retired to Italy.[30]

But, despite this favourable turn of events, Curthose suddenly decided that it would be better to postpone the Maine campaign and travel to England instead. For Rufus had become a very unwilling ally.

Orderic has a story that demonstrates just how precipitately the brothers left Normandy. On 1 June, a synod had chosen Abbot Serlo of Saint-Evroul, Orderic's monastery, to be the new Bishop of Séez, a key political appointment in view of previous Bellême family influence in the diocese. On 23 July, five days after the Caen inquest, Serlo had gone to Saint-Evroul to help the monks choose a new abbot. Three days later, the decision was made and the abbot-elect set off to the ducal court to be invested. But when the party of monks arrived, after perhaps a two-day journey, they found to their astonishment that Curthose had left. Word had come that King Malcolm of Scotland had made a raid into Northumbria in May, and Rufus had insisted that he must first deal with this threat to his northern border before returning to attack Maine. At the beginning of August, the two brothers crossed to England, leaving Henry prowling the borders of Normandy.[31]

Curthose and Rufus organised a joint expedition into Scotland, their army supported by a fleet hugging the North Sea coast. Such an undertaking had seldom been attempted before, and the logistical difficulties were immense. Small wonder then that, as the autumn weather worsened, so their problems increased. The army paused in Durham in mid-September for the formal reinstallation of Bishop William, who had returned to England with the royal party, laden with books and altar goods for his cathedral.[32] Then they continued north, but most of the fleet was wrecked and its flotsam washed onto the shores around Tynemouth. The army too was severely depleted by bad weather before the end of the month. Eventually they struggled on to Lothian, where King Malcolm met them, together with Edgar Ætheling, who had lost his Norman lands to Rufus's supporters and had returned to his brother-in-law's court.

Curthose and Edgar were able to negotiate a peace between the two kings. Malcolm was resentful at first of Rufus's claims of overlordship, pointing out (according to Orderic) that he had only ever sworn homage to William the Conqueror and to his eldest son. Robert persuaded him that his homage must now be paid to Rufus, and in exchange Rufus restored to Malcolm his English lands and undertook to pay him an annual allowance of 12 gold marks. Curthose also effected a reconciliation between Edgar and Rufus.

Malcolm soon discovered the quality of the English king's promises. The money was not forthcoming, and two years later he again crossed the border. He stayed briefly at Durham to lay the foundation stone of the new cathedral, and then continued south and met Rufus at Gloucester. Gaining no satisfaction, he returned home and mounted a raid into Northumbria in November 1093, in the course of which he and his eldest son Edward were ambushed and killed. Reactions to the death of the Scottish king were mixed. Symeon, the chronicler of Durham, believed that the world was well rid of an inveterate raider who had disturbed the peace since the reign of Edward the Confessor; Edgar Ætheling lost one of the few places he could call home; but Queen Margaret, Symeon noted, a saint who had fed the poor, endowed monasteries and taken travellers into her own rooms, died three days later of a broken heart.[33] After a brief period of civil war, Malcolm was succeeded by his son Duncan, whom Curthose had freed and knighted in 1087.

Meanwhile, duke and king returned to Windsor in early winter 1091, where the emissaries from Saint-Evroul found them. Curthose willingly agreed to the election of their new abbot and invested him with the temporalities of his office. But after a month at the English court it became apparent that King Malcolm was not the only one to be deceived by Rufus's easy promises. The king had no intention of returning to Normandy to fulfil his side of the bargain and help his brother regain Maine, nor of granting him any land in England. So Curthose refused to stay for the Christmas court, and instead left conspicuously on 23 December, sailing from the Isle of Wight together with Edgar Ætheling. There is some evidence that he tried to abide by his side of the treaty, witnessing a charter for Bec Abbey that reserved certain rights 'for his brother King William as well as for himself'.[34] But, without Rufus's support, successful military intervention in Maine was increasingly unlikely. Bishop Hoel was beginning to work with Hélias of La Flèche, who started issuing charters as 'Count of Maine'.[35]

Although Robert had resolved the immediate threat from Rufus, he could not relax, for two related problems now flared up in the south-west of the duchy demanding his attention. There were a series of disputes between Robert of Bellême and his neighbours that threatened to spiral out of control, although the importance of this has probably been exaggerated because the land across which the skirmishes were fought was well known to Orderic Vitalis, the only source for many of these events. The other problem, however, was all too real, for Prince Henry had taken advantage of his brother's absence in England to return to his old territory near the Cotentin.

Robert of Bellême had built a new castle at Fourches, close to the centre of power of his traditional enemies the Giroie-Grandmesnils, and this had stirred them to renewed hostility. At the same time, he faced a series of attacks from his cousins the Counts of Mortagne, who laid claim to much of his maternal inheritance. Chief among the disputed castles was Domfront, in a frontier region notoriously independent of ducal control.

Even today Domfront is an impressive citadel, standing high on a crag above the River Varenne, with sweeping views on all sides. It had first been fortified by Robert of Bellême's great-grandfather, and had been in his family for over sixty years. With their other major castles at Alençon and Bellême, and the family abbey at Lonlay, it was a cornerstone of their power. By some means, during the winter of 1091–2, Henry had managed to gain access to this stronghold. Orderic names 'Achard' as the man who let him into the heavily fortified town and then into the castle. Possibly this was Henry's old tutor, who may also have been a member of a Bellême vassal family: there is evidence that Henry later rewarded this man's family with land in England.[36]

Once he was established at Domfront, Henry began to construct a massive stone keep, and made a succession of raids into Norman territory. In this he was helped by the power vacuum resulting from the death of his uncle Robert Count of Mortain, whose lands had come close up against Domfront. Likewise, Bishop Geoffrey of Coutances, another of Curthose's staunch supporters, had fallen ill early in 1092 and died in February 1093.[37] Orderic, for all his bias in favour of Henry, speaks of arson, plunder, abductions and wrongful imprisonments. As his booty accumulated and he extended his control over the surrounding land, Henry linked up with Hugh of Avranches, and began to reward his old followers with tangible gifts. At the age of 23, he had finally achieved the vital springboard of a secure castle and land, and was determined never to lose it. The disturbances he caused can be glimpsed in a survey of the lands of the abbey of Holy Trinity Caen, where his sister Cecilia was in charge in the declining years of its first abbess. Many are listed as having been reclaimed or despoiled by the family of the original donor (a common enough occurrence), but it also names 'Count Henry unjustly taking foot-tolls from Quetthou and all of the Cotentin, and forcing the men of the countryside to work on building his castle'.[38]

While Henry raided and despoiled the Holy Trinity lands, a scandal of a very different kind began in France. Bertrada of Anjou, the helpless virgin bride used as a bargaining counter by Robert Curthose and William of Evreux, began to fear that her husband Fulk would repudiate her as he had done his other wives. So she formed a liaison with King Philip of France, who became infatuated with her and abandoned his own wife. Orderic accuses Odo of Bayeux of performing the 'marriage' ceremony, while William of Malmesbury blames the Archbishop of Rouen. In fact, a French bishop conducted the service. 'So the absconding concubine left the adulterous count and lived with the adulterous king.'[39]

Perhaps in response to the loss of Domfront, Curthose joined with Robert of Bellême to construct a new castle at Château Gontier, as protection from Henry's incursions. Robert of Bellême also made an unsuccessful assault on the Giroie castle at Saint-Céneri. Although Robert Giroie had been restored there as a counterweight to Bellême influence in the region, he was now giving Curthose cause for alarm by his increasing ties to Geoffrey of Mayenne, whose lands stretched far into Maine and whose loyalty to Normandy had never been secure.

Whatever his present intentions towards Normandy, Rufus was unable to do anything in the first part of 1093, for he fell gravely ill at Gloucester after the Christmas court. For many weeks he feared for his life, and was even moved to promise reform, including filling the archbishopric of Canterbury, which had been vacant for four and a half years while its revenues were siphoned into the royal treasury.[40] Curthose was, therefore, able to take an army down to the borders of Maine, where the private war between Robert of Bellême and Robert Giroie was spilling over into more general lawlessness. He invested an illegally raised Giroie castle at Montaigu, and captured and destroyed it. Then he held a court, and found in favour of Giroie to the extent that he allowed him to retain possession of Saint-Céneri, and also to regain more of his family lands.

By now it must have been obvious that Rufus, although fit and well again and already making life difficult for his new archbishop, had no intention of coming to Curthose's assistance in Maine, and without him nothing more could be achieved. Moreover, the Count of Eû went openly to England, 'bought over by his great greed of gold, and the promise of great honours . . . and, prince of traitors, placed himself under the king's lordship'.[41] In disgust,

Robert sent an emissary to Rufus's Christmas court, which was again held at Gloucester, demanding his brother's goodwill in observing their treaty, or else requiring him to come to Rouen and explain his refusal.

Rufus decided that this was the moment to throw off his treaty with Robert and make a new attempt on Normandy. He went to Hastings in early February, intending to cross the Channel, but was delayed for six weeks waiting for a favourable wind. When he landed, he met Robert near Rouen, in the presence of the twenty-four magnates who had witnessed the treaty between them two years earlier. Perhaps he hoped to gain some condemnation of Robert that he could use to justify a campaign against him, but this trial of the conduct of king and duke reached a unanimous decision: the magnates on both sides blamed everything on the king, 'but he would not assent to it, nor further keep to the agreement, and therefore they separated with much dissention'.[42]

Rufus had taken the precaution of bringing with him a large store of treasure, his best weapon in the past, and with it he was able to buy an army of mercenaries. In many ways the two brothers were right back to where they had been three years before, except that Henry was now secure in Domfront. Rufus began this 1094 campaign by targeting Bures, one of Hélias of Saint-Saëns's castles. Having captured it, he took the garrison prisoner and sent some of them to England. But Curthose had alerted King Philip, who was close by with his army, and together they moved south. Philip attacked Argentan, which was held by Roger the Poitevin, Robert Bellême's brother, and the castle and its garrison (including 700 knights, according to Orderic) submitted in a single day. Curthose threatened another (unidentified) castle, which fell with comparable ease, and William Peverel and a second large body of knights abandoned Rufus. In one swift campaign, Rufus had lost two important strongholds, the loyalty of his partisans was in doubt, and Robert Bellême had been persuaded to throw in his lot unreservedly with his duke.

But Rufus was not finished yet. He sent word to Ranulf Flambard in England, who called out a huge army (20,000 foot soldiers, according to the Anglo-Saxon Chronicle) to meet at Hastings. Each man brought ten shillings for his keep for the coming campaign. Then, acting on the king's instructions, Flambard took the money and sent the men home. He shipped the coin over to his royal master, who had thus benefited from a novel tax, with minimal effort and without the need to transport troops across the Channel.[43] With this enormous addition to his treasury, Rufus again approached King Philip, who was already advancing against Eû, and yet again he took the bribe and returned home to his new paramour.

Rufus now tried to summon Henry to assist him. But, although the king's messenger reached him, Robert's grip on the duchy was secure enough to prevent the prince from travelling across Normandy, so he and Hugh of Avranches took boat from the Cotentin, and sailed direct to England, where they waited for Rufus. For once things had not gone the king's way. He had spent vast sums, but had achieved very little. The year ended with Robert still securely in control of the great majority of Normandy. The magnates on both sides had declared in a formal court that the English king was faithless and forsworn, and the Bellême-Montgomerys were again in the ducal camp. After spending the first part of the Christmas season at Wissant waiting for a fair wind, Rufus crossed to England on 29 December.

The only thing that Rufus had really gained in 1094 was that Henry had abandoned his ambiguously neutral stance and had come openly onto his side. This was just as well for Rufus, because the following year he faced another major rebellion. Robert Mowbray, Earl of Northumbria, refused to appear at the Easter court in March 1095, and it soon became apparent that there was a plot to assassinate the king. It was organised by a group of magnates, including Mowbray, Odo of Champagne (the third husband of the Conqueror's sister Adelaide, who had hitherto supported Rufus), and that 'prince of traitors' William of Eû, whose loyalty seems to have been rather more easily swayed. The aim was to replace Rufus with Stephen of Aumâle, Odo and Adelaide's son and hence the king's cousin. Stephen had been one of the first barons to defect to Rufus in Normandy, and it is not clear what he thought about this plot.[44] Nevertheless, it was a very real danger for Rufus, who was forced to remain in England to face the rebels. All he could do to harass Curthose was to dispatch Henry to Normandy with a supply of money to prosecute the war alone.

In the summer, Rufus lead his army north, and besieged Mowbray and his family in Bamburgh castle. In late September he was forced to leave the siege in response to Welsh raids into Shropshire, and returned north only at the end of the year. Robert Mowbray had meanwhile been deceived into leaving Bamburgh, and had been captured. Rufus took him from his prison and paraded him before the castle walls, threatening to have his eyes put out if his wife did not immediately surrender. After a brief consultation, the countess and the family steward agreed to submit. Once they were in the king's hands, it was easy to extract the names of the other traitors. The alarm that Rufus felt at this second uprising can perhaps be seen in the treatment meted out to the plotters. Robert Mowbray was taken to Windsor and kept imprisoned for the rest of his life. William of Eû was tried by combat, and lost, whereupon he was blinded and castrated. Many of the conspirators, including Odo of Champagne, Rufus's uncle, were deprived of their lands in England. Some, such as Philip Montgomery, were imprisoned for a while and then released, while the lesser men were 'taken to London and there destroyed'.[45] Only Bishop William of Saint-Calais escaped punishment. Nothing was ever proved against him in connection with this plot, for he died at court on 2 January, while awaiting the king's pleasure.[46]

Almost nothing is known of Curthose's actions this year. One charter dated 15 August 1095 at Rouen records a ducal grant to the cathedral.[47] Orderic seldom reports good things of him, so we can perhaps take this as a sign that, with Rufus occupied elsewhere, a sort of peace descended on Normandy. Henry does not seem to have been energetic in spending his brother's money in Normandy, unless he used it on his dramatic building programme at Domfront, where a stone keep 80 feet high, a curtain wall and a new priory were all constructed in a very few years.[48] Orderic seems to give the impression that unrest continued unabated, but the disputes to which he refers relate to an earlier period, and are inserted out of chronological order.

What we do know is that, in the late summer of 1095, Pope Urban II began a year-long progress through France, from the Italian border to Maine and back again. At Clermont in November he held a Council, culminating in what has become known as 'the preaching of the First Crusade'. When a Norman council met at Rouen in February 1096, the call for a crusade found eager listeners among the aristocracy of the north.

Chapter 5

SOLDIER OF CHRIST

Nobody could have guessed in 1095 that the echoes of what became known as the First Crusade would still be reverberating painfully a millennium later. But even at the time it was an uncomfortable amalgam of diverse motivations: political, cultural and spiritual. With a generation's hindsight, the undertaking came to be described with a suspicious clarity and theological exactitude, and those versions of events must now be read with due caution. But several participants also wrote about their experiences, in 'histories' and in letters home, and these, together with the surviving evidence of arrangements made before crusaders set off on their journey, allow a more human narrative to emerge.

Pope Urban II personified the underlying tension in the crusading concept. He had served as a cardinal at Rome under Gregory VII, the great reforming pope who worked so hard to increase papal power, free the Church from lay control and improve standards of clerical behaviour, and Urban aimed to continue these reforms. But he was also by birth a member of the French knightly class, with an innate sympathy for them. Their society was dominated by martial achievement, with an assumption that arbitration or central government was seldom able to right wrongs. Self-help and vendettas in support of a flexibly defined kin-group and network of feudal obligations were the inevitable consequence. Yet, as a side effect of the reforms, this society was increasingly permeated by notions of a different standard of behaviour. Men were becoming aware of their shortcomings well before the conventional deathbed moment of contrition, and with this came a profound fear of hell. Aristocrats could enter monasteries, as Simon de Crépy did, or found and endow them, but other than this the Church had no ready answer to the questions in people's minds. Although the parish system was expanding rapidly, and many aristocratic households had several chaplains, there do not seem to have been remedies available for these men of the world who were also anxiously aware of their spiritual dilemma. Confession, lay devotions and the necessary theological framework were all as yet unavailable. The only clearly understood hope lay in pilgrimage.

Pilgrimage, penitential travel to a place imbued with particular holiness, where prayers were especially effective, was a well-established part of Christianity by the eleventh century. Hundreds of local sites, the emerging shrine of St James in Spain and above all Rome and Jerusalem, were the focus of innumerable personal and group journeys. The Holy Land remained a popular destination even after it was overrun by the Muslims in the seventh century, not least because of a shared reverence for many of the holy sites. This seemed to change in 1009, when the Holy Sepulchre was desecrated by the Fatimid Caliph Hakim of Egypt. But this proved to be only a temporary setback, even though Hakim subsequently descended into madness and began persecuting his fellow-Muslims. Rebuilding was quickly begun by Hakim's Christian mother, and interest in the Holy Land was fuelled by the millennium of the resurrection in 1033.[1] Count Fulk Nerra of Anjou returned from one of his four pilgrimages with a piece of rubble from the Holy Sepulchre, and other pilgrims brought other relics, further stimulating interest. These pilgrims gained personal benefits. As well as a strong belief in the forgiveness obtained, there could be more tangible results: Fulk's notorious temper was noticeably improved for a while after his return.

In the 1070s, the situation became more confused when Turkish tribes spread into Anatolia and Syria, defeating the Byzantine army and pushing the Christian border back almost to the Bosphorus, and capturing Jerusalem from the Fatimid Caliphate of Egypt. Now, to all the existing difficulties of the journey were added the perils of crossing lands inhabited by mutually suspicious and semi-nomadic clans, with no tradition of interaction with Christians. But with long-distance sea voyages restricted, and shipwrecks commonplace, there was little alternative.

It may have been Gregory VII (1073–85) who first encouraged the idea that knights might become 'soldiers of Christ', although earlier popes had already used the Norman adventurers who were settling in southern Italy to defend the papal territories. But Urban II was the pope under whom all the disparate elements came together to generate the idea of crusade. Urban seems to have been considering some sort of expedition to ease the situation in the Holy Land, when an embassy came to a council at Piacenza in spring 1095 from the Byzantine emperor Alexius. He asked for help (presumably he had in mind mercenary troops of the kind that already fought so successfully in his army) to drive back the Seljuk Turks, who were now dangerously close to the Bosphorus and Constantinople itself. With this specific appeal, the crusading movement began its inexorable momentum, swiftly taking on a life of its own until neither emperor nor pope could control it.

By late summer 1095, Urban had begun a year-long tour of French territories, to promote the Reform and to preach his crusade. The whole progress was carefully organised and included three major church councils. Urban began with several stops in Provence, celebrating the Feast of the Assumption (15 August) at Le Puy, a major Marian shrine and pilgrim centre where it is almost certain that he took Bishop Adhémar into his confidence and chose him as the papal representative and spiritual leader of the forthcoming expedition. Then the papal party made its way up the Rhône valley by stages to Cluny and then on to Clermont for the first great council of church leaders in November.

At Clermont, a series of reformist canons were passed,[2] and then on 27 November Urban closed the council with a sermon in which he announced the idea of the expedition to the East. He spoke passionately of recent events, in a cleverly stage-managed appeal for commitment. The actual text of the sermon is not recorded, but recollections of it written afterwards, in the light of the outcome of the crusade, and letters he wrote at the time, give an idea of the content. The pope called for a band of 'pilgrim knights' to form, who would be forgiven as if they had undertaken more conventional penances. They would journey to the Holy Land without the need to lose face by travelling unarmed, and blood they shed in a just cause would not be held against them. This was revolutionary new doctrine, and the theologians had great difficulty explaining it. These new Soldiers of Christ were to be set apart with a cloth cross on their garments, and an oath taken before God, just as they habitually took oaths to their feudal lords, not to turn aside from the pilgrimage until it was complete. The pope's pilgrims were to make war on God's behalf, to free the Holy City and their suffering fellow-Christians in the

East from the yoke of the infidel. When Urban had finished speaking, Bishop Adhémar stepped forward and publicly announced that he would be the first to join this new movement. Crosses were already to hand, and the bishop was given one to sew onto his clothes.

Everywhere Urban went on the remainder of his tour, he preached in the open air, wrote letters to places he could not visit in person, and in every way possible he spread his vision of the crusade, asking for able-bodied young knights to take the cross. He asked them to assemble at Le Puy and be ready to depart in August 1096.

Among the hundreds of bishops and abbots at Clermont were Odo of Bayeux, Gilbert of Evreux (called The Crane because he was so tall) and Serlo the new Bishop of Séez.[3] On their return to Normandy, the Archbishop of Rouen summoned a council for February 1096, at which the decrees of Clermont were promulgated and a call was made for pilgrims to join the pope's expedition. The archbishop had been to Jerusalem as a young man, and was able to speak from personal experience of the difficulties involved and the merits of the cause. The resulting zeal for action against pagans sparked an anti-Semitic riot in Rouen as the council ended.[4]

Curthose soon determined to take the cross, as did his brothers-in-law Count Stephen of Blois and Duke Alan Fergant of Brittany, his cousin Robert II of Flanders, and Hélias of La Flèche, the new Count of Maine. There may have been communication between these courts from an early stage, since it seems that all five rulers intended to travel together. There is some evidence that King Philip also wished to take part, but he was barred from doing so because he remained excommunicated for his adulterous relationship with Bertrada, which had been publicised and reaffirmed at Clermont. Urban avoided preaching in the royal territories, but no objection was made when Philip's younger brother Hugh 'The Great' joined with a contingent of French knights. The concept of the crusade was quickly adopted by the men at whom it was aimed. Robert of Flanders stated in a charter that he was 'going to Jerusalem on the authority of the apostolic see, to liberate the Church of God which has been trampled underfoot by savage peoples for a long time'.[5]

Why did these Frankish aristocrats, many of whom left great lands behind them at the mercy of unreliable relations, so wholeheartedly embrace the idea of Urban's pilgrimage? Certainly it was cleverly marketed, but, much more than this, it fitted closely with their aspirations. Knightly prowess was for them the prime virtue; it was what they were trained for and it was their main occupation. The chief among them were near the top of their own social hierarchies, but they could readily make parallels with notions of service to Christ as their 'lord'. Undoubtedly Urban was aware of this and used imagery and language that would connect with his audience. Many of the crusaders also had close relatives in the Church, and the two worlds were very close at this level: Curthose's uncle Odo was Bishop of Bayeux, while the Conqueror's uncle Mauger had been Archbishop of Rouen, and his cousin Nicholas (who had died only in 1092) had been Abbot of Saint-Ouen's.[6] Moreover, many of these men, however worldly, were also deeply religious, and not merely through fear of the pains of hell. The new pilgrimage promised a real sacrifice, without a permanent commitment to a monastic vocation with all the complications that entailed. These parallel streams are clear in the donation charters made by crusaders before their departure, where the words for pilgrimage and military expedition are used interchangeably.[7]

Despite its novel aspects, the pilgrimage Urban called for had potent links with existing concepts, and the crusaders were often drawn from families with a tradition of pilgrimage. Robert of Flanders's father, for example, has been a Jerusalem pilgrim; Curthose's great-grandfather Richard II had donated 100 pounds of gold for the rebuilding of the Holy Sepulchre and financed a pilgrimage of 700 people there in 1026; his grandfather Robert I had died on pilgrimage, and his father's cousin Nicholas had been to Jerusalem in 1091.[8] But such traditions were no guarantee that men would enlist: Count Fulk Le Rechin elected not to join the crusade, even though his grandfather had been to Jerusalem four times and Urban had spent six weeks in Anjou during his progress around France. Likewise William Rufus refused to be drawn in and may have actively discouraged his associates from becoming involved.

The crusade may have seemed a simple idea to Urban when he proposed it, but it soon became clear that it was not possible to organise and equip the numerous men who responded to his appeal and move them to Le Puy in the timescale he envisaged. Instead, it became a series of quasi-autonomous regional contingents, owing allegiance to local noble commanders. Urban's vision of an army of fit young knights fighting for Christ and St Peter shaded imperceptibly into a more complex movement, including poor pilgrims of both sexes, old men making their way to Jerusalem in the hope of dying there, and landless younger sons eager to carve out a reputation or even a fiefdom for themselves.

Curthose was in his mid-forties, with a lifetime's experience of warfare, when he took the cross in early 1096. The journey would last more than a year, and so he began the complex task of equipping his entourage, not just of household knights but of all the other crusaders who wished to travel with him. There had been a succession of poor harvests in northern France, and reserves were low, which made finding suitable mounts and pack animals difficult. Then there was the question of spare weapons and armour: lance, sword, mailcoat, saddle, helmet and shield were all specialist tools, and correspondingly expensive. Each knight would have several warhorses with him, as well as his palfreys, and perhaps three grooms and squires. All these people and animals would need to be fed, so cooks, grain supplies, huntsmen, falconers and their animals were added to the burgeoning commissariat. Every extra pack animal or draught team needed more fodder, or money to purchase it as the cavalcade made its way across Europe. All told, it has been estimated that the leading crusaders spent about four times their annual income equipping their contingents.[9]

Where no wealthy overlord was willing or able to pay these expenses, private arrangements had to be made. Family land was pledged, often to monastic houses, in a contract known as *vifgage*. The monastery demanded no interest, but instead occupied the property until the loan had been repaid or there was certain news that the crusader was dead, whereupon they took full possession. Many of these *vifgages* were very small – for example, a knight called Hamo pledged a plot of land to Saint-Vincent-du-Mans Abbey for twenty solidi.[10] Some idea of the value of these sums, and of the importance of pack animals, comes from another pledge of land for 200 solidi in coin and a mule valued at 100 solidi.[11] The wealthiest monasteries, especially Saint-Jean-d'Angéley, Saint-Vincent-du-Mans, Cluny and Marmoutier, obtained large additional estates in this way, and were able to supply many crusaders with much-needed money and animals.

There are only a few Norman charters of this type, which probably reflects Curthose's ability to provide for a large contingent himself. He could not supply funding on this scale unaided, and so he pledged the duchy to Rufus, in a *vifgage* drawn up by the papal legate.[12] The arrangement suited both brothers well. Rufus was eager to rule Normandy, and prepared to tax England heavily for it, and Robert was eager to participate in the crusade. If Curthose died on the journey, he would have gained the inestimable benefit of remission of his sins, and Rufus would acquire the duchy. They agreed a pledge of 10,000 marks, an enormous sum that few could have contemplated finding. Rufus imposed a geld of four shillings per hide but was still forced to demand that the abbeys make their contributions, by melting down their treasures if necessary. The Abbot of Malmesbury ordered the stripping of the silver and gold from his altar furnishings, gospel books and reliquaries, but still failed to find the sum the king had demanded. Archbishop Anselm was unwilling to do this, and instead borrowed 200 marks from the Canterbury treasury, at his own expense.[13] Lesser rulers used similar methods, but on a smaller scale: Godfrey of Bouillon pledged his duchy to the Bishop of Liège for 7,000 marks, and the bishop was forced to plunder the altars and shrines of the diocese to raise the money, while Odo Arpin, Vicomte of Bourges, later pledged his lands to King Philip.[14]

Curthose himself seems to have made no other arrangements to raise money, but he did make at least one donation, to Rouen Cathedral, and he witnessed the donations of three other men who were intending to join him on the crusade. These charters were just as important as the *vifgages*, because they ensured the prayers of the religious community to which the donation was made. They also demonstrated that the donor was in good standing with the Church. Once the crusader vow had been taken, there was considerable pressure to fulfil it, and this in turn entailed setting your house in order before you left. It is not surprising, therefore, that there are records of substantial endowments of land from the period of the First Crusade, mostly with clear expressions of penitence and humility from the donor.[15] Pilgrimage was a dangerous undertaking, and the crusade was even more so. It is not always clear whether these donations are from crusaders, or from conventional pilgrims, but sometimes the context and the level of anxiety felt shine through. Thus Robert of Flanders settled a dispute with an abbey 'for the remission of my sins and my safety and the safety of my wife Clemency', while Stephen of Blois made a donation of an area of woodland to Marmoutier Abbey: 'So that God, at the intercession of St Martin and his monks, might pardon me for whatever I have done wrong and lead me on the journey out of my homeland and bring me back healthy and safe, and watch over my wife Adela and our children.'[16]

By September, Rufus had at last collected the money together. Such large sums as this were transported across the Channel in barrels: 67 barrels each weighing 100 pounds. The king came in person to Rouen to hand over the coin and formally take possession of the duchy. Also in Rouen was a contingent from Maine, led by Count Hélias. Orderic Vitalis is clear that many Manceaux served under Curthose on the crusade, and several crusader charters survive from the area. But Rufus refused to guarantee the safety of Maine in Hélias's absence, for he now had an incentive to reconquer it for Normandy and rule it himself. According to Orderic, Hélias then redefined his crusading vow into a sacred duty to defend Maine, 'for fear of leaving God's people at the mercy of predators, like shepherdless sheep among wolves', and returned home. Whether such an advanced concept of 'holy war' existed in 1096 may be doubted, but at the time that Orderic was writing, forty years later, a bishop of Le Mans wrote to the Count of Anjou to dissuade him from joining a later crusade in very similar terms as these, and Orderic probably knew of this.[17]

Curthose's actual date of departure is not known, but it is likely to have been mid-September. The last known crusader charter from Normandy is that of William of Le Vast, who pledged his land to Fécamp for three silver marks on 9 September. William arranged to take the 1096 harvest from the fields, presumably to help supply his outward journey, and, if he failed to return, his sisters or other near relations were to have the option of redeeming the pledge.[18] By September, the harvest, which was much better in 1096, was gathered, and reserves of grain, fodder and fit animals could be obtained, while a later start would risk heavy snow in the Alps, the first major hurdle on the journey. Orderic states that Rufus took control of the duchy in September, and after that Curthose left. Most manuscripts of Fulcher of Chartres's account give a September departure; one later one gives October.[19] A possible date would be immediately after the 14 September celebration of the Feast of the Exaltation of the Cross, a long-established festival with clear resonances with the crusade.

The names of those known to have accompanied Curthose are intriguing. Some had obvious reasons to avoid Normandy with Rufus in control, in particular their uncle Odo of Bayeux, who had been a leading player in the 1088 rising and had taken personal responsibility for the imprisonment of Prince Henry. Eustace of Boulogne, Philip Montgomery and Stephen of Aumâle had also rebelled against Rufus, as had Arnulf of Hesdin, who had held lands in ten southern counties. Although Arnulf had been formally cleared of his guilt when a vassal won a duel for him, Rufus had forced him into exile.[20] Several men whose castles in Normandy had come into Rufus's hands early in his reign also elected to take the cross. This group included Gerard of Gournay and his wife Edith, and Walter of Saint-Valéry and his son Bernard.[21] The presence of these men, who had contributed to many of Curthose's recent difficulties, in the Norman contingent may be coincidental, or it may reflect their anxiety about Rufus's plans for governing the duchy. In either case it indicates the leadership skills needed if the party was to cohere as a fighting unit.

Other Anglo-Norman crusaders had been associated with Curthose in his youth, but were now linked to Rufus's administration. Notable among these were Ivo and Aubrey Grandmesnil, whose brother William was living in Constantinople; Ivo had probably by this time succeeded their father as Sheriff of Leicestershire. Ralph Montpinçon, a brother-in-law of the Grandmesnils, was the son of a royal steward. Another brother-in-law, William of Bayeux, was the great-nephew of Hugh of Chester and Avranches, and son of Hugh's heir Ralph, who was given some of Odo's forfeited estates and the hand of the twice-married heiress Lucy Bolingbroke. William Ferrers was the son of the Sheriff of Derbyshire, and Ilger Bigod was a relation of the Roger Bigod, who had supported Curthose in 1088 but was by this time serving Rufus as Sheriff of Norfolk.[22]

Still others fit into no obvious category, such as the elderly Bishop Gilbert 'The Crane', William Percy of Yorkshire, and the youthful Payen Peverel, protégé of Bishop Gilbert Maminot of Lisieux. Aged about 16, a younger son of a minor family, Payen survived the crusade, acting as Curthose's standard-bearer when the others had died. In 1112 he founded Barnwell Priory and presented it with relics brought back from the East. He died in about 1135.[23] Rotrou of Perche, the son of Count Geoffrey of Mortagne, was from a family deeply hostile to Curthose's ally Robert Bellême. Count Hugh of Saint-Pol and his son Enguerrard were from Artois but elected to join the crusade in Normandy. Richard of Aunou-le-Faucon, by contrast, was from a junior branch of the ducal family.[24] Others may just have been conventional pilgrims who set off at about the same time as the crusade – for example, William of Colombières, whose son Henry confirmed in 1103 'all that his father had given and granted before he went to Jerusalem'.[25]

In Curthose's personal entourage was his chaplain, the Fleming Arnulf of Chocques. Despite the unflattering comments of the Provençal historian of the crusade, Arnulf was a well-known and scholarly teacher, to whom Ralph of Caen dedicated his history as 'his most learned teacher'. The anonymous Italian chronicler calls him 'a most wise and esteemed man'. Arnulf had been chosen as a chaplain by William and Mathilda, and given special responsibility for the education of their eldest daughter, Cecilia, who became abbess of Holy Trinity Caen and was herself noted for her learning.[26]

Also in the Norman contingent was a group of Bretons, led by their duke, Alan Fergant, who was married to Curthose's sister Constance until her death in 1090. Alan seems to have partly funded his expedition with money from the Breton ducal abbey of Sainte-Croix de Quimperlé. An exchange of land with Sainte-Croix dated 27 July 1096 indicates that at this time the Breton contingent had still not set off. Other Breton crusaders included Archbishop Baldric of Dol's steward, who was Arnulf of Hesdin's son-in-law; Conan, the second son of the lord of Lambale; Duke Alan's steward; Hervey fitz Dodman; Riou of Lohéac, a married man who left behind his wife and son but who, like the Grandmesnils, already had a brother in Norman Italy; and Simon of Ludron, who brought back the relics collected by Riou and presented them to Lohéac parish church on his behalf. Last but by no means least, and one of the oldest of the Bretons, was Ralph Gaël, who had briefly been Earl of Norfolk but had been deprived of his English lands for rebelling against the Conqueror in 1075. He went on the crusade accompanied by his wife Emma and one of their sons.[27]

Finally, although Count Hélias had returned to Maine, a group of Manceax persisted in their pilgrimage, among them Guy of Sarcé and two of his brothers. Guy's charter to Saint-Vincent-du-Mans dated 22 June 1096 cites Urban's visit and his call for a 'journey on behalf of God to Jerusalem against the unbelievers'. William of Braitel witnessed Guy's charter and soon after made a donation of his own as he prepared to set out. A Manceaux clerk named Robert also went to Jerusalem, leaving behind his wife and at least one son as well as several brothers. He pledged his tithes from a church and received a modest sum in exchange. Hamo of La Hune made a donation at the end of July 1096 and another a few days later, in exchange for 20 solidi, and his wife witnessed the charter. Two other Saint-Vincent charters may also be from crusaders lower down the social scale: a man identified simply as Ingelbald referred to the weight of his sins and his desire to seek 'the Holy Sepulchre, from which our Redeemer overcame death and rose again'. Another charter, which refers to a journey to Jerusalem, describes the ceremony used in such contracts. Payen de Chevré here 'placed his pledge on the altar of the church' and, having received three shillings already, one for himself and two for his family, he was given a further 'three coins, one to buy a knife, one to buy a scabbard and the third to arm a crossbow'.[28]

This, then, was the heterogeneous contingent that Curthose found himself leading as they began their journey south in September 1096. Rich and poor, friend and foe, knights, foot soldiers, common pilgrims, wives and the many other non-combatants needed to feed and administer a large group on the road. They varied in age from small children to men such as Odo, Gilbert of Evreux and Ralph Gaël in their sixties, and were united only by their desire to take part in the crusade and their willingness to be part of Duke Robert's army. The numbers who participated in the First Crusade are notoriously hard to determine, but this was one of the largest contingents, and may well have been 6,000 strong as it left Normandy.

For the first part of the journey, they were accompanied by the papal legate and the chronicler Hugh of Flavigny. They headed south-east 600km to Pontarlier, where they effected a junction with the two other northern contingents, from Blois and Flanders, with their leaders Count Stephen, married to Curthose's competent younger sister Adela, and Count Robert II. Both men had left their lands to be administered by their wives. Stephen of Blois was accompanied by the priest Fulcher of Chartres, who later wrote an account of the expedition while living in Palestine.[29] At Pontarlier the legate left them, and the cavalcade, now about 10,000 souls in all, headed up into the Alps.

An expedition of this size could not move fast. It was limited by the speed of the many unmounted people, but even more by the width of the roads, the time it took to pack up and leave each morning and the time needed to pitch camp and eat in the evening. By October there were barely eleven hours of daylight, and that decreased daily. The aristocracy and senior clergy could expect to be accommodated in monastic houses and travellers' hospices, but the rank and file and lesser knights would have to camp. If carts were being used for carrying bulky goods, space was saved on the road, but they were more vulnerable to accidents and becoming bogged down in the mud. Odo of Deuil, who went on the Second Crusade (1147–8), observed that 'the carts delivered more in hope than reality. We say this to caution those who come after, for . . . if one broke down, all were equally delayed. But if they found alternative roads, all used them indiscriminately, and in short by avoiding the blockages they ran into something worse. Thus many horses died and many men complained at the shortness of the day's march.'[30]

Fulcher gives no information about how goods were transported, but another contingent, which came down from Germany across Hungary, is known to have used carts. In view of the need to cross the Alpine passes as winter approached, it would be safe to assume that Curthose obtained as many pack-mules as he could, and kept the use of carts to a minimum. Even so, daily distances of about 25km would be the most that could be expected, with at least one day per week for rest and reprovisioning.

These speeds, averaging at best 150km a week, fit well with those estimated for other crusader armies.[31] They also agree with information on other early journeys, allowing for the fact that these usually relate to much smaller groups of people, who could travel further each day. In the Roman Antonine Itineraries, a standard day's journey was between 25 and 40km. The tenth-century Archbishop Sigeric of Canterbury travelled from Pontarlier over the Alps to Lucca in thirty-one days, averaging 22km a day, while the twelfth-century Icelandic Abbot Nikulas of Munkathvera, who joined this route at Lake Geneva, took twenty days from there to Lucca, an average of 30km.[32]

The route from Pontarlier lay along a well-travelled road, the *Via Francigena*, which carried the pilgrim traffic from northern Europe to Rome and beyond. As such, it was a relatively well-maintained and largely paved survivor of the old Roman road network, equipped with numerous hospices and monasteries. Near the *Mons Iovis* alpine pass, Archbishop Sigeric had stayed at the hospice of St Peter (now Bourg-Saint-Pierre), but by Abbot Nikulas's time this had already been superceded by the new house built by St Bernard, on the pass itself. Down in Aosta, two days further on, an Irish saint had founded the first hospice in a flourishing city. Once out of the valley, the army could make better time, on the broad Roman road, wide enough for carts to pass each other, across the River Po flatlands. Pavia was a strongly walled city that until 1024 was a royal capital, with over forty monasteries, churches and hospices for travellers, including the ancient Anglo-Saxon *St Maria Brittonnorum*. On to Piacenza, another important city, with a bridge over the Po, and then near Parma Curthose would have turned south to cross the Apennines, reaching Lucca in mid-November.

Lucca, set on the northern edge of the marshy plain of the Arno Valley, was a major political and economic centre. Not only was it the principal city of Tuscany, and becoming increasingly independent of its ruler Countess Matilda, but it dominated the *Via Francigena* and the routes inland from the growing port of Pisa, with which it was frequently at loggerheads. It was a pilgrim centre in its own right, housing the fabulous Holy Face of Lucca, a larger than life size Christ in Majesty on a huge wooden cross, which was believed to have been carved by an angel while Nicodemus slept at the tomb on Easter Eve. William Rufus habitually swore 'By the Holy Face at Lucca', and the image was well known in Northern Europe because of the pilgrim traffic.[33]

By the time of the crusade, Lucca had expanded beyond its Roman walls, and the newly founded city hospice of St Martin was complemented by at least three extramural establishments.[34] This was an ideal place to regroup after two months on the road, and near Lucca Curthose and the other nobles met Pope Urban, who had spent the middle of October at Cremona, where he remained until at least the 17th.[35] The pope, who was also making for Rome, could therefore have reached Lucca at the end of October, but not before, and Curthose would have had word of his movements along the road. The nobility, and even Fulcher himself so he tells us, received the pope's personal blessing, and then they continued down towards Rome, via Siena and Viterbo, a journey that Sigeric reckoned at twenty-five stages, or about a month. But this section, being a major artery of travel, was relatively easy, and the crusaders could have made rather better time here, perhaps arriving at the gates of Rome in the second week of December.

Rome in 1096 was a deeply divided city and a shadow of its former self. Only a small fraction of the area within the walls, that part closest to the Tiber, was then inhabited, the rest being a jumble of ruins of the imperial past, interspersed with farms, vineyards and orchards. Even so, the population was about 50,000, greater by far than any city the Normans had seen. Despite frequent fires that destroyed the poorer wooden houses, the city was still 'Wondrous Rome', with a 35km circuit of walls, and innumerable churches and shrines, many of them extramural. The greatest shrine of all was Constantine's Basilica of St Peter on the Vatican hill, within its own walls outside the city, across the Sant'Angelo Bridge and through the Saxon Quarter where many English expatriates had settled and where English pilgrims were still catered for. Within its outer courtyard, St Peter's façade was decorated with mosaics of the cities of Jerusalem and Bethlehem, peculiarly appropriate for the crusaders coming to pray there. Inside, the basilica was immense, some 120m long and 64m wide, with a ceiling 32m high, supported on a double row of columns each side. At the top of the nave walls, among frescos of Old Testament scenes, ran a walkway normally used by lamp lighters.[36]

His audience with Urban would have prepared Curthose for the presence of the anti-pope's supporters in the city, but Fulcher was deeply shocked by what they found in St Peter's itself:

The Devil . . . spurred on a man named Wibert, Urban's adversary . . . supported by the impudence of the emperor of the Germans . . . and this man usurped the papal office . . . and exiled Urban from the monastery of St Peter . . . So two popes ruled over Rome, and many did not know whom to be subject to, or whom to petition . . . And when we had entered the Church of St Peter, we found before the altar men of Wibert the false pope, who with swords in their hands wrongly snatched the offerings placed on the altar. Others ran up and down on the timbers of the church itself, and threw down stones at us as we were prostrate praying. For whenever they saw anyone faithful to Urban, they immediately longed to massacre them. In one part of the vault of the church were Lord Urban's men, who carefully guarded it loyally for him, and resisted their adversaries as best they could. We were sorely troubled when we saw such a great disgrace . . .[37]

Fulcher notes that some people were dismayed at what they saw, and turned back for home. These, however, may have been conventional pilgrims, who never intended going further than Rome, travelling with the crusaders for protection. Refraining from becoming embroiled in the conflict, the rest of the contingent reassembled and continued south, past the Abbey of Monte Cassino, the birth place of the Benedictine Order, and into Apulia. Southern Italy had in the previous generation been captured from the Lombard princes and the Byzantine Empire by the Norman adventurer Robert Guiscard and his numerous relations. His brother Roger 'The Great Count' had similarly conquered Sicily from its Muslim rulers. On Guiscard's death in 1085, his son Roger Borsa had succeeded as Duke of Apulia, while his eldest son by a previous marriage had seized a small principality around Taranto in the

heel of Italy. This man, who had been christened Mark but was so tall he
was always known as Bohemond, after a mythical giant, was to play a key
role in the crusade.[38] Duke Roger Borsa was married to Robert of Flanders's
sister, and welcomed the crusaders, perhaps meeting them at his new capital
of Salerno. He presented his brother-in-law with relics of St Matthew and
St Nicholas, and the hair of the Blessed Virgin, which Robert sent back to his
wife in Flanders for safe-keeping.[39]

Hoping to cross over to the Balkans without delay, the cavalcade turned
east, and came to the coast at Bari, a prosperous and multicultural port that
had been captured from the Byzantines only in 1071. A new church was
being built there to house the shrine of St Nicholas, whose remains had been
removed from Myra on the Turkish coast ten years before. By now it must
have been early January, and, although they approached the port with joy,
and prayed there, they found new obstacles in their path.

Several contingents of crusaders had been this way before them. First had
come a party led by Hugh 'The Great' of France, a rather pompous, self-
important man of about 40, King Philip's younger brother. He had attempted
to cross the 250km of sea in early October, but had been caught in a terrible
storm, and only a few ships, including his own, had struggled to the Balkan
coast. The Byzantine coastguards found him, bedraggled and almost destitute,
and gave him a fresh horse and equipment. They then escorted him to their
headquarters at Durazzo (modern Durrës), at the start of the *Via Egnatia*, the
imperial highway across the southern Balkans. Hugh was given an armed
escort, and taken with the remnant of his followers to Constantinople, where
he was treated with great distinction but kept under surveillance, while
the emperor considered how best to manage these foreign armies that were
entering his lands.[40]

A contingent of Normans from southern Italy had also crossed. These were
led by Bohemond of Taranto, now a cunning, quick-witted man in his mid-
forties, immensely tall, lithe and slightly stooping, clean-shaven and with
his blonde hair cropped close about his head. With him were several of his
nephews and cousins, including the audacious young Tancred and his two
teenage brothers. With their local knowledge, they had made the crossing
without mishap, apart from a brief engagement with the imperial navy.[41]
This south Norman army was relatively small, but had been drawn from
the forces of Duke Roger and his uncle Roger of Sicily, who had been jointly

engaged in putting down a rising in summer 1096: Count Roger let it be known that Bohemond had thereby deprived him of some of his best fighters. The result was a compact, disciplined and well-equipped force, apparently unencumbered by supernumerary pilgrims. They had sailed a few weeks after Hugh, and had taken advantage of Bohemond's knowledge of the Balkans as well; he had fought a prolonged campaign there for his father fifteen years earlier and defeated the Emperor Alexius several times, although he had ultimately failed to gain a foothold. If Bohemond resented this, he also appreciated that the crusade would need to cooperate with the Byzantines if it was to have any hope of success, and he was prepared to hide his enmity. Reassembling his army well south of Durazzo, he set out on a minor road up into the Pindus mountains.

Fulcher reports that the sailors at Bari were unwilling to cooperate. The army was reliant on local ships and their crews for transport, and the losses from Hugh's ill-fated venture had been heavy. The winter of northerly storms was upon them, and time was not on their side. Curthose and Stephen therefore turned back inland to see out the winter, while Robert of Flanders pressed on and made the crossing, taking his soldiers with him. Unlike Hugh, he made it safely. Fulcher notes that 'many people' felt they had been deserted by their leaders and so abandoned their weapons for pilgrim staves, and returned home. But, as with the desertions at Rome, it is not clear whether these were conventional pilgrims, or members of the Flanders contingent who had been abandoned by their count.

Curthose has been castigated for this delay, and some modern historians have assumed that the deserters were Normans expressing their frustration at his timidity. But it was already mid-winter, well into the season during which Mediterranean shipping almost came to a standstill, both by legislation and by choice. It is clear from the monthly pattern of letters sent by the papacy that the Adriatic was seldom crossed from November to February or March, and in January scarcely at all.[42] Winters in southern Italy can be cold and are as wet as in Normandy. Fulcher says that they came to Bari expecting to cross without delay, but were prevented by the sailors and adverse conditions. This is entirely plausible. A disaster like Hugh's would seriously deplete a port even as big as Bari and deter the crews from making another winter crossing, even supposing the ships were available. Moreover, Curthose's Normans had now been on the road for almost four months, and people and animals alike must have needed rest. A winter halt offered time to restock, repair and purchase reliable new animals for the journey ahead. Men in Apulia could tell them that the *Via Egnatia* was a good road and that they would be able to make up for lost time in the spring. It is true that Normans admired reckless leaders, but only if they were also lucky. Rufus was praised for his bold daring, because he got away with it. If Robert of Flanders had come to grief as Hugh had done, he would have been called foolish and Curthose prudent.

So Curthose and Stephen 'withdrew into Calabria and spent the harsh winter weather there'. Fulcher gives no more detail, but there is a charter of Duke Roger Borsa dated March 1097 from Bisignano, a ducal residence near Cosenza part way down the 'toe' of Italy.[43] One could speculate that the pilgrims spent at least part of the winter in this area, as guests of the young duke. It is also quite likely that, while they were at Bari, Curthose was entertained by the wealthy Count Geoffrey of Conversano, one of Guiscard's many nephews, and may have met his beautiful daughter Sibyl.

What is certain is that Bishop Odo left Curthose's contingent and travelled to Sicily. His reasons are impossible to determine. Perhaps he was merely going to visit some of his numerous relatives: his cousin's daughter had been Count Roger's second wife, and several of her brothers seem from charter evidence to have had estates there. One of the new Sicilian bishops was from Rouen, and Odo may have wished to visit this land of opportunity. Perhaps he was envious of the success of Bishop Geoffrey of Coutances, who had made a lucrative fund-raising trip to the Italian Norman states and used the proceeds to restore Coutances Cathedral.[44] Or it is possible that Odo had never intended to continue to Palestine. He was present at Clermont, but did not necessarily take the cross, and his destination may always have been Sicily. Whatever his intentions, once he reached Sicily, he quickly fell ill. He died with Bishop Gilbert 'The Crane' at his side, and was buried in St Mary's Cathedral at Palermo. Count Roger had a splendid tomb made for him, but it was removed when the cathedral was rebuilt in the twelfth century. There is no evidence that Bishop Gilbert continued on the crusade after this, and he was certainly back in Normandy by November 1099 for the dedication of the new church at Saint-Evroul, a fact for which we can rely on Orderic if for few others.

The actual date of Odo's death is a matter of some controversy. It was commemorated on various dates in early January at Bayeux, Canterbury and

Jumièges, while Orderic gives February. It seems very unlikely that he could have reached Palermo by January unless he went there direct from Rome, which would strengthen the case for him merely accompanying the crusade thus far. February, on the other hand, fits well with Curthose's timetable, and would leave open the question of Odo's motives.[45]

So ended the varied career of Curthose's most loyal adviser. From humble beginnings as the son of an obscure Norman knight whose only fortune was to have married the mistress of his duke, Odo was promoted swiftly by his half-brother William. A bishop from a young age, of relatively chaste behaviour (only one illegitimate son is known[46]), he fought at Hastings, held vice-regal powers in England, endured a dramatic fall from grace and was forgiven on the Conqueror's deathbed. After his unsuccessful advocacy of Curthose's claim to the throne in 1088, he occupied himself with restoring the fortunes of his foundation of Saint-Vigor, where he intended to be buried, until finally after a journey halfway across Europe he was laid to rest in an ancient basilica that had served as a mosque for two and a half centuries.

Chapter 6

THE CONQUERING HERO

With the return of more clement weather in late March, Curthose returned to the Adriatic coast. While overwintering in Calabria, he had been joined by additional Normans from Italy: one who was to play a prominent role in the coming campaign was Roger of Barneville, who had been a significant landholder in Sicily since at least 1086.[1]

This time, Curthose sailed from Brindisi, a port in the lordship of Geoffrey of Conversano, on Easter Sunday, 5 April. At first it seemed that his crossing would be as ill-starred as Hugh's. One of the first ships to launch cracked apart just off the shore, and most of those on board were drowned. The few survivors struggled ashore, amid consternation at the losses of valuable animals, equipment and coin. Fulcher reports still more faint-hearted pilgrims turning back at the sight. But someone had the presence of mind to examine the bodies as they were washed ashore, and it was seen that they bore the mark of the cross – a sure sign that their deaths had not been in vain! Now the trumpets were blown, and the rest of the army embarked. The winds were light, and the crossing was slow, but at last on the fourth day they landed safely at two harbours close to Durazzo.

The imperial officials told them that, as well as Hugh and Robert of Flanders, another much larger contingent had passed that way during the winter. Led by the white-haired, one-eyed Count Raymond of Toulouse, who was accompanied by his young Spanish wife, they had endured a terrible journey. After crossing the Provençal Alps and northern Italy, Raymond had taken the overland route around the head of the Adriatic.[2] They had suffered from poor roads along the Dalmatian coast, and frequent bloody skirmishes with the inhabitants, and had seldom been able to buy food. They had reached Durazzo hungry, ill-disciplined and exhausted. After resting and being resupplied, they had been sent off towards Constantinople in mid-February, with a vigilant escort.

The main road across the Balkans from Durazzo to Constantinople, the *Via Egnatia*, had a good infrastructure of accommodation and supply depots for travellers and the imperial administration. The road skirted to the north of the high Pindus Mountains via Bitola, and crossed the River Vardar to the Aegean coast at Thessalonica. Curthose's contingent were escorted in Raymond's tracks; they made very good time, and, after a four-day rest at Thessalonica, they pressed on through Macedonia and came to Constantinople in mid-May.

There they found that their winter halt had paid off. Raymond had left Durazzo nearly two months ahead of them, but had travelled at barely half the speed, and his army had been involved in several clashes with their escort, in the course of one of which Bishop Adhémar had been injured and had been left behind at Thessalonica to recover. As they approached the capital, Raymond had been invited to meet the Emperor Alexius, and had gone on ahead, whereupon discipline had broken down in his army, which had attacked and been severely mauled by a Byzantine force. Although Raymond refused to take a full oath of allegiance to the emperor, he swore to respect the peace between them and to act in Alexius's interests. Once Bishop Adhémar had arrived, relations between Raymond and the emperor improved noticeably, and, two days after the oath-taking, the Provençals were shipped across the Bosphorus to a well-stocked imperial camp, about a week before Curthose arrived before the city.

Raymond's crusaders were the latest in a series of foreign armies to reach Constantinople. First, in November 1096, Hugh and his small group had arrived, had taken an oath to Alexius and had been showered with presents. Just before Christmas, a large contingent under Godfrey of Bouillon, a younger brother of Count Eustace of Boulogne, had arrived via the land route through Hungary. They had used another old Roman military road, but it had proved to be barely passable in places through lack of use, and they had arrived at Constantinople in an ugly mood. After several misunderstandings and some serious disorder, Godfrey had taken the oath, and his army was shipped over to Anatolia. With him, as different as chalk from cheese, was his young brother Baldwin, with his Anglo-Norman wife and small children.

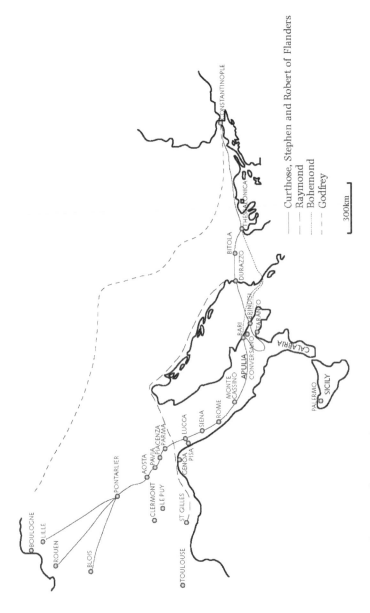

Major crusader routes to Constantinople

The Eastern Mediterranean, c. AD 1096

Whereas Godfrey was fair, gracious and sober, Baldwin was dark, haughty and ambitious. Their eldest brother, Eustace, travelled either with them or with his close associate Curthose. Next, Robert of Flanders had arrived with his men, and then early in April Bohemond came, having taken a circuitous route through the Pindus and overwintered on the road. In this way he had delayed his contact with the imperial authorities, perhaps in order to gather information on the progress of the other contingents. When he neared Constantinople, he went on ahead, leaving the army under the control of the youthful Tancred, and took the oath. Knowing that Raymond's army was not far behind, Alexius had the South Normans shipped over as quickly as possible, lest they unite against him. The very next day, Raymond's Provençals had arrived.[3]

Alexius greeted Curthose with cautious courtesy. The army was allowed to camp outside the walls for two weeks while the nobility were entertained by the emperor, and lesser folk were escorted inside the city in small groups. The massive landward walls, built by the Emperor Theodosius II, enclosed a large area of open land beyond the old Constantinian walls, and protected a city of fabulous magnificence. The wealth of the emperor, and the splendour of the palaces and churches, with their glorious mosaics, left visitors breathless. Fulcher was amazed: 'It is an onerous burden to recite what an abundance of all kinds of goods are found there, of gold, silver, holy relics . . .'. Stephen of Blois wrote home to Adela, his effusiveness perhaps overcoming his domestic judgement:

> My Countess, my sweetest friend, my wife . . . By the grace of God, we came with boundless rejoicing to the city of Constantinople. The emperor received me with dignity, honour, and the greatest care, as his son, and showered me with the most generous and costly gifts. In this whole army of God there is no duke, no count nor any other person of consequence, whom he trusts and befriends above me. My dearest, his imperial majesty has even several times offered to take one of our sons into his service . . . Truly I tell you, there is no other such man alive under the heavens . . . your father, my beloved, gave many great gifts, but his generosity was as nothing compared to this.[4]

Curthose and Stephen took the required oath, and, after they had rested and listened to Alexius's advice, they too were shipped over the straits. They caught up with the rest of the crusade at Nicaea (Iznik), the city where Curthose's grandfather had died, in the first week of June. The whole army, including non-combatants, camp-followers and hangers-on, was now of the order of 60,000.[5] Among them were the remnants of an earlier mass movement, the so-called People's Crusade, a ramshackle horde of some 20,000, led by the preacher Peter the Hermit. They had plunged into an attack on the Seljuk Turks at Nicaea the previous autumn, with tragic results. The survivors, consisting chiefly of the 500 knights attached to the group, had been rescued by the Byzantines, while the bones of their companions littered the road to Nicaea, striking fear in the hearts of the new arrivals.

Nicaea was a strongly fortified city in a fertile basin, protected by its lofty Roman walls and by a lake to the west. The city had been captured by the Seljuks only twenty years earlier, but was already being established as the capital of Kilij Arslan, the most powerful of the Anatolian Turks. The recapture of the city was a strategic imperative for Alexius, and it stood in the way of the crusaders' advance to Syria. Although disappointed that the emperor did not lead them in person, the Westerners could have no complaints at the help he gave, including generous provisions, light boats that could be dragged to the lake, and a force of crack imperial troops to assist in the siege.

Kilij Arslan was taken by surprise by the launch of a second attack on Nicaea. Having destroyed the People's Crusade, he had left his family at Nicaea and withdrawn east to intervene in the complex politics of northern Syria. The whole region was on the dividing line between the Sunni Caliphate of Baghdad, which since the 1050s had been under Seljuk control, and the Shi'ite Fatimid Caliphate of Egypt. In between these two power blocks, the recently arrived and still largely nomadic Turkish clans vied for autonomous power and personal advantage, exploiting family feuds and local jealousies for short-term advantage. Indeed, at the time of his death in 1086, the previous ruler of Baghdad had been negotiating a marriage alliance with the Byzantines, against his fellow Sunnis in Anatolia. Alexius for his part had used Seljuk mercenaries against Robert Guiscard.[6] While Byzantium continued a careful policy in a complex and rapidly changing situation, the crusaders struggled at first to moderate their Holy War to local needs. In fact, as they soon came to appreciate, the political realities were remarkably like the feuds and power-broking they were familiar with at home.

Recalled by the news of the arrival of a new and much larger Christian army in Anatolia, Kilij Arslan rapidly returned to Nicaea. There his scouts reported that the crusaders were fanned out around the eastern and northern walls, with Raymond's recently arrived contingent in the act of setting up camp to the south. Using their favoured tactics, the Seljuks massed on the hills above the city and launched squadrons of swift, lightly mounted archers against Raymond's position. The repeated showers of arrows, falling like sharp rain, killed many of the westerners' horses, and terrorised the soldiers. Men used to clashes between strongly armed knights now suffered torments like swarms of flies or angry wasps on a hot day, which repeatedly return to the attack as soon as they are brushed off. The archers pulled back only when more crusaders moved round the perimeter in support. Kilij Arslan then withdrew to seek allies, and the crusaders gained a respite.

A regular siege of Nicaea was then put in place, joined after two weeks by Curthose and Stephen with their sizeable contingent. Raymond's chronicler merely notes 'The Count of Normandy had come', but Fulcher says with pride: 'When those who were besieging Nicaea had heard it was told that our leaders, the Count of the Normans and Stephen of Blois had arrived, they came rejoicing to meet them and us on the road, and escorted us to the place where we stretched our tents outside the city, to the south.' Bohemond's chronicler particularly remarks on the presence of the Sicilian Roger of Barneville among Curthose's men.[7] With no sign of Kilij Arslan returning to the attack, the screws were tightened on Nicaea. Well supplied by Alexius and able to build siege towers, mangonels and other engines of war, and with boats operating on the lake, cutting off that remaining free side, the crusaders soon brought the defenders to capitulate. After a seven-week siege, Nicaea negotiated a surrender to Alexius in mid-June, according to which all the inhabitants' lives would be spared and Kilij Arslan's wife would be treated honourably in captivity.

There were grumblings in the crusader camps that the usual perks of plunder had been denied them, but Alexius needed to live with the Seljuks as neighbours. As some compensation, it was reported that the emperor would set up a hospice and monastery in Nicaea for Western pilgrims, and he also made conspicuously generous gifts to the poor among the crusader armies. Even so, there was a sense that an opportunity had been missed to revenge the massacre of the People's Crusade. Despite their losses, notably

Count Baldwin of Ghent who had brought a party of knights with Robert of Flanders, there was elation at this first significant and relatively easy victory, which augured well for the rest of the campaign. Stephen of Blois ended his letter to his wife on a wildly optimistic note: 'God is victorious, Nicaea is restored . . . I tell you, my sweet one, we shall accomplish the journey from Nicaea to Jerusalem in five weeks, unless Antioch should happen to delay us for a while.'[8]

Now, in the heat of full summer, the crusade prepared to cross Anatolia, accompanied by a senior Byzantine officer who knew the area well, and a corps of imperial troops. Their local knowledge would be essential as the army pressed further into a hostile hinterland. The old Roman roads were still easy to follow, but the pilgrims faced the searing heat and drought of summer, and, if they were much delayed, the risk of cold weather in the mountains. Kilij Arslan might attack again, but there were other men, both Christian and Muslim, whom with care they might be able to cultivate as allies. In particular, Alexius was negotiating with the Fatimids of Egypt, who had recently lost control of much of Palestine and Syria to the Seljuks, and on his advice emissaries were sent to them as well. Ideally, the crusade would push quickly on to Jerusalem. But with voyages largely restricted to short-distance coastal routes, their communications with Constantinople would always be threatened if they could not secure a land corridor along their path.

Leaving behind a small detachment to repair and garrison Nicaea, the crusaders moved on in late June in their separate contingents.[9] Their immediate objective was the city of Dorylaeum (Eskisehir), an important road junction. From there, the traditional Pilgrim Road went on to Ankyra before branching south. Another road cut across the arid, salt desert of central Anatolia, while a third route, itself made up of several good roads, skirted the desert's southern edge.

Unknown to the pilgrims, Kilij Arslan had arranged a temporary peace with a rival, and returned west with their combined forces, supplemented by a vassal army. Anticipating which way the crusaders would come, he waited in ambush near Dorylaeum. Perhaps in order to facilitate the movement of such a large army, the crusaders were travelling in two columns, a day apart. The first, composed of the contingents of Bohemond, Curthose, Stephen and Robert of Flanders, together with the Byzantine guides, encamped on 30 June in a broad valley just short of Dorylaeum. The following morning, the Seljuk

Anatolia and the First Crusade

archers sprung the trap. The crusaders' scouts had given a brief but crucial warning, and the knights seem to have been able to begin forming the camp into a defensive position; they also managed to send a message to the second column, urging them to move up in support. Then they were surrounded by a swarm of mounted attackers, who loosed an unending storm of arrows into the camp. Fulcher cowered among the tents with hundreds of others: 'such fighting was unknown to any of us . . . huddled together like sheep in a fold, trembling and terrified.'[10]

For several hours they were penned into the camp, while the knights repeatedly fought off the closest of their enemies. Their losses included two teenage aristocrats, Tancred's brother William and Geoffrey of Conversano's great-nephew. At last the second column came into sight, and now it was the Seljuks' turn to be amazed: they were apparently unaware that they had caught only part of the crusade. As they began to fall back, they left behind many horses and camels, which were a welcome addition to the western army. The decisive moment came when a small column of knights was seen breasting a small hill to one side of the valley. Fearing a third large column was upon them, the Seljuks fled in panic, although this was only a mounted group led by the resourceful Bishop Adhémar. As Kilij Arslan retreated, he was forced to abandon part of his treasury and, vital for the status of a nomadic ruler, his royal tent. With his prestige badly damaged and his confidence shaken, he pulled back far to the east, opening the way for the crusade across Anatolia.[11]

Two crusader leaders in particular shone in this crucial battle: Bohemond and Robert Curthose. The anonymous South Norman chronicler is unsurprisingly effusive in his praise for Bohemond. But Fulcher was also present in the vanguard, and he is conspicuously silent about the conduct of Stephen of Blois, with whom he was travelling. Ralph of Caen, who collected an assortment of stories after the crusade and is often critical of Curthose, notes that it was the Duke of Normandy who rallied a group of knights after an impetuous charge from the safety of the camp early in the engagement. He turned them around, forcing them to re-engage with the enemy in a cohesive way. Apart from their similar ages, Bohemond and Curthose could hardly have presented a greater contrast: the short, stocky duke with his cheerful voice and good nature, quick-witted, brave, respected as the grandson of a Jerusalem pilgrim and son of the great King William; and

Bohemond, immensely tall, lean, youthful looking, but calculating, cunning and avaricious, the portionless son of a repudiated wife. But they both showed their mettle at Dorylaeum, quickly grasping the need for new tactics in a novel situation, sharing the command between them and holding firm until reinforcements came.

After recovering somewhat, the cavalcade set off again. They feared a repeat attack from Kilij Arslan, and their guides would have warned them that the independent-minded tribes to the north remained a threat, while the loyalty of the Christian population was fragile. The short road across the arid region was too dry for their large and slow-moving host, so they headed south, skirting around the dry lands. Alexius's priority was almost certainly to regain control over as much of the Mediterranean coast as he could, and for this purpose too their route was logical. Although this was a fertile region, the Seljuks employed a scorched-earth policy as they fell back, and after decades of warfare the farms and wells were poorly maintained. The landscape was a mixture of high steppes and rolling hills, and the heat was intense. Keeping well south, the crusaders obtained fresh supplies at Pisidian Antioch (Yalvaç), a small but important city in a fertile rolling plain ringed by high mountains. Then they entered a drier area, and animals and men alike began to suffer from exhaustion and thirst. Fulcher especially notes the torment caused by the alternating hunger and plenty, and how people were prone to die from drinking too much after a long period of thirst. First the finest horses died, then the pack animals began to succumb, and the knights began to ride mules and captured animals, using anything they could as beasts of burden: even goats and dogs were pressed into service.

In mid-August, at about the time Stephen had optimistically predicted they would be at Jerusalem, the cavalcade wound up into the hills to a high bleak plateau dominated by the city of Iconium (Konya). Despite the hardships the travellers had endured, spirits were quickly restored when it was found that the Seljuks had abandoned the city at their approach. So far there had been no more ambushes, and at Iconium they found generous supplies, streams, orchards and fertile fields. Here they were rejoined by two small detachments that had taken different roads, perhaps as scouts: Tancred had followed the shorter but much drier road to the north of the hills via Philomelium (Aksehir), while Baldwin (Eustace and Godfrey's younger brother) had led another small group through the mountains. They halted at Iconium for a while, and the nobility amused themselves hunting, during which Godfrey was injured pursuing a bear. Raymond suffered a mysterious illness and received extreme unction, but he gradually recovered. The population of the neighbouring villages were Armenian Christians, more favourably disposed to a Byzantine-coordinated Christian army than to the Seljuks, and they advised the crusaders to take as much water with them as they could for the next part of the journey, which ran along the fringes of the desert.

With the details of the journey blurring into a haze of heat and unfamiliar names, always watchful for another attack, they pressed on over difficult terrain of soft, deeply eroded rocks, ringed to the south by fearsome mountains. At the end of August, they came to another fertile valley, and the city of Heraclea (Erégli), where they at last found the Seljuks waiting. But Arslan's power base was badly shaken, and, when the crusaders attacked, the Turks refused to give battle and retreated, leaving the city open.[12]

The way was now barred by the mighty Taurus Mountains, their peaks rising to over 3,000m, the only passes being precipitous narrow gorges, overshadowed by hostile crags. The short route, which carried the main Roman road, ran through the Cilician Gates, a pass so narrow that a handful of men could block it in places. The alternative was to make a long detour up to the north-east via Caesarea-in-Cappadocia (Kayseri) before approaching Antioch from the north. The Cilician Gates were so vulnerable to ambush that the large numbers of the crusader army would be useless in the event of an attack. The road also entailed a steep ascent to 1,000m, but the pass itself should be free of snow for several more months, and it gave quick access to Tarsus and the cities of the low-lying Cilician coastal region. The road via Caesarea, on the other hand, involved a long slow haul up to about 1,700m, and increased the risk of running into early snowfalls. Besides this, the passes through the Taurus were nearly as narrow as the Cilician Gates in places.

Both Cilicia and Cappadocia were predominantly Armenian Christian areas, with many semi-autonomous cities that had owed allegiance to the emperors before being over-run by the Muslim tribes. Moreover, the local Seljuk emir was deeply hostile to Kilij Arslan, and had even briefly held Nicaea against him. This gave the Byzantines an opportunity to reassert their hegemony over the Armenians, or at least to use them as allies. Perhaps not surprisingly, the crusaders decided to divide their forces at Heraclea and explore both regions. The main body, accompanied by their Byzantine guides and some local Armenians, prepared to follow the road to Caesarea, while two small companies, again led by Tancred and Baldwin, crossed into Cilicia.

The long uphill road to Caesarea, taken by Curthose and the other princes, proved uneventful but draining, the days still hot but the nights starting to turn chilly as September drew to a close. The city, impressively set below the towering Mount Erciyes, was occupied without any trouble, and a nearby stronghold was handed over to the control of an Armenian who had been travelling with them.[13] Then their road entered more mountainous country, where the population was eager to throw off the Seljuk yoke, and the garrisons of several small towns, including the stronghold of Coxon (Göksun), surrendered as they approached. At one Christian town, they found a Seljuk army that fled as they approached. Elated by these easy victories, Bohemond set off with a group of knights in pursuit, but their quarry melted away and it became a fruitless quest.

Near Coxon, where the crusade rested for a few days to resupply, a rumour reached them that the great city of Antioch was being deserted by its garrison. A contingent was therefore sent ahead to investigate, and if possible seize it. The rumour proved false, but their confidence was still running high and the detachment was able to capture and hold the small city of Rusa.

The main army now had to cross the highest part of the Taurus, through to Maras. The road proved a terrifying ordeal:

> We began to climb a cursed mountain which was so high and confined that none of our men dared to pass another on its paths. Horses and pack-animals plunged over the cliffs, one after the other. The wretched knights stood everywhere wringing their hands, overcome with fear and shock . . . they sold their shields, expensive breastplates and helmets if they could . . . or threw them down and went on.[14]

After this harrowing experience, and by now desperately short of animals, they came down from the 'cursed mountain' to Maras, in a well-watered and fertile landscape at the start of the long valley that runs down to Antioch and the sea. The garrison again fled at their coming, and the previous Armenian ruler was reinstated. Here they were rejoined by Bohemond, returning from his unsuccessful pursuit through the highlands. The predominantly Christian population advised the crusaders that the inhabitants of Artasia, a town between Aleppo and Antioch, would also welcome them, but there was a strong garrison holding it for the local emir. This strategic site – later known as the Shield of Antioch – was chosen as a preliminary target, and Robert of Flanders went ahead with a strong vanguard of knights to attack it. As they approached, the population rose and massacred the garrison, and opened the gates to Robert and his men. But no sooner were they safe within the walls than a large force of Seljuks surrounded the town, and lured a group of knights out into an ambush. A determined charge by Robert and the remainder of his force rescued them, but their losses were heavy. The Flemings remained bottled up in Artasia until relieved by reinforcements and then the arrival of the main army.

As the crusade prepared to attack Antioch, they were rejoined by Tancred and Baldwin, bringing the remains of their detachments over the Ammanus Mountains. Tancred had taken a very small mounted party through the Cilician Gates, followed a few days later by Baldwin with a larger group. At first things had gone well. Tancred had captured Tarsus, which controlled access to the pass and was within easy reach of the sea, and sent a messenger back to the main army requesting reinforcements to garrison it. But when Baldwin came up he seized control of the city, forcing Tancred to move further east. The reinforcements arrived, but Baldwin refused to admit them, and while they were camped outside the walls, a Seljuk raid fell upon them, massacring them to a man. Tancred meanwhile had taken over Adana, a key river crossing, Mamistra (Misis) and, most important of all, the port of Alexandretta (Iskenderun). In each case the Seljuks fell back as he approached, leaving the predominantly Armenian population as free agents.

Baldwin decided to leave a small garrison to hold Tarsus for him, and he too now moved east. He met Tancred at Mamistra, and they had a violent disagreement before making an uneasy truce. As autumn came, the humid weather in the low-lying malarial coastal belt was deteriorating, and fast losing its appeal. So Baldwin abandoned Cilicia and, presumably with a local guide, took his men through the passes back to the main army. There he found that his wife and children were seriously ill, and soon after his return they died. Fulcher glosses over the reception Baldwin had, but stories of the debacle at Tarsus must have spread through the army, and it may have been this that made Baldwin decide to leave the crusade, and seek his fortune in the Armenian lands further east. For an ambitious younger son, the crusade must always have offered the possibility, however remote, of some opportunity for advancement. And now his wife and children were dead, there was nothing to tie him to the main army, except his crusading vows. What is more surprising is that Fulcher now decided to leave Stephen of Blois with whom he had set off, and transfer to Baldwin's party. There is no explanation given, and it is not clear what position Fulcher may have had in Stephen's household, but hereafter his description of events in the journey towards Jerusalem is more confusing, and clearly second hand.

Tancred, too, returned to the main army, with his handful of men. This Cilician interlude, although expensive in manpower lost or diverted to garrison duties, had borne valuable fruit. The Turks had been pushed back; the Armenians had been given new confidence in the expedition and were more disposed to lend it assistance; the crusaders themselves were elated by the rescue of so many eastern Christians from the Muslim yoke; and the port of Alexandretta promised contact with the West and a supply route after many months of isolation. Indeed, while Baldwin was at Alexandretta, he had made contact with a freebooter who had some connection with Boulogne, and was willing to use his fleet to support the crusade.[15]

Antioch was a formidable city, dominating traffic through Syria. Here the crusaders faced new enemies, not nomadic tribes but settled regimes although still nominally under Seljuk control. The area was riven with petty feuds, especially between the mutually hostile successors of Tutush, the ruler of Damascus who had been killed in 1095. Chief among these were the factions gathered around Tutush's two sons, one based at Damascus and the other at Aleppo.

One of the main figures in the local balance of power was Kerbogha, the ruler of Mosul, who was nominally responsible for protecting Antioch. But he was unable to dominate the deeply fragmented situation, with its internecine wars and cultural, political and religious divisions. Within the Christian population, too, there were divisions, between the Orthodox who had traditionally backed the Byzantine emperors, and the many 'heretical' churches, some of which preferred Muslim rule to the Byzantine Orthodox. In particular, there was great animosity between the Syrian Christians, the Orthodox and the Armenians.

Only when the western army appeared south of the Taurus Mountains did the semi-independent governor of Antioch appeal for help. Not knowing which way to turn, he sent his sons to Damascus, Mosul and the Anatolian leaders, but no one was in a hurry to respond, and the westerners were able to make their way down the valley towards Antioch unopposed.

The first sight of Antioch was awesome. Stephen of Blois in another letter home called it 'a very great city, stronger than one can imagine, and utterly impregnable'. Its walls enclosed an area about 4km long and 2km wide, along the side of a steep hill near the top of which was a strongly defended citadel. A large part of the area within the walls was rough and uninhabited, with the city itself down at the bottom of the valley, close to the walls along the River Orontes. The road to the coast ran along the far side of the river and was reached by a single bridge. About 25km upstream, a bridge known to the crusaders as the Iron Bridge carried the Aleppo road back over the river. Built in the sixth century and strongly fortified, this was the first objective, to prevent Antioch being relieved from the east.

Curthose led the vanguard with a strong body of knights and a corps of foot soldiers, and while other groups attempted to ford the Orontes to attack the Iron Bridge from behind, he engaged the defenders in a stiff fight before capturing the bridge. The fords were then taken, and the area of the bridge was secured. With their backs better protected, the crusaders moved closer to Antioch and began to invest the city. It was now the end of October, and while they were expecting a delay because there was a sizeable garrison and little chance of taking the city by storm, it seemed likely that Antioch would soon capitulate, as all previous garrisons had done. Meanwhile it was necessary to tighten the noose as much as possible and deprive the defenders of supplies.

The crusaders moved into the low land to the north and west of the walls, and camped in sections, according to their place of origin and language. They built a bridge of boats over the Orontes to facilitate communication along the central section, where there was no gate from which they might be surprised by a sally. From the start there seems to have been some disagreement between the leaders; Bohemond favoured a cautious approach, knowing that the city had recently fallen to the Seljuks by treachery from within, while Raymond wished for a swift all-out attack.[16] But their camp was well provisioned, and the district had abundant supplies of food, and to start with their situation was good. Gradually, however, the defenders became bolder, and took to attacking their foraging parties, causing a steady trickle of casualties and a gradual sapping of morale. Among those who were noted for warding off these attacks were Hugh of Saint-Pol and his son Enguerrard, who had travelled from Normandy with Curthose.[17]

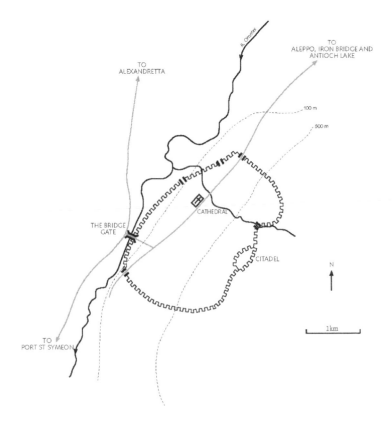

TO
ALEXANDRETTA

TO
ALEPPO, IRON BRIDGE AND
ANTIOCH LAKE

R. Orontes

100 m

500 m

THE BRIDGE
GATE

CATHEDRAL

CITADEL

N

1km

TO
PORT ST SYMEON

Antioch

= land over 1,500m

200km

Syria, Palestine and the First Crusade

The food reserves of the immediate hinterland of Antioch could not feed the army indefinitely. Despite their losses, through desertions, casualties and the garrisons left at the many captured cities, there were still about 30,000 mouths to be fed. By December, the weather had become cold, with frequent rain. Mud covered the roads and slowed movement down. Warfare in Syria, just as in northern Europe, normally came to an end during the winter. At Christmas 1097, the shortage of food was becoming acute, and a foraging party was sent off up the Orontes valley under the joint command of Robert of Flanders and Bohemond. As soon as they were safely out of range, the defenders sallied out and attacked Raymond's camp. They were driven off, but with heavy losses.

Meanwhile Robert and Bohemond made their way up the valley as far as Hama, where they were surprised by a large army coming from Damascus to relieve Antioch. Robert was nearly captured, and only just saved by the quick thinking of Bohemond. Although the crusaders claimed a victory and forced the Muslims to retreat, they returned empty-handed, which greatly depressed the pilgrims' spirits.

In January the weather became still worse, the torrential rain making life in the tents a misery. Foraging parties went as far as the Taurus, but supplies could be bought only in small quantities. The local population may have preferred the crusaders to the Seljuks, but not to the extent of supplying them free of charge. Stephen grumbled to his wife:

> We have borne many toils and countless sufferings up to this present time. Many have used up all their own resources . . . Truly, very many of our Franks would have died from starvation if the mercy of God and our money had not rescued them. We have suffered for our Lord Jesus Christ before this city of Antioch throughout the whole winter, from excessive cold and great deluges. What some say about the impossibility of bearing the heat of the sun throughout Syria is untrue, for the winter there is very similar to our winter in the west.[18]

Some help came from the sea. At about the same time as the crusade reached Antioch, a Genoese fleet of thirteen ships put in to St Symeon, the harbour at the mouth of the Orontes. They had set sail from Genoa in July, and must have called in at several places along the way to gather information about the progress of the army. There would have been time for the ships to go to Constantinople, and then via Cyprus to Alexandretta and still arrive at St Symeon in October or November.[19] An English fleet also arrived off the Syrian coast in late 1097: Raymond of Aguilers says thirty English boats had sailed into the Mediterranean and captured both St Symeon and the port of Laodicaea before the crusade reached Antioch, and Anselm of Ribemont, another eyewitness, refers to Laodicaea as if it was captured at about the same time as Tancred took Tarsus. An Arabic source may be referring to this English fleet when it speaks of twenty-two ships from Cyprus arriving on 19 August and pillaging Laodicaea. Bishop Adhémar seems to have visited Cyprus soon after the crusade's arrival before Antioch, whence he wrote a letter back to the West jointly with the exiled Orthodox Patriarch of Jerusalem.[20] It seems, therefore, that when the crusaders reached Antioch, if not before, they were aware that St Symeon and probably also Laodicaea were in Western hands. Adhémar presumably sailed to Cyprus to establish contact with the West and Constantinople, and to spearhead the dispatch of supplies of food and equipment.

Unfortunately for the crusaders, the Mediterranean was even more hostile than the land in winter. The winds were variable, and frequently too strong for galleys to put to sea. An army of this size would need several good-sized grain ships a week, and materials for building siege engines and the other paraphernalia of war would also take up valuable space. The Genoese fleet, for example, is reported putting into St Symeon in mid-November, perhaps after delivering Bishop Adhémar to Cyprus. It seems to have brought a cargo of timber, and with it a watchtower was built to control the main gate of the city.[21] After Christmas, another tower was built, with wood brought in by the English fleet.[22]

The road from the port to the crusader camp was particularly vulnerable, winding uphill for 30km to the Bridge Gate. There are several reports of attacks on supply convoys as they came up the valley, and, in view of the increasing need for food, it would not be surprising if senior princes had taken charge of the commissariat. This seems to be exactly what happened. Stephen of Blois was given the ambiguous title of 'leader, planner and manager' of the army, and he told his wife with pride that he had been put in charge of the treasury, so he now had far more wealth at his disposal than she had entrusted to him when he left home. What Stephen's functions were is not clear, nor is there any indication of how the logistical nightmare of protecting the ports, coordinating the arrival of ships and arranging escorts for the transport of their cargoes up to Antioch was undertaken.

In late December 1097, Curthose was not in the camp, but he was present again six weeks later.[23] Ralph of Caen explains the duke's absence in rather hostile terms:

> the Norman count, exhausted by the miserable circumstances . . . went to Laodicaea . . . which the English were holding at that time, guarding it for the emperor. . . . Therefore the Norman count entered Laodicaea and spent his time in slumber and idleness. This was not entirely useless, however, because he found substantial supplies there and gave them out generously to those who were in need. Cyprus, abounding in wine, grain and great numbers of cattle, supplied Laodicaea and its needy Christian hinterland . . . and was the only place which was both Christian and held for Alexius . . . But this did not excuse his idleness, and the aforementioned count twice failed to heed the summons to return to the camp, and at last came with great reluctance under threat of anathema.[24]

Ralph of Caen is the only source for this story, which is clearly imperfect, since St Symeon and Alexandretta were also in Christian hands at the time. Laodicaea was a full two days' journey further down the coast, well into enemy-held territory, so it is unlikely that Curthose would have chosen it as a safe haven from the rigours of winter siege warfare. Ralph was not an eyewitness of the crusade, arriving in Syria only in 1108, where he served Bohemond and Tancred. He based his *Gesta Tancredi* on the anonymous South Norman history, with additional material that he gleaned from other sources in the East. This account of Curthose's activities therefore needs to be treated with caution.

It is possible that Curthose was based at the ports to supervise the transmission of supplies. Anselm of Ribemont comments in a letter that on one occasion when extra manpower was needed a message was sent to recall those who were stationed at the coast, so Curthose may have had a significant contingent of soldiers with him. Although there were about forty ships operating between the Syrian coast and Cyprus during this winter, the army was coming close to starving and the supply chain was crucial. Anselm noted that by February 1098 as many of his friends had died of sickness as in battle, and both Godfrey and Raymond were seriously ill at times.[25]

So we were left in the greatest possible need, for the Turks were wearing us down on every side, so that nobody dared to leave the camp. For they attacked us in one way and starvation tormented us in another. All help and aid had abandoned us. The lowly and poor fled to Cyprus, to Anatolia or up into the mountains. We did not dare to go to the sea for fear of those terrible Turks, nor was there any way out for us.[26]

Taken as a whole, the descriptions of the siege of Antioch through that winter make it clear that there were sporadic shipping movements between the coast and Cyprus, a sea voyage of three or four days in good conditions, bringing in supplies, ferrying out deserters and transmitting information. Given the dangers on the road inland to Antioch, it would be an important duty, delegated presumably to a reliable leader, to be based at one or other of the ports to oversee the transmission of material to the camp. Reading between Ralph of Caen's lines, one can discern just such a strategy in place, submerged beneath the envy of a man stuck in the camp, where discomforts were greater, but where opportunities for glory were correspondingly more frequent.

As with so many other moments of his life, a close analysis of the sources for Curthose's actions shows that it is only after his cause was publicly lost that a negative twist is introduced, although his natural good nature and lack of the thrusting ambition of many of his contemporaries cannot be denied. Few commentators are as transparent as Guibert of Nogent, writing in northern France in about 1106–9:

It would hardly be right to remain silent about Robert, Count of Normandy, whose bodily indulgences, weakness of will, prodigality with money, gourmandising, indolence and lechery were expiated by the perseverance and heroism that he vigorously displayed in the army of the Lord. . . . he should now be forgiven, since God has punished him in this world, where he now languishes in jail, deprived of all his honours.[27]

At first, morale in the army besieging Antioch was maintained, and desertions were few. But as the weeks dragged by and conditions in the camp deteriorated further, more prominent people began to leave. First, the Byzantine officer who had accompanied them from Nicaea took ship to

Constantinople, perhaps to consult Alexius, or possibly because of rumours that he was in danger of being poisoned by disaffected crusaders. After he had gone, Bohemond spread the word that he had fled through cowardice, suggesting that the Byzantines were unreliable allies. One morning, it was discovered that Peter the Hermit had escaped with a group of followers; Tancred furiously dashed after them and apprehended them on the road to the coast, bringing them back in disgrace. Bohemond meanwhile began suggesting that he should be rewarded for his part in the crusade with a principality centred on Antioch, hinting that he might otherwise pull out.

In early February, reports reached the crusaders that the ruler of Aleppo was at last coming to rescue Antioch. His army numbered perhaps 12,000 men, against which the crusaders could now muster only some 700 warhorses. A council of war agreed to an audacious plan proposed by Bohemond, that he and Robert of Flanders should fling the full weight of the remaining knights in a surprise attack on the enemy near the Iron Bridge, to try and prevent them reaching the city, while Curthose, Eustace and Bishop Adhémar commanded the infantry and the many knights who no longer had mounts, to defend the camp and maintain a tight siege, against any attempted break-out. Using information gleaned by scouting parties led by Walter of Saint-Valéry, the knights waited until the Aleppan army had encamped close to the Iron Bridge, and then they took up their position behind a low hill, during a night of heavy rain. Early in the morning of 9 February, they charged and took the relieving army completely by surprise. After a brief but fierce battle, in which Conan of Brittany was killed, the Seljuk army was routed and fled in disorder back towards Aleppo, being harried by the native Christians as they went.[28]

A group of Egyptian ambassadors with the crusade witnessed this victory and were so impressed that they proposed a mutual partition of Palestine. The crusaders sent their envoys back to Cairo for further negotiations.

Early in the spring of 1098, the English fleet with its valuable cargo of timber put into St Symeon. Raymond was temporarily restored to health and becoming increasingly suspicious of Bohemond, so the two of them led a party down to the coast to escort the supplies up to the camp. On the way they were fiercely attacked by a sortie from Antioch, and both narrowly escaped with their lives. Orderic Vitalis and other derivative accounts suggest that this fleet was under the control of Edgar Atheling, but there is no support for this in the contemporary sources. The Anglo-Saxon Chronicle places him with an army on the Scottish border soon after Michaelmas 1097, after which he returned to England. He cannot, therefore, have provisioned a fleet that sailed across Biscay and along the entire length of the Mediterranean to arrive off the Syrian coast in spring 1098. If Edgar had wished to hurry to join his foster-brother Curthose in the Holy Land, he would have done better to cross Europe overland and take a Genoan or Pisan boat that summer. There is, however, definite evidence for several northern fleets assisting the crusade, since another contemporary letter describes English (or perhaps 'North Sea') ships going to Syria from northern Italy at this time. A much later saga about Anglo-Saxon exiles also speaks of a large fleet from England that reached Constantinople shortly before the crusade.[29]

The new supplies of good timber enabled the crusaders to build another much-needed watchtower, to protect the road down to St Symeon. Raymond claimed ownership of this tower, and therefore garrisoned it with a group of his Provençal soldiers. In April, a third tower was built.

By early May, the crusade had been halted before Antioch for six months, in an increasingly dangerous stalemate. Supplies were running low in the city, but as yet it showed no signs of capitulating. Reports were now arriving that Kerbogha of Mosul was marching to relieve the city, and also that Alexius had set off across Anatolia, supported by a fleet. For Bohemond, who was intent on taking over Antioch for himself once it had fallen into Christian hands, the worry was that Alexius would arrive before that was accomplished. The other princes knew that if they did not take the city before Kerbogha arrived, they would be trapped between his army and the walls, at the mercy of the garrison they had besieged for so long. For all, it was now a matter of the utmost urgency to devise a plan to take Antioch, by whatever means. Fortunately, or by the grace of God as the crusaders saw it, Kerbogha made a fatal error in his calculations, which gave the crusade a vital breathing space.

While the main crusader army had headed south to Antioch the previous autumn, Baldwin had set off with a small company of mounted followers and an Armenian guide, into the lands bordering the River Euphrates. In this region of precariously independent Armenian principalities, he had quickly managed to take advantage of the internal feuds in Edessa, and set himself

up as its ruler. Perceiving this western enclave as a threat, Kerbogha diverted
the first part of his assembling army to besiege Edessa for three weeks, before
resuming his march on Antioch and joining up with the remainder of his
allies.

This critical period gave Bohemond the time he needed. He had been
cultivating contacts among the multiethnic, multicultural population of
Antioch for some time, and in particular he had established a link with an
Armenian inhabitant. Although this man was trusted by the city rulers,
he was more than willing to betray it to the crusaders. For the time being,
Bohemond kept his counsel, while perfecting his plan in private.

As Kerbogha's army, swelling with additional allies, drew closer day by day,
desertions in the crusader camp increased, until on 2 June Stephen of Blois's
nerve broke and he fled to the coast. Fulcher of Chartres seems embarrassed
to discuss his reasons, while some eyewitnesses frankly say he was afraid.
Albert of Aachen, who collected many stories from crusade participants
some years later, says Stephen made his way to Alexandretta (he would
thereby avoid meeting those who were in charge of the main ports), where
he was joined by many other deserters, who managed to board ships back
towards the West. The anonymous chronicler also mentions Alexandretta,
and implies that Stephen took the survivors of his Blois contingent with him,
ignoring pleas from Antioch to return. Attempts have recently been made to
rehabilitate Stephen, to justify his actions as a considered withdrawal rather
than an emotional collapse, but this is hard to sustain in the light of the
evidence. He was clearly in breach of his crusading vow, excommunicated
and publicly shamed. It was perhaps this more than the terrible nagging he
endured from a humiliated and infuriated Adela that drove him back to the
East three years later.[30]

The departure of Stephen was a significant setback for the crusade.
He had never shone as a major contributor, but he was a conspicuous
figure, whose absence was noticed, and he had presumably taken with
him desperately needed knights with their precious horses. There is some
suggestion that he had been ill for some time, although other sources
declare this was feigned. He may also have been considering abandoning
the crusade for some weeks, waiting for a convenient fleet of ships and
favourable weather. The letter he wrote to his wife in late March ended
with a curious postscript:

Dearest, I write to you about few, indeed, of many matters, and, dearest, because I cannot express to you what is in my mind, I bid you act well, and order your children excellently to your call, and treat your men fairly, as befits you, because you will certainly see me as soon as I am able. Farewell.[31]

Poor Stephen, if only he had waited a little longer, he might have been saved from the consequences of his ignominious flight. That very evening, Bohemond revealed his plans to the remaining princes, chief among them Curthose, who was emerging as a mediator in their disputes. The plan was simple if typically audacious and seems to have been readily accepted. In the twilight, visible to the defenders on the walls, a detachment made off as if on an expedition, and then under cover of darkness crept back towards the city gates, while Bohemond's picked followers scaled the walls into the tower commanded by the betrayer. After a vicious scuffle, the Christian inhabitants were roused, the gates were flung open and the crusaders poured in. Bruno of Lucca, who came to Antioch with the English fleet, later reported that Bohemond, Curthose and Robert of Flanders had engineered the plan between them.[32]

A swift and bloody massacre ensued, the half-starved inhabitants slaughtering the Seljuk garrison, supported by the pent-up fury of the crusaders. By nightfall on 3 June, hardly a Turk in Antioch remained alive, apart from a remnant under the governor's son, who had raced up to the citadel and barricaded themselves in, taunted by Bohemond's purple banner, which now flew from the adjacent high point of the walls. The governor himself had escaped, only to be thrown from his horse and discovered lying stunned on the ground. His head was hacked off and taken to Bohemond as proof that he was dead. Meanwhile local Christian bands rampaged around the surrounding villages, in an orgy of pillaging.

No sooner had the victorious crusaders begun clearing up the outer city the next morning than the advance detachments of Kerbogha's army appeared. The besiegers now found themselves besieged, trapped in a walled area denuded of almost everything edible, but mercifully well supplied with drinking water, watched by the remnant of the Seljuk garrison, holed up in the citadel. An Armenian monk living in Antioch at the time wrote:

This year the Lord visited his people, as it is written, 'I will not abandon you or leave you.' . . . They took the city and with the sharpness of a two-edged sword

they destroyed the overweening dragon and his battalions. And after one or
two days, a mighty army gathered, promising safety to its people . . . insolent as
pharoah. . . . For two weeks, reduced to extreme fear, they were brought low in
their affliction, because they lacked the most basic food for man and mare.[33]

Kerbogha captured the Iron Bridge, and his main army camped nearby,
while a mounted squadron advanced close to the city walls to test the resolve
of the crusaders. They were unable to resist the challenge, and a group
of about fifteen knights, including Roger of Barneville, by now serving as
Curthose's standard-bearer, dashed out. As always, an ambush was sprung,
and Roger was unseated, hit in the back and then decapitated, all within
clear view of the city walls. No one dared venture out until nightfall, when a
party crept out, and brought back his mangled remains for burial in St Peter's
Cathedral.[34] Pushed onto the defensive, the crusaders inside the city could
only wait for Kerbogha's next move.

Over the next three days, the Muslim alliance moved up and camped about
5km up the valley, where a river draining a large lake flowed into the Orontes.
Detachments spread round the city, forcing the crusaders to pull back from
their wooden towers into the safety of the walls. Then Kerbogha sent a
contingent up the steep hill to the east of the city and formed a small camp
from which he could communicate with the defenders of the citadel.[35]

Fearing that Kerbogha would reinforce the citadel, the crusaders (led by
Bohemond, Curthose, Godfrey and Robert of Flanders) staged a pre-emptive
strike against this upper camp, but were driven back with heavy losses. The
fighting raged for two days, pausing only when darkness fell, until mutual
exhaustion forced a lull. Kerbogha then abruptly changed tactics, and withdrew
his men from their exposed and waterless camp, back into the valley. The
crusaders seized the opportunity to build a defensive wall across the lower
ground between the citadel and Bohemond's tower, and then, leaving the
invalid Raymond to watch the citadel, moved back down the slope to the city.

That night, there were further high-profile desertions. Bohemond's brother-
in-law William Grandmesnil, with his brothers Aubrey and Ivo, Count
Lambert of Clermont and several others, lowered themselves over the walls of
the city and escaped on foot to St Symeon, where they readily persuaded the
sailors to abandon the harbour. As with Stephen, their flight became a lasting
reproach, and they were known to the Norman world as 'the rope dancers'.[36]

Within Antioch, hunger and fear rubbed shoulders. 'The leaves of figs, vines, thistles and any tree were cooked and chewed . . . others stewed the skins of horse, camels, asses and oxen.' The knights dared not kill their few remaining horses, but some were reduced to bleeding them and cooking the blood with cumin and pepper discovered in the spice market. Then, on the morning of 11 June, a priest named Stephen of Valence reported to Bishop Adhémar that he had received a vision, promising divine aid. Adhémar wisely used this as an opportunity to shore up the army's morale, and staged a public ceremony at which the remaining princes swore not to desert the cause. The Armenian monk wrote: 'And thus terribly weakened and fearful of the pagan multitude, they gathered in the Basilica of the Apostle St Peter, and with a great cry and lamentation they cried to the Lord . . . and then they encouraged one another, saying, "The Lord will give strength to his people."'

Two days later, a poor Provençal named Peter Bartholomew ('almost the lowest of the low', according to Bruno of Lucca) also had a vision, telling him that the Holy Lance lay hidden in the floor of St Peter's Cathedral. At his direction, the floor was excavated, and Peter leaped into the hole, producing a piece of metal, which he said was the Lance. The effect on morale was electrifying. Not only Raymond and the Provençals but all the disparate groups that made up the crusade were united in rejoicing and new-found hope. Anselm of Ribemont wrote 'all our spirits were revived'; the anonymous chronicler saw it as the turning point: 'From that hour, we began planning for war.'[37]

It was clear that the crusaders could not endure a long siege, especially in the heat of summer. First Raymond and then Adhémar fell seriously ill again, and it seems to have been agreed that Bohemond should take overall command of the army. The acute shortage of horses severely restricted their options, and at first a trial by combat with twenty mounted warriors from each side was offered and rejected. Estimates of the numbers of mounted knights available seem quite realistic by this stage in the campaign: a total of only about 700 animals, many of which were in a severely weakened condition or were mules and asses. There was therefore need to plan a new style of attack, and it was perhaps this that delayed the sortie from Antioch for two weeks, despite the great morale boost provided by the finding of the Lance.

On the morning of 28 June, the Eve of St Peter and Paul, the crusaders formed up inside the Bridge Gate, clearly visible to the defenders of the citadel, who hoisted a black flag to warn Kerbogha of the coming break-out. He allowed them to emerge before closing for battle, relying presumably on his greatly superior numbers and fresh horses to achieve a clear-cut victory. Raymond was still too ill to participate, and was left with a small body of men to prevent a sortie from the citadel. The other contingents came out as quickly as they could, led by Hugh, Curthose, Robert of Flanders and Eustace. Godfrey brought his men out next, and these groups spread out from the walls towards the middle of the wide valley, facing up towards Kerbogha's camp in the distance. Adhémar, by contrast, marched the Provençals quickly across the valley, aiming for the higher ground on the other side. Bohemond emerged last, keeping his men in reserve to respond as events unfolded. Each group of infantry had a small group of knights at the rear, directing operations and ready to charge if needed.

The advantages of this strategy are obvious. By emerging from the Bridge Gate, near the seaward end of the walls, the crusaders had only a small enemy force behind them, and they could engage those guarding the nearest parts of the walls first, before other groups came up. The main enemy camp was about 8km away, so Kerbogha was unable to control the movement of his army. Moreover, by sending out Curthose and the other northern crusaders in the first cohort, they were assured of a relatively cohesive group who could communicate easily and act quickly and forcefully in the initial attack.

The plan worked to perfection. The enemy closed with the crusaders piecemeal, and lost their advantage of superior numbers, while the desperation of the westerners far outweighed the mutual suspicions and half-hearted participation of many of Kerbogha's allies. A body of mounted archers did attack, causing some casualties, but the crusaders had an answer this time, as Hugh led up a group of bowmen, protected by a roof of shields. The brunt of the fighting was felt by the groups of northerners closest to the city walls, where Curthose was positioned, with the few mounted knights inspiring their men to stand firm. At least, after ransacking the city, they were now well supplied with weapons. Some Turks came round to the rear, but Bohemond was able to fight them off. The engagement was fierce and bloody, with many losses on both sides, but Kerbogha's men were the first to break, turning and running back up the valley, hampering their reinforcements and giving the impression that the day was lost. A general retreat soon began, and Kerbogha assumed that his army was defeated, before it was even engaged. Although the crusaders were unable to give chase for want of horses, the great army was soon in full flight. 'They charged against the wicked enemy,' wrote the Armenian monk; 'they dispersed them; they put them to flight and slaughtered them to the setting of the sun. This was a great joy to the Christians, and there was an abundance of wheat and barley.'

When they saw they were abandoned, the defenders in the citadel gave themselves up to Bohemond, who took it over as his headquarters. His relationship with Raymond, who was still ill but holding out for the rights of the emperor over Antioch, now declined swiftly. Raymond installed an armed guard in the old Palace in the lower town, creating a dangerous and divided atmosphere. The other princes meanwhile sent Hugh and Count Baldwin of Hainault back to intercept Alexius, with the news that Antioch was finally in their hands. But on the road through Anatolia they were attacked, and Baldwin of Hainault and his men were never heard of again. Hugh reached Constantinople too late to avert the growing crisis.

The army, although victorious, now desperately needed a period of rest, to recover from the terrible deprivation of the winter, obtain more horses and resupply. Some contingents had already been on campaign for two years, and Bohemond was in no hurry to move. It was generally assumed that Alexius would soon arrive, the disputes could be settled, and they would then move on to Jerusalem. The Genoese fleet soon reappeared at St Symeon, and on 14 July Bohemond staked his claim to Antioch by making a trading agreement with them, arrogating the rights of a ruler to grant them houses in the city. This not only demonstrated his determination to establish himself at Antioch, but it gave him a powerful link with Italy, a potential source of reinforcements. His isolation among the princes by this time is apparent, since all four lay witnesses of the charter were minor members of his entourage.[38]

On 1 August, Bishop Adhémar died. He had been the respected spiritual leader of the crusade, the pope's personal representative and a non-partisan voice among the fractious princes. Without his guidance, the rifts between them deepened, while the spiritual vacuum was filled by the Provençal Peter Bartholomew, whose prestige was high after the finding of the Lance. On 11 September, the princes, probably at the urging of Bohemond, sent an open letter to the West, describing the capture of Antioch in terms highly critical of

Alexius. Hugh meanwhile had decided not to rejoin the crusade, and slipped quietly home to France. Like Stephen of Blois, he returned to the East in 1101, where he died.

Through the heat of late summer and into the autumn the crusade was halted. An epidemic killed many people and caused the princes to disperse, perhaps also wishing to emulate Bohemond and Baldwin and establish power bases for themselves. It may have been at this time that more of Curthose's companions died, notably Philip Montgomery, youngest brother of Robert of Bellême, and Gerard of Gournay. Gerard's widow Edith later returned to Normandy and married a French crusader.[39] Godfrey went up to Edessa and joined his brother Baldwin. Bohemond visited Cilicia and strengthened the garrisons left there, further depleting the main army. Tancred may have tried to hold some small cities on the road to Aleppo. Of Curthose there is no clear evidence. He may have gone to Laodicaea, but by the time the crusade finally moved south the port had probably been handed over into imperial control.[40] Raymond moved to Rusa and made forays to the south-east. Raymond Pilet, one of Raymond's knights, crossed the Orontes and tried unsuccessfully to capture the city of Ma'arra, assisted by the local Christians.[41]

The Provençal actions in particular may have been intended as a foil against Bohemond, but there were other good reasons for the princes to disperse, apart from the epidemic. They were, for the first time, inactive in an area with an essentially friendly population, which made obtaining supplies very difficult, since plunder and requisitioning were discouraged. The immediate hinterland of Antioch had been scoured clean of food, and the fields had been largely idle for a year because of the siege, so it was necessary to fan out and locate new sources. The army was so short of animals that it was impossible to contemplate a further campaign until more mounts and pack animals had been procured. Lastly, it was vital to keep the soldiers busy, lest disaffection should grow.

In late summer, news arrived that Alexius would not be coming. Stephen of Blois had crossed to Anatolia, and found the emperor at Philomelium, which he had reached after a successful naval and military operation recapturing territories isolated by the crusader victories. Whatever Alexius's original intentions (and both the Byzantine and Crusader sources assert he was on his way to join the crusade), Stephen's tale that Antioch had fallen to Kerbogha, wiping out the entire crusade, resulted in the imperial army turning back for

Constantinople. Now Bohemond had more justification for his view of Alexius, and anti-Byzantine feeling grew.

Eventually voices began to be heard, led by Peter Bartholomew, demanding a resumption of the march on Jerusalem. On 1 November a council was held at Antioch. As before, the main division was between Bohemond, who now demanded that Antioch be handed over to him, as he had masterminded both its capture and its subsequent deliverance from Kerbogha, and Raymond, who still held out the hope that Alexius would either come in person or arrange for Antioch to be formally handed back to the empire. The difficulties were made worse because, although the crusade clearly depended on Alexius's goodwill for the supplies from Cyprus, Raymond never seems to have excelled as a military leader, had been ill for much of the campaign, and lacked charisma.

The November council resulted in what Raymond of Aguilers, Count Raymond's chronicler, aptly called the *discordem pacem* : the disharmonious peace. The princes agreed to resume their march on Jerusalem, while allowing Raymond and Bohemond to maintain their fortified enclaves in Antioch. After this, the crusade fissured still further, and, with only one chronicler in each party, it becomes very hard to discern what actually happened, among the hostile reporting and innuendo.

Rather than start for Jerusalem, the Provençals and Flemings returned to attack Ma'arra, perhaps to increase their zone of influence close to Antioch. Bohemond followed them there, and their combined forces threatened a direct assault. After two weeks, during which Enguerrard, son of Hugh of Saint-Pol, was killed, the city fell, was plundered and endured a wholesale massacre.[42] Inevitably, Raymond and Bohemond immediately argued over the future control of the city. Bohemond returned to Antioch and expelled Raymond's garrison from the Palace, in breach of the peace terms. Disgusted, Raymond announced that he was leaving for Jerusalem.

On 13 January 1099, a much-reduced crusade finally set off again towards Jerusalem. Raymond and Curthose, together with Tancred, who had taken service with Raymond, marched off with perhaps 1,000 knights and about 6,000 foot soldiers, on the inland road to Homs, accompanied by the survivors of the English fleets, who had abandoned the last of their boats. Godfrey and Robert of Flanders showed no inclination to continue, and Bohemond was determined to occupy Antioch.

As they went, the crusaders made peace with the local Islamic rulers, who allowed them to buy food and horses, so that despite the wet and muddy conditions, they were in increasingly good shape. A vigilant rearguard warded off the occasional skirmishers. Near Homs, they turned west towards the coast, and encountered some opposition when their foragers were attacked from a fortress on a seemingly impregnable hill. In the ensuing skirmish, the Muslim shepherds fled to the safety of the fort, and the crusaders were diverted into rounding up the flocks, only to be attacked again. That night the defenders unexpectedly withdrew, and their fortress fell into the crusaders' hands: a huge and unanticipated bonus, giving them a valuable defensive site, where the mighty castle of Krac des Chevaliers would soon be built. Appreciating its potential, Curthose and Raymond halted at Krac for three weeks, to celebrate the Feast of the Purification and enjoy their haul of booty and provisions, while they planned their next move.

From Krac several routes were open to them. They could return to the inland road and aim for Galilee via Damascus; they could contact the Fatimids, who had taken advantage of Kerbogha's defeat to recapture Jerusalem, and negotiate a peaceful takeover of the city without resorting to a military attack; or they could continue to the coast road and link up with Laodicaea, which was only a few days' journey to the north. If they took the coast road, they still had the choice of continuing to make peace with the local emirs, or of attacking one or more of the cities on the way, to give themselves a stronger bargaining position. One obvious target for such a strategy was Tripoli.

The Emir of Tripoli sent envoys to the crusaders at Krac, and in return emissaries visited him, bringing back such stories of his wealth that they decided to make a show of strength in his territories in the hope of forcing his hand. They therefore moved on Akkar, near the coast, while sending a small detachment under Raymond Pilet to try and take the port of Tortosa by stealth. Arriving after dark, Pilet had fires lit round the landward perimeter of the port, persuading the occupants that they were surrounded by a huge army. The governor promptly evacuated his garrison by night and sailed to Tripoli, leaving the population to open the gates in the morning. This brilliant success reopened communications with Antioch and Cyprus.

The army meanwhile closed on Akkar, on 14 February. News of their progress was taken north by sea, by Curthose's chaplain Arnulf of Chocques, and it prompted the princes at Antioch to move.[43] Bohemond brought a contingent as far as Laodicaea, but then he turned back, perhaps fearing Alexius might come to Syria now that spring was approaching. Godfrey and Robert of Flanders continued down the coast road and joined the siege of Akkar. This was not going well. Raymond, having a larger treasury than Curthose, may have had nominal control, but he lacked the charisma of Bohemond, and already Tancred was regretting taking service with him. Raymond of Aguilers defends Count Raymond, saying Tancred was deliberately stirring up trouble, but, as soon as the reinforcements arrived, Tancred switched his allegiance to Godfrey.

Akkar was built on a steep spur of land projecting above the coastal plain, protected on one side by a ravine that at this time of year was a rushing torrent. Curthose and Raymond had divided the army between them, separated by a narrow bridge. The defenders were determined, and hurled ballista stones into the crusader lines, causing many casualties including Anselm of Ribemont, who received a fatal blow on his head. It became increasingly apparent that a successful assault might be nearly as costly in time and manpower as Antioch, and to little purpose. The Emir of Tripoli was still willing to consider terms, and the crusade was so depleted and weary that it could not endure another long period of attrition.[44]

But now Raymond, with his one eye perhaps on his conquests to the north, was beginning to step into Bohemond's shoes, demanding that the siege be complete, while the other leaders urged that the dispute with Tripoli be resolved and they move on Jerusalem. The division was accentuated when an envoy came from Alexius at Easter, saying that he would come in person in June and lead them into Palestine. Peter Bartholomew experienced a suspicious resurgence of visions, increasingly obviously in line with Raymond's wishes, and doubts about the authenticity of the Holy Lance began to be voiced more openly, despite Raymond's continuing strong support. Peter, perhaps foolishly, was convinced by the genuineness of his visions, and volunteered to undergo trial by fire to justify himself. The results were inevitable. Peter dashed through the flames, emerging horribly burnt. He died in agony twelve days later, leaving Raymond clinging to his belief in the Lance and claiming that Peter had emerged unscathed but had been pushed back into the flames by the eager crowd who had witnessed the miracle. The trial resolved nothing, except further to erode Raymond's credibility.

Curthose, Godfrey and Robert of Flanders now took things in hand, and launched a separate attack on the outskirts of Tripoli, and then quickly negotiated an accord with the emir. It was just as well that they did so, for, unknown to them, Alexius was actively negotiating with the Fatimids, playing down his links with the crusade in the light of Bohemond's seizure of Antioch.

Leaving their dead at Akkar, the northern crusaders burnt their camp and marched to Tripoli, accompanied by part of Raymond's contingent, who had decided to abandon him. The desire to complete their pilgrimage and reach Jerusalem was now paramount, and Raymond was reluctantly forced to follow. As they prepared to leave Tripoli, their ambassadors to Egypt returned, having witnessed the Fatimids' capture of Jerusalem and been taken on a tour of the city.[45] But whereas the Fatimids had previously offered to divide Palestine, with Jerusalem going to the crusaders, much had now changed, and their new offer was less favourable. They were in control of Jerusalem, and knew that Alexius was not fully behind the crusaders. They were also negotiating secretly with the Seljuks of Syria. For its part, the smaller and vastly more experienced crusader army was now confident of its abilities, and was focused on capturing Jerusalem. The princes were consequently unimpressed when the Fatimids offered safe conducts for unarmed pilgrims to Jerusalem and the Holy Places. They therefore concluded a detailed and very favourable treaty with the emir, including guides, supplies and protection as they moved down the coast. He even offered to convert to Christianity and place Tripoli under crusader control if they defeated the Fatimids.

On 16 May the crusade, now numbering some 1,200 knights and 12,000 on foot, moved on. By now, the relationships between the princes had shifted again. Raymond still controlled the largest contingent, but he was to a considerable extent discredited, and Curthose and Godfrey had emerged as two key players. Their march down the coast, with access to friendly fleets, including the ships of the Emir of Tripoli, but hemmed in by high ground, was accomplished very quickly. They took twenty-three days to cover the 360km from Tripoli to Jerusalem, including making treaties with Beirut and Acre, encountering no resistance as they passed Tyre, Haifa and Caesarea (where they rested for four days for Pentecost) and meeting trouble only at Sidon, where they halted for three days and were harassed by the inhabitants and attacked by snakes. The land was nominally under Fatimid rule, but the population comprises Maronite and Jacobite Christians, who were mostly willing to help the Christian army. At Acre, the narrow coastal road widened out, and they rested for three days again, having escaped without any serious ambushes.

At Arsuf, they turned inland for Ramla, while Jaffa was abandoned and its defences destroyed as they approached. This gave them a port close to Jerusalem. At Ramla, the enemy melted away as they approached, and they camped in a well-provisioned site, where they rested until 6 June. All along the coast of Lebanon and Palestine, their journey had been accomplished with less trouble and more ease than they could have dreamt possible. At Lydda, on the edge of the Judaean hills near Ramla, the crusader leaders visited the shrine of St George, and appointed Robert of Rouen, perhaps another of Curthose's chaplains, as Latin bishop, and left a garrison to guard the Jaffa road. That day, they moved up to the place they believed was Emmaeus, half a day from Jerusalem.

In the evening, they received an appeal for help from Bethlehem, to which many of the Christians of Jerusalem had gone when the city was captured. Tancred, who was still not reconciled to Raymond, took some knights, and at dawn they were welcomed into the city by a rejoicing procession from the Church of the Nativity. He left a small garrison there and returned to the main army, which moved up on 7 June to the hill of Montjoie, and saw Jerusalem spread out before them, its great walls and bastions protecting the domes and towers within. Peter Bartholomew had urged them to approach the city as penitent pilgrims, but

seeing Jerusalem they halted and worshipped God, and kneeling they kissed the holy ground; all would have walked barefoot, but fear of the enemy made them advance fully armed. They went weeping, and those who had come together to pray, having first to join battle, first carried weapons. Thus they wept at that for which Christ also wept.[46]

The crusaders were aware that Jerusalem was far from an easy target. Although the city had been captured only a year before, the walls had been repaired, and the defences were formidable, with a succession of walls, bastions and towers, including a partial double wall around much of the more vulnerable northern side. To the east, a steep valley divided the city from the Mount of Olives, and a second valley impeded access from the south-west. In preparation for the expected attack, the defenders had disabled the water supplies outside the city, and destroyed all the useful timber for miles around. The Fatimid garrison served a great power, not suffering from the factional fighting that so impeded the Seljuks. With a supply base 80km away at Ascalon, they could be quickly relieved. For their part, the crusaders were more united than they had been in the past, although Raymond's camp was still troubled by infighting, and he and Godfrey were deeply hostile. Not only had Tancred persisted in his adherence to Godfrey, but a Gascon nobleman, Gaston of Béarn, had transferred to Curthose's camp, where his knowledge of engineering would soon be put to good use.

In this situation, and not knowing whether a supply fleet would reach them before the Fatimids came up to attack, the crusaders decided to launch an early assault. The contingents spread around the walls, with Curthose and Robert of Flanders on the north, then Tancred and Godfrey, with Raymond on the west, beyond the high point that carried the Tower of David. But Raymond soon decided that this position was not suitable, and moved his force much further round to the south, so he was separated from the others. Although the place he selected was close to a relatively weak section of the walls, his camp was exposed to fire from within the city. Many of his men deserted and joined the other contingents, so he was forced to dig into his substantial treasury to pay soldiers to serve with him.

On 13 June, an attempt was made to storm the city, but only Tancred had access to any wood (which he had found hidden in a cave, to which he had retreated during a bout of diarrhoea), and so the entire army had only one ladder. Unsurprisingly, the attempt was easily beaten off. Fortunately for morale in the camp, they received news on 17 June that six ships had put in at Jaffa, including two Genoese vessels, bringing a range of supplies, including a good stock of timber for siege engines. The ever-resourceful Raymond Pilet led a mixed group of knights and infantry down to the coast as an escort, but on the way they were attacked by a Fatimid raiding party. There were significant losses, compensated for by the capture of many precious horses. Because Jaffa could not be defended, the fleet later became trapped in harbour by a Fatimid squadron. One ship escaped, and took the news to Laodicaea, but the remaining five were dismantled and burnt to prevent their capture. The sailors joined the crusade as foot soldiers, where their expertise with timber and ropes made them a valuable addition to the force.[47]

Raymond used the Genoese sailors and conscripted Muslim labourers to construct a strong mobile tower in his camp to the south of the city. Curthose and Godfrey meanwhile relied heavily on Gaston of Béarn's knowledge for the construction of a second tower, but they also made a massive battering ram and three mangonels, dividing the tasks between them and giving every appearance of working together well as a team.[48] In the first week of July, the quarrel between Raymond and Tancred flared up again, and on 8 July it had to be settled publicly, ending with a procession around the walls of Jerusalem and a sermon preached by Arnulf of Chocques, 'that most respected clerk', on the Mount of Olives.[49]

The siege machinery was now ready, and on the night of 9–10 July Curthose and his colleagues laboriously moved their great three-storey tower about a kilometre to the east, so it was close to a section of the walls that had not been strengthened. This remarkable feat astonished both the defenders and the Provençals. Raymond had no such opportunity for surprise, with his every movement on the small area of ground where he was camped watched by the Fatimids inside. Over the next three days, Curthose and his group worked furiously to fill in enough of the ditch to enable them to roll up their battering ram, and then they began swinging it against the outer walls. Godfrey set fire to the bales of straw lowered down to protect the masonry, and the soldiers repeatedly put out fires lit on the ram. It took two days to make a large enough hole in the walls to enable them to bring up the tower, and then they found that the ram had become stuck and could not be withdrawn. So the game was reversed, with the crusaders desperately trying to burn the ram and get it out of the way, while the defenders equally desperately tried to extinguish the flames. At last the tower was moved slowly up, amid an incessant storm of arrows, mangonel stones and flaming missiles.

In this final assault, communication seems to have been the key. The brothers Godfrey and Eustace led the men on the top floor, so high that they could see down into the city far below them. On the middle floor a company from Flanders were led by Lethold and Engelbert of Tournai, while at the bottom men heaved and pushed the unwieldy structure inch by inch up to the walls. Further back, Curthose and Tancred supervised the archers as they loosed off volleys of arrows, forcing many of the defenders off the parapet. At one point, a flaming tree was dangled over the walls in an attempt to set fire to the tower, requiring a party of men on the ground to get hold of it somehow, pull it down and drag it away. With covering crossbow fire from Godfrey and Eustace, and from the massed weapons of those on the ground behind, the brothers from Tournai then broke through the front of their platform and made a rough bridge of tree trunks onto the walls. They scrambled across, followed by Bernard of Saint-Valéry leading swarms of euphoric crusaders, exhausted and taut-nerved after five days of constant effort.[50]

Once into the city, they fanned out, opening the gates as they went and admitting the rest of the northern part of the army. Raymond and his men were still trapped close to their camp, making little headway against a stout resistance. Perhaps he was unable to improvise adequately, or perhaps his exposed position gave him a serious disadvantage, but the role of this second attack from the south in diverting and dividing the efforts of the defenders should not be underestimated. As they considered whether to withdraw, a knight was seen up on the Mount of Olives, waving his shield in victory and urging the Provençals to push forward. Setting ladders against the walls and using climbing ropes, they too now poured in over the parapets and joined in the rampage against Muslim, Jewish and Christian inhabitants alike. Raymond made his way to the Tower of David, and took its surrender, seizing the horses of its elite guard.

After a day of consolidation, during which throngs of jubilant crusaders visited the Holy Sepulchre to pray, the princes met on 17 July and ordered the removal of the corpses of the defenders and the countless civilians who had been caught up in the massacre. They knew only too well that their victory was not yet assured, and as a precaution against a counter-attack from Egypt, the surviving Fatimids were sought out and killed.

There were also more immediate problems to overcome, for Tancred, Raymond and Godfrey were again coming to blows. Tancred was accused of placing his standard over the Church of the Nativity in Bethlehem 'as if it were an ordinary house'; he in turn was enraged that hostages he had taken and protected in the Dome of the Rock had been murdered in cold blood; Raymond refused to give up the headquarters he had established in the Tower of David. A ruler for Jerusalem was urgently needed, and the council of princes offered the job to Raymond, who turned it down. His intentions had always been unclear, for he had left an adult son in charge of his county,

1. Robert Curthose, 1050–1134. Duke of Normandy 1087–1106. Polychrome thirteenth-century wooden effigy on a fourteenth-century tomb chest. Duke Robert was originally buried before the high altar at Gloucester, but the tomb was moved at the Reformation and now stands in the south ambulatory. *(Photography by R.J.L. Smith of Much Wenlock)*

2. William the Conqueror and his two half-brothers, Bishop Odo of Bayeux and Robert, Count of Mortain. Both Odo and Robert became supporters of Duke Robert after Rufus came to the throne. *(Detail from the Bayeux Tapestry, wool embroidery on linen, eleventh century. © Musée de la Tapisserie, Bayeux, France/The Bridgeman Art Library)*

Notum sit omnibus catholice fidei cultorib; qđ ego Simon Radulfi comitis
filius. terram que vocat̃ Guser. quam pater m͂s de dono Maurilii archiepi
ceptit. ea condi tione ut post morte ei͂ in dominio Archiepiscopatus
restituerem. qđ contra hanc conditione eui͂ usurpaui penitens. psate
ecc͂le Rotomagensi Sc͂e Đi genitric̃ Marie. reddo. et restituo. et ab
omi clamore libam et quietam uoco. Hanc redditione et libertatem
hoc Signo ✠ Sc͂e crucis corroboro. Hec redditio atq; restitutio
oͬbͬ facta. e. de manu Simonis comitis in manu Iohannis archiepi
presente Machilde. nobilissima ac gloriosissima regina. astante
Rogerio baimonterii. et qplurib; nobilibus uiris Scilicet Hugone picterna
Sudone de oillei Rogerio de blosse uill̃. Ex parte t̃ archiepi
Benedicto archidiacone. Arnulfo pisillo. Nobes detola. Ex parte
Simonis comitis. Isdia de gerondreit. Hugo de bauorcio. Petro beluacensi.
Hanc etiam redditione psitellū sup altare Sc͂e Marie posuit psātis
uiris assistentib;. et eundis̃ eam canentis̃. quoͬu un͂ fuit Rotb͂e decani.
alii eiusdem ecc͂lesie archidiacoñ. Goisleni archidiacoñ. Hugo etiā de silde uill̃.
et Goisldi fil̃ buardi. et Rogeri batdn͂. et Guillin fil̃ osbn͂. et quam
plurris etiam familie archigii. Et hac redditione dedit psāt̃ archiepi
Iohannes. trecentas libras rotomagensis moneta psato comiti Simoni.
Fac͂ta. e. aut hec redditio Anno incarnationis đnic; M. LXX. V.
indictione v iii. Psidence romane ecc͂le. papa Gregorio. de monarchia
regente cesare Henrico. Regni qq; francie Philippo. Anno ducatus
Guillini ati. Regni qq; X ✠

3. *Opposite:* An original charter of late 1075, by which Simon de Crépy, son of Count Ralph, restores the border land of Gisors to Rouen Cathedral. The restoration was made in the presence of Queen Mathilda ('presente Mathilde nobilissima ac gloriossissima regina') and the charter is witnessed by Robert Curthose ('signum+Roberti comitis') and Robert Beaumont ('signum+Roberti Belmontensis'). This charter shows Curthose taking an active role in ducal government when William the Conqueror was still alive. The date is given in a number of ways, including Anno Domini and the regnal years of the Emperor Henry, King Philip of France and King William. *(Seine-Maritime Archives: ADSM G 8739)*

4. Building ships. Any large-scale sea-borne invasion would involve the construction of new vessels. The portrayal of tree-felling on the Bayeaux Tapestry suggests that the 1066 invasion may also have exhausted supplies of seasoned timber. *(Detail from the Bayeux Tapestry, wool embroidery on linen, eleventh century. © Musée de la Tapisserie, Bayeux, France/with special authorisation of the city of Bayeux/The Bridgeman Art Library)*

5. Transporting horses by sea was a difficult logistical technique, developed by the Normans in southern Italy. A well-equipped knight would expect to travel with four horses. *(Detail from the Bayeux Tapestry, wool embroidery on linen, eleventh century. © Musée de la Tapisserie, Bayeux, France/with special authorisation of the city of Bayeux/ The Bridgeman Art Library)*

6. The Royal Seal of William the Conqueror, reverse or 'equestrian' side, bearing the inscription + HOC NORMANNORUM WILLELMUM NOSCE PATRONUM SI (By this sign recognise William, protector of the Normans). The other side shows a king enthroned, with the legend HOC ANGLIS REGEM SIGNO FATEARIS EUNDEM (By this sign acknowledge him as King of the English). *(British Library: Doubleday Cast A11)*

7. The Royal Seal of William II Rufus, reverse side. Both sides of Rufus's seal carry the inscription + WILLELMUS DI GRATIA REX ANGLORUM (William by the grace of God King of the English). The obverse shows a king enthroned. *(Eton College Archives)*

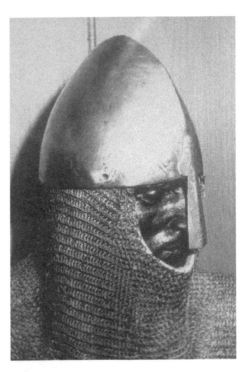

8. Early twelfth-century helmet, with a broad-based nasal and a chevron decoration. *(Private Collection)*

9. Elephant ivory chess piece showing two knights using couched lances. Chess has been played in northern Europe since at least the tenth century. The outline shape of this piece is Arabic in style, but the decorative detail is Western Christian. Late eleventh or early twelfth century. *(The Louvre, Paris, 083297)*

10. Domfront Castle dominates the surrounding countryside from a crag high above a loop in the River Varenne. A Bellême family stronghold for many years, it was captured by Henry in about 1092, and became a thorn in Curthose's side. The keep Henry built still stands. (*Ann Nissen-Jaubert*)

11. The Cilician Gates, a vulnerable pass through the Taurus Mountains, carrying the main road from Anatolia to Tarsus and the Cilician coastal plain. *(Sonia Halliday Photographs)*

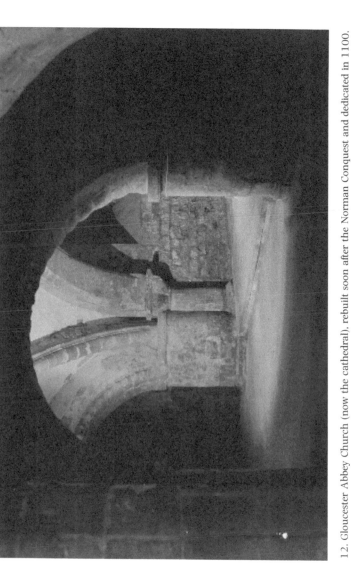

12. Gloucester Abbey Church (now the cathedral), rebuilt soon after the Norman Conquest and dedicated in 1100. Gloucester was used for many Christmas Courts in the reigns of William the Conqueror and Rufus, but ceased to be a royal centre under Henry I. It is the final resting place of Robert Curthose. (*Paul Lack*)

and brought his new Spanish wife with him, but had not formally abdicated his claims in Provence. Now he spoke of his intention to remain in the East 'until Easter', and his need for a suitable base for his men in the city. The princes next offered the crown of Jerusalem to Godfrey, who also refused to be called king there, but accepted the title of 'Advocate of the Holy Sepulchre'. He asked Raymond to yield up control of the Tower of David, and the other princes and many of Raymond's men supported the request, but Raymond relinquished it only most reluctantly, claiming he had been tricked. He then took the remaining loyal Provençals down to the Jordan to bathe in the sacred water. The other crusaders elected Arnulf of Chocques, Curthose's chaplain, as the new Latin Patriarch. There is no suggestion whatsoever, in these contemporary sources, of the story that emerged in England in the 1120s that Curthose was the first to be offered the crown but refused it through laziness.[51] This version of events appears only long after his fall from power, and becomes increasingly colourful as time goes on.

In the first week of August, foraging parties saw unmistakable signs of the Fatimids bringing up a large army against Jerusalem. Godfrey, accompanied by Eustace and Robert of Flanders, took their contingents down towards Ramla, and sent messengers back to request Curthose and Raymond to join them. The first messenger was captured by the enemy and never seen again, and, when the request did reach Jerusalem, even his own chronicler suggests that Raymond may have been inclined to hold back through a desire for revenge over Godfrey. But when they had obtained independent information about the size of the gathering Fatimid army, which was approximately twice the total crusader strength, the Normans and Provençals set off on 10 August for Ramla. Raymond carried with him his talisman the Lance. In Jerusalem, Peter the Hermit led anxious prayers for a Christian victory.

As the united army moved south, they captured a large herd of animals, and the herdsmen told them that the Fatimid army was camped before the walls of Ascalon, close to the sea, with limited manœuvring room. The crusaders launched a frontal attack, with over a thousand well-mounted knights providing a powerful weapon against the Egyptians, who fought en masse and thus presented an easier target than the Seljuks did. From the centre of the crusader army, Robert of Flanders and Tancred led a thunderous charge. Then Curthose led another, aiming straight at the Fatimid leader's marvellous golden standard, fashioned 'like an apple on a spear encased in silver'. The standard was captured and a combination of the loss of this rallying point and the penetration of the Fatimid camp by other crusaders caused resistance to collapse. The Fatimids turned and fled, hundreds of them dying as they attempted to seek shelter within the city. Crusader losses seem to have been few: one casualty among Curthose's contingent was probably the Breton Riou of Loheac, whose collection of relics from Jerusalem was carried back to Brittany in his memory.[52] After the battle, Curthose presented the standard to the Church of the Holy Sepulchre.[53]

The aftermath of this great victory was as sour as the other crusader triumphs. Despite the huge quantities of booty collected from the abandoned enemy camp, Raymond was not satisfied and demanded the right to negotiate the surrender of Ascalon, and then rule over it himself. Godfrey refused, and the result was that the city remained in Fatimid hands, a thorn in the side of the nascent kingdom of Jerusalem for years to come and the cause of many more deaths. An all-out war between Raymond and Godfrey was only narrowly averted.

At last, at the end of August, almost exactly three years after beginning his pilgrimage to Jerusalem, Curthose turned for home. He led the remnant of his Norman contingent, together with those men who had joined him along the way, back up the coast road, accompanied by Robert of Flanders and Raymond. Godfrey was left with an army of about 3,000 with which to defend his new kingdom.

They found Bohemond trying to wrest Laodicaea from imperial control, aided by a fleet of Pisan ships, which had brought a new papal legate to the East. Bohemond was forced to halt his siege, and Raymond took over the port on behalf of Alexius. The two Roberts then embarked with those men who wished to return north, and, despite the lateness of the season, made a safe passage to Constantinople. William Percy of Yorkshire was one who remained, and established a lordship in Syria.[54] The two princes were received with great distinction by the emperor, who must have felt both gratitude for the part they and their contingents had played in turning the Seljuk tide in Anatolia and relief that the crusade had not caused any more harm. He made arrangements for their return journey through the Balkans, and some time presumably in late winter 1099–1100 Curthose crossed the Adriatic to Italy. Robert of Flanders is next heard of back in his county in autumn 1100.[55]

In Apulia, Curthose was treated as a conquering hero. Any pilgrim to Jerusalem was accorded exalted status, but the crusade was already being seen as a miraculous event, a demonstration of God's guiding hand and overarching mercy. A series of Western Christian states had been established in the Muslim heartlands, and Jerusalem had been won back for Christ. The subtle distinction between capturing the Holy City from the wild Seljuks, which had been the original purpose of the crusade, and taking it from the Fatimids, allies of Byzantium, would have been largely lost on the people of the West, and they were unlikely to be too troubled that relations with Byzantium had been further damaged in the process. These men, who had fought and starved for three years across Anatolia and Palestine, endured freezing winter campaigns, suffered searing heat, seen countless companions die slowly of wounds and disease, and participated in bloody massacres, were changed in the roots of their being. But for the people to whom they returned, they were the victorious soldiers of Christ.

Curthose spent the remainder of that winter in Italy, and during it he became familiar with the family of Geoffrey of Conversano, Duke Roger Borsa's older cousin. Geoffrey had a daughter Sibyl, a beautiful, intelligent and able young woman, and at the age of almost 50, Curthose fell in love with her. He was doubtless encouraged in this by her family's great wealth, stemming from the largest lordship in Norman Italy, and the prospect it offered of a generous dowry with which he could redeem his pledge to Rufus and repossess his duchy. For the elderly Geoffrey, the acquisition of the Duke of Normandy as a son-in-law was a tremendous coup.[56] Curthose and Sibyl were married, and as summer came they took to the road, heading for Rome and the *Via Francigena* north.

Chapter 7

A FATAL ARROW

News of the astonishing, miraculous successes in the East preceded
the returning crusaders. Bruno of Lucca brought home stories of the fall
of Antioch, and the people of Lucca wrote an open letter to northern
Christendom in late 1098 describing his exploits. This letter not only
named Curthose, but described him as one of the three chief men to whom
Antioch surrendered. In stark contrast, the letter stigmatised poor Stephen
of Blois, 'thoroughly terrified' and retreating to Constantinople. Copies
of this letter could have been in northern France by early 1099, making
Stephen's homecoming still more uncomfortable.[1] The Archbishop of
Canterbury, too, had been in Italy, attending the Council of Bari, and there
was communication between Italy and the East and between the pope and
the English court in late 1098 and into 1099. By December 1099 detailed
accounts of the fall of Jerusalem and the victory at Ascalon were circulating
in the north. A letter from Archbishop Manasses of Rheims lists some of the
chief casualties, including Anselm of Ribemont, asking for prayers for their
souls. Against all the odds, Curthose had survived the crusade, and was
coming home.[2]

For Rufus, this must have been a serious disappointment. He seems to have
relished ruling his ancestral lands, although he avoided styling himself duke.
One of his first actions after Robert had left for the crusade was to recover his
father's regalia from St Stephen's Caen: Rufus was a king who felt entitled to
wear a crown in Normandy. As events turned out, he had many opportunities
for ceremonial crown-wearings in the duchy. Despite Orderic's opinion that
Normandy was 'ground down relentlessly' during his tenure,[3] and despite

the impression of efficient and successful governance, it was still not easy to rule, nor had the problems fundamentally changed. For much of the previous five years, Rufus had been trying unsuccessfully to wrest control of the Vexin from King Philip of France and his more active heir Prince Louis, and had orchestrated an initially successful but ultimately indecisive intervention in Maine. As a result, up until Easter 1099 all but two of his crown-wearings had taken place in Normandy.[4] Rufus had been an active ruler there, and if he were to retain the duchy, he would now have to fight Robert for it all over again.

For Henry, however, the news of his oldest brother's survival and imminent return was surely a devastating blow. There is nothing in the evidence of his later years to suggest that he was content with a subordinate role, and with Rufus still unmarried after thirteen years on the throne (despite wealth that could have bought him any wife he desired), one must assume that Henry had become accustomed to the idea that he would in due course succeed not only to England but to Normandy as well. He was now in his early thirties, unmarried but with a growing family of illegitimate sons and a significant power base in western Normandy. Now, however, came tidings that Curthose was not only on his way home, but at the age of 50 was unexpectedly bringing a bride with him, who for all Henry knew might already be carrying a child. Suddenly, Henry's place in the royal family had changed radically, and not for the better.

While Curthose had been away, Henry had kept a low profile. Apart from one reference in Orderic, which may refer to 1097, there is no suggestion that he spent time with Rufus in Normandy, and he seems to have been at court in England only once, at Whitsun 1099.[5] This was the first time that the Great Hall at Westminster was used, a hall built at the cost of much suffering by the English who were conscripted and taxed to create it, but which was the architectural glory of Rufus's reign. The roof has since been replaced, but its scale is still awesome. This court was a grander affair than normal, with the King of Scotland present to demonstrate his vassalage to Rufus.

After five years in the shadows, though, Henry suddenly reappeared at Rufus's side, on a hunting expedition in the New Forest in high summer 1100, at just the time that news of Robert and Sibyl's approach would have been confirmed. It is in the light of this remarkable piece of timing that subsequent events must be seen.

The basic story was told soon after the event by the Anglo-Saxon Chronicler and by Anselm's faithful scribe Eadmer, and is supported by the somewhat later account of a monk of Battle Abbey.[6] On Thursday 2 August, after eating, William Rufus went out into the New Forest to hunt and was shot by an arrow fired by one of his own household. Eadmer adds that, in his opinion, it was 'by the just judgement of God he was stricken down and slain', and notes that there was some dispute over whether the arrow struck the king directly or if he somehow stumbled and fell onto it. The implication is that there was significant discussion and confusion about the detail. These three English accounts are broadly supported by the Le Mans episcopal records, which note that the King of England was hunting in a wood and was shot by one of the knights who were with him.[7]

Two new elements were introduced into later versions of the story, although it is not clear at what stage they gained currency. William of Malmesbury's *Gesta Regum* (first written in about 1124) provides far more detail, and places considerable emphasis on the fact that a knight from the French Vexin named Walter Tirel, who had married into the influential Clare family and held a manor in Essex, was responsible for firing the arrow. Tirel's brother-in-law, Gilbert fitzRichard of Tonbridge, had rebelled against Rufus in 1088 and was implicated again in 1095, although on both occasions he had quickly made peace. William of Malmesbury also says that it was late in the day by the time the hunt got under way, so the sun may have been low and visibility poor. He specifies that only Tirel was present when Rufus was shot (although one must assume the presence of some huntsmen). Tirel is clearly described, shooting the king by accident but in such a way that he died without uttering a word. Upon seeing this, the French knight fled, and escaped over the Channel. There is no mention of Henry I here, nor for many pages thereafter.[8]

Also in the 1120s, John of Worcester repeated the assertion that it was Tirel who shot Rufus, but he supplied much less detail. Instead he added that it was commonly said that the death of Rufus, that of his nephew Richard (Curthose's illegitimate son who was shot in a similar accident in May 1100) and even the death of his brother Richard thirty years previously were all the result of divine retribution. The cause was the formation of the New Forest, and the suffering inflicted on the people who used to live there and were dispossessed by the Conqueror.[9] Later still, the emphasis of the story changed yet again. Orderic, now writing after Henry I was dead, still had Tirel as the instrument of Rufus's death, but Henry is immediately involved in subsequent events.[10]

Another strand of evidence, however, seems to exonerate Tirel. John of Salisbury, writing in the 1160s, said that, although Tirel was blamed for the shooting, he had denied it on his deathbed, and nobody knew who had really fired the fatal arrow. And Abbot Suger of Saint-Denis, Paris, said that those who asserted that Tirel had shot the king were wrong, for he, Suger, had often heard Walter Tirel swear on oath that he had never been near Rufus in the forest that day.[11]

Is it possible to make any sense of these varying accounts by looking at the later events of Henry I's reign? The starting point must be that by 2 August 1100 Curthose was almost home. He was apparently welcomed back into the duchy with great public rejoicing in August, or September at the very latest. The Anglo-Saxon Chronicle gives 'harvest time', which traditionally began on 7 August.[12] From Henry's point of view, this death in the forest was only just in time: with two older brothers alive, his prospects would again be severely limited. At first, a simple story seems to have been enough. Men did die in hunting accidents, just as they died in jousts and battles, and the death of Curthose's son Richard just three months earlier was a reminder of what a dangerous pastime it was. But in 1120, when he seemed relatively secure on his throne, all Henry's plans came to nought when his only legitimate son was drowned in the *White Ship* off Barfleur. Is it a coincidence that it is only after this tragedy that Tirel is named as the guilty party, as if to divert attention away from Henry himself? Could it be that there were whispers that asked whether the deaths of his queen and now the heir were divine judgement on his occupation of the throne? Tirel had himself conveniently gone on a pilgrimage on which he died, and had only been a minor figure in England, so was an easy target. The unpopular Forest Laws were another.

It is impossible now to say whether any suspicion was attached to Tirel at the time, but for a French knight at the scene of the shooting of the English king, flight was the obvious option, whether guilty or not. What is extraordinary is that nobody was punished in any way for the regicide, regardless of whether it was thought to be assassination or accident. To put it down to the hand of God and leave it at that is to ignore the political realities of the situation. When Curthose's son, a young man with few prospects of a crown, was shot, the knight responsible had fled to St Pancras Priory at

Lewes, and become a monk.[13] In stark contrast, not only did Walter Tirel keep his manor in Essex, but no attempt seems to have been made to pursue him, even though Prince Louis paid a courtesy visit to Henry's first Christmas court.[14] Tirel's English relations were conspicuously rewarded at the start of the new reign, and this has been developed into a regular conspiracy theory by several writers.[15] William Giffard, Tirel's wife's uncle, who was Rufus's last chancellor, was immediately appointed to the vacant see of Winchester, a crucial post that involved responsibility for the royal treasury. Walter Giffard, the bishop-elect's brother, may have received the earldom of Buckingham at Henry's coronation, since he first attests a charter using the title on that day.[16] And Richard of Clare, Tirel's brother-in-law, was summoned from Bec, where he was a monk, and installed as Abbot of Ely.

At the time of Rufus's death, as far as one can tell from the sources, there was a strong belief that he had got his just deserts, and the human intermediaries were of little account. As Eadmer noted, 'the Just Judge by a death sharp and swift cut short his life in this world'.[17] The Anglo-Saxon Chronicle immediately goes on to enumerate the late king's injustices, especially against God's Church. The hand that drew the bow, it seemed, was the Hand of God. Even Henry of Huntingdon in his *De Contemptu Mundi*, which is generally hostile to Henry, has no hint of fratricide. But then, one would hardly expect such a thing to be suggested openly in an age when the merest opposition to the royal will could be met with extreme penalties.

Divine justice need not, however, be the sole lens through which a modern assessment is made. Now we are at liberty to look at the evidence from a broader perspective. Various theories have been advanced over the twentieth century to explain this shooting. Most propose a conspiracy of some sort between Henry and the Clare family, and it has recently been noted that Gerald of Wales, writing in about 1200, names a knight called Ranulf de Aquis, perhaps a retainer of Tirel's, as the man who shot the king.[18] More outlandish ideas include a suicide pact, perhaps involving witchcraft or the occult.[19] A variant on the Clare conspiracy theory suggests that Rufus was indeed assassinated, by Tirel or one of his men, working as a double agent for the French king-elect Louis.[20] Tirel's lands were mostly in the French Vexin region, and he remained in contact with Louis, but it must be noted against this idea that rulers have always been reluctant to encourage regicide and rebellion among their own subjects, lest the habit spread.

It may be that one hint does survive in the medieval sources, deeply buried in the *Roman de Rou* written by Wace when Henry was long dead but his grandson Henry II was on the throne. Wace, whose aim is to tell the history of the Norman dukes and who lost favour with Henry II, relates how a youthful Henry was teased by William Warenne, because he was such an expert huntsman. Warenne taunted the prince with the nickname 'Stagfoot', saying that he was so well versed in the hunt that he could even tell from looking at their tracks how many tines a stag had on its antlers. Could this be a sly allusion to Henry's possible involvement in bringing down the ultimate in royal quarries?[21] A hunting accident would be the ideal cover for regicide.

Rulers, though anointed, were not immune from treacherous death, and in 1095 Rufus had escaped an assassination attempt. Two recent examples among the Spanish royalty would have been known to Henry. King Sancho of Leon and Castile was murdered by his own brother in 1076, and a few years later the King of Catalonia was also a victim of fratricide. Closer to home, there were still rumours circulating that Henry's own grandfather had attained the Duchy of Normandy by similar means. In both the Spanish cases, however, the conspirators had not been sufficiently careful, and the new king was severely compromised. If Henry was involved in Rufus's death, he would have been well aware of the imperative need to cover his tracks.[22]

At this distance in time, and with so little evidence to go on, the details of what happened on that Thursday afternoon will unfortunately never be known. But this does not mean that some conclusions cannot be drawn. There certainly were some very odd things going on, then and over the next few days, and the assertion that it 'cannot be regarded as a usurpation' is altogether too much special pleading.[23] Henry's reaction to the shooting was typical of the man. He had already shown in his disposal of Conan at Rouen that he was capable of decisive and brutal action. His actions in later life demonstrate that he could be hard-hearted, brutal and determined beyond the standards of his day. While Rufus's death might have been nothing more sinister than an accident that Henry took advantage of, it was such a fortuitous and well-timed accident from Henry's perspective that it must continue to arouse suspicions of having been helped on its way.

Only the later accounts give details for the sequence of Henry's actions, so one cannot safely extrapolate as much as one would like, but where these can be checked against contemporary letters and charters there is a substantial level of agreement. Throughout, there is a sense of great urgency. One's mind is inevitably drawn back to the events of September 1087, as Rufus galloped for the coast. As then, there was no external threat to the kingdom, and no likelihood of an immediate insurgency. The only threat to Henry's bid for the throne was Curthose, or an assembly of nobles loyal to him. Henry's letter recalling Anselm to England says 'the need was so urgent because enemies were intending to rise up against me', and Eadmer, who was probably an eyewitness when the archbishop and king met in September, suggests that Henry 'was afraid that Anselm would approach his brother Robert . . . and make him King of England'.[24] This is surely what was driving Henry over these hours.

Henry rode as fast as he could for Winchester, leaving the servants to load Rufus onto a cart and bring him to the city overnight. Henry's first objective was the treasury, and only with some difficulty did he obtain possession. Orderic says that William of Breteuil (inheritor of the Norman estates of William fitzOsbern and brother-in-law of the crusader Ralph of Gaël), who had followed Henry to Winchester, demanded that they should wait until Curthose arrived, since they were all homage-bound to him. Henry responded by drawing his sword. Henry, Earl of Warwick took Henry's part, and William was out-voted and silenced.[25]

If he had not already laid his plans, Henry was extremely busy that night. He appointed William Giffard, Rufus's chancellor, to the see of Winchester, set in train arrangements for the royal burial below the crossing of the Minster, and probably drafted his Coronation Charter, a crucial propaganda document in which he promised radical reforms of the abuses of Rufus's reign, 'all the evil customs by which the kingdom of England has been unjustly oppressed'. Eadmer noted that this document was quickly and widely distributed, perhaps to every shire: he 'had promised that he would maintain good and strict laws . . . confirmed by a solemn oath to be published throughout the kingdom with, by way of lasting memorial, a written document authenticated by his seal'.[26]

The following morning, Rufus was buried beneath the tower of the Minster, with minimal ceremony and the utmost speed. Interestingly, William of Malmesbury seems deliberately vague as to when exactly the king died. He avoids saying more than that he was found 'unconscious and speechless', and later describes the royal corpse being brought to Winchester, 'with blood dripping freely the whole way'.[27] Is this another example of Malmesbury's 'subtle undercutting'? It is about 35km from Brockenhurst to Winchester: ample opportunity for a wounded man to bleed slowly to death while being bumped along the rutted tracks of summer on a cart. Again, the parallels with 1087 are intriguing. As Rufus had left his father to die at Rouen, did Henry abandon Rufus in the forest, confident he would soon be dead, while he made his dash for Winchester?

With Rufus buried, the next part of Henry's plan had to be executed, yet more swiftly. It was now Friday morning, and he was still about 110km from Westminster, where a coronation should traditionally take place on a Sunday. Anselm was far away in exile in Lyons, and might take two months to be found and recalled, but Archbishop Thomas of York was, as Henry may have known, in Ripon. The Archbishop of York had crowned both Harold and William the Conqueror, and it would have been quite reasonable in the circumstances for Henry to accept the rite at Thomas's hands. Indeed, the archbishop began a hurried journey south as soon as news of Rufus's death reached him. But rather than risk even one week's delay, Henry rode hard for London, apparently arriving that same evening: an astonishing feat that William of Malmesbury describes with laconic understatement as 'done with all speed'.[28]

Over the next twenty four hours, a small group of barons gathered in Westminster, chief of whom were the Beaumont brothers Henry and Robert, Simon Earl of Northampton, Walter Giffard, Robert de Montfort and Robert Malet, together with Eudo dapifer, Roger Bigot, Robert fitzHaimo, Abbot Gilbert Crispin of Westminster and the chaplain William Warelwast. The senior bishop present was Maurice of London, who had been a royal chaplain and chancellor since about 1078, and bishop for fourteen years, and the only others who seem to have been in Westminster were bishop-elect William Giffard, Gundulf of Rochester and Gerard of Hereford. The latter two may have been intercepted returning from the consecration of the new abbey church at Gloucester.[29] This group was chiefly conspicuous for including neither of the archbishops nor any of the three leading lay magnates, William Count of Mortain, Robert of Bellême and William II Warenne, who between them controlled a large area of the country. Of William of Breteuil, who had pleaded Curthose's cause at Winchester, there is no sign.

While these men were assembling, Henry persuaded Bishop Maurice to proceed with the coronation himself, rather than wait for Anselm or even Thomas of York. He presumably also completed drafting the Coronation Charter, since he took an oath to abide by it as part of his coronation. And, in all probability, a letter was written to Anselm, explaining what had happened.

On Sunday 5 August, barely three days after Rufus had been shot, Henry was crowned. Copies of the Coronation Charter were probably sent out that same day, announcing the change of regime and the promise of better government. And messengers were sent overseas with a letter from the new king, urging Anselm to return, but begging him to avoid Normandy and to cross to England from Wissant. Henry's scramble for the throne was unprecedented, undignified and hard to justify. Even Louis VI of France, faced with a hostile stepmother and her sons, left five days between his father Philip's burial and his own coronation.[30]

All that was now needed to establish Henry on the throne was a queen, to give him legitimate heirs. At once he set about obtaining the hand of Matilda, the daughter of King Malcolm and Queen Margaret of Scotland, who offered him the legitimising influence of Anglo-Saxon royal blood, being the great-granddaughter of King Edmund Ironside and the niece of Edgar Ætheling. The negotiations took longer than Henry might have wished, but even so they were married, and Matilda crowned, in November.

Thus it was that when Curthose returned to Normandy to a hero's welcome, he was confronted with the astonishing news that Rufus was lately killed, and for the second time in his life he had lost the crown of England to a younger brother.

Chapter 8

THE THWARTED KING

Curthose was furious. Not only had his brother usurped the throne, and in so doing broken his oath of homage, but, as he explained in a letter to the pope asking for his assistance, Henry was occupying part of the duchy as well, centred on the castle at Domfront.[1]

Curthose's first recorded action on his return to Normandy was to take his duchess on a pilgrimage to Mont-Saint-Michel. This served several purposes. It involved a ducal progress through the length of their lands, demonstrating very publicly that he had returned, and it showed Sibyl to her new people; the route went through Henry's heartlands between Domfront and the Cotentin; and Mont-Saint-Michel was the principal shrine of the duchy, as important as the shrine to the archangel at Monte Gargano in Apulia. On their way back to Rouen, they probably also visited Caen, the burial place of both Curthose's parents, where he presented a trophy from the crusade to his sister's abbey of La Trinité.[2]

Soon after this, messengers came from a contingent of Rufus's troops in Maine, still holding out against Hélias of La Flèche, asking what Curthose wished them to do. Since he had relinquished control of Maine to Hélias before going on the Crusade, he declined to become involved. An embassy to Henry in England produced a similar response, so by October Hélias was able to consolidate his position as count, beneath the overlordship of Fulk of Anjou, a position he maintained with considerable success until his death in 1110.[3]

By autumn 1100 Curthose had more important things on his mind than relieving Rufus's men in Maine. He was already planning for an invasion of

England, to depose Henry and claim his birthright, the throne of England. Henry was almost twenty years his junior, was homage-bound to him and had been a party to the treaty with Rufus that acknowledged the oldest brother as heir to the kingdom. Moreover, Curthose had reliable information that not only the Norman magnates but all three of the chief men of England were opposed to Henry's usurpation, and ready to welcome him. The 1088 rising against Rufus had failed because it had been discussed too openly in England, and the arrest of William of Saint-Calais had forced a premature start from which it had never recovered. This time, a key element would have to be that Curthose's supporters would keep their counsel until he was actually in England.

Wealthiest among these supporters was Robert Bellême, who had by now inherited his father's earldom of Shrewsbury and many other English lands, including Arundel with its harbour. He also held the Montgomery-Bellême lands in Normandy, and in October 1100 his father-in-law died, making him Count of Ponthieu in right of his wife, with control of the Somme estuary. Almost as powerful as Robert was the young William, Count of Mortain, Robert of Mortain's son. He was both the first cousin of Duke Robert and King Henry and the nephew of Robert Bellême. He too held a strategic castle, Pevensey, with a good harbour.[4] Thirdly, William II Warenne, Earl of Surrey, held Lewes and the family lands near Dieppe. All these three magnates were in England in late autumn 1100. Eustace, Count of Boulogne, whose lands bordered the narrowest part of the Channel, also supported Curthose. One more key player was Henry, the new Count of Eû, whose father had taken part in the failed 1095 plot against Rufus, for which he had been brutally mutilated and blinded, dying soon after of his wounds. Although most of the family lands in England had been taken under royal supervision, young Henry still controlled the large harbour of Tréport near Dieppe. It was here that Curthose ordered his invasion fleet to assemble.

Why did these magnates, who had so much to lose in England if the rising failed, back Curthose in 1100? Many of them, or their fathers, had also done so in 1088, and this, together with their enormous combined wealth, is a conspicuous feature of the duke's following. In part, it was probably because serving two lords one either side of the Channel had already proved so difficult, and these great magnates may have felt especially vulnerable for this reason. They were perhaps also expressing a desire to be 'king-makers'.

No one could seriously claim that Henry had been elected by his barons, no matter what his propaganda said. The coronation had been far too hasty for anything like a representative group of lords to assemble. Then again, Curthose was a tried and tested ruler and warrior, with all the glamour and status attached to a returned and victorious crusader. Henry, by comparison, was a virtual unknown in England, and even the barons of Normandy had seen little of him in action. Both Eustace of Boulogne and Ivo Grandmesnil had served with Curthose in the East, and they now joined his party, as did William Ferrers and many more whose names are lost. But it is important not to overlook the fact that many men may also have felt that Curthose had a genuine grievance, that even though the succession traditions were ill-defined, he was the one who should have been king, not least because he was the eldest son.

On Henry's side, by contrast, there were just two senior members of the nobility, Henry Beaumont and his older brother Robert, now in his sixties, who had inherited most of the Beaumont and Meulan lands in Normandy. The long-standing and increasingly bitter hostility between the Bellême and Beaumont families no doubt partly explained their backing of the different brothers' claims to the throne. Henry came to rely on several long-serving sheriffs and royal counsellors from his father's reign, some of Rufus's servants (particularly Robert fitzHaimo) and the group of young men he had gathered about himself in the Cotentin, most notably Richard Redvers.[5]

The Winchester Annals speak of Curthose's fleet numbering 200 ships.[6] This is about a third the size of the one that had sailed in 1066, but the Conqueror had been invading an enemy country, while Curthose was going to join his allies in England. Even so, it was a considerable undertaking to find or construct so many vessels, gather together the troops, horses and supplies for the crossing, and move them from the various Channel harbours to Tréport. There was no possibility of the invasion being mounted until well into 1101.

Henry, meanwhile, had not been idle. It seems he was anticipating that Curthose would not take his demotion lying down: despite the steadfast propaganda of later years, the duke was seen from the start as someone who was liable to take vigorous action to regain his inheritance. From the day of his coronation, Henry was aware of this danger, begging Archbishop Anselm to avoid Normandy and make a detour north, returning to England through

Flanders.[7] In a move calculated to win widespread support, he also arrested Ranulf Flambard, Rufus's financier, who had recently been intruded into the see of Durham, and imprisoned him in the Tower of London.[8]

In accordance with the opening clause of his Coronation Charter to restore the rights of the Church, Henry made new clerical appointments, although these were carefully calculated. Rufus had left two bishoprics and as many as eleven abbacies vacant, as well as taking most of the Canterbury income after Anselm had been forced into exile. Henry had immediately appointed a new Bishop of Winchester, who controlled the royal treasury, but Salisbury remained vacant. He also filled four of the abbacies, but two of his appointees were scions of important lay families: a bastard son of the Earl of Chester, and a Clare, a member of a family whose loyalty to the Crown had been uncertain in 1088. There was also a military side to these appointments. Bishops and abbots were responsible for supplying a specified number of knights to the king when demanded, and it is conspicuous that the four abbacies Henry chose to fill were those that owed the largest service, a total of 170 knights between them. Glastonbury alone owed 60. The only other abbey that owed a large number of knights, Peterborough, was not vacant. The value of having a reliable man in post as abbot was clearly demonstrated when Henry did have to call up his army in 1101, for when one of the Abingdon Abbey tenants refused to supply the knight he owed, the newly appointed abbot made up the deficit himself. Richard of Clare, the new Abbot of Ely, by contrast, failed to supply his quota, and Henry took his revenge by having him deposed the following year.[9]

The income that was lost to the treasury from these four abbeys was significant (Glastonbury's Domesday valuation was about £800, most of which was being creamed off under Rufus), but Henry's pressing need in the months following his coronation was for allies at home and not the income to pay for foreign mercenaries. Moreover, William Giffard may have been appointed to the see of Winchester, but he continued to serve as chancellor for about twelve months, and was not consecrated until 1107, after a period in exile. And when Archbishop Thomas of York died at Christmas, Henry chose Gerard of Hereford, who had transferred his allegiance very firmly to the new regime, to fill the vacancy. In this way, the income from Hereford now came into his hands and he gained a reliable and amenable royal servant in one of the archbishoprics. Overall, Henry was able to pursue a policy calculated to improve relations with the Church, while strengthening his own political situation.

Henry also made several diplomatic moves. Having welcomed Anselm back into England in late September, he made sure that his marriage to Matilda, and her subsequent coronation, were celebrated by the archbishop. Henry also recognised the importance of his cousin William of Mortain, and attempted to bind him to the royal camp with a marriage to the portionless but blue-blooded Princess Mary of Scotland, Matilda's sister. But William refused the offer.[10] Thirdly, Henry took the highly unusual step of entertaining the designated heir to France, Prince Louis, at his Christmas court at Westminster. Responsibility for the government of France was beginning to be shouldered by the young prince, while his stepmother Bertrada schemed to have him replaced by one of her own sons by King Philip. There was thus ample opportunity for a deal to be struck between Henry and Louis, to their mutual advantage.[11]

At the beginning of February, Ranulf Flambard smuggled a rope into his quarters in the Tower, and escaped to Normandy. With him he took his detailed knowledge of the royal finances, and information about the loyalties of the nobility. The following month, Henry took further steps to contain the threat from the Continent, renewing the treaty made between Rufus and Robert I of Flanders, which was itself based on a treaty between William the Conqueror and Count Baldwin at the time of the Conquest. Henry's new treaty with Robert II required him to supply an enormous contingent of 1,000 mounted troops from Flanders and Boulogne, each with two spare horses, to be held ready at the Flemish ports for transfretation to England whenever Henry summoned them. They were also, significantly, to be ready to fight for him in Normandy, and a safe passage was to be guaranteed through Flanders for any mercenaries Henry might obtain. All this was to be in exchange for an annuity of £500. While there is no evidence that Robert II ever supported Henry against his old crusading companion Curthose, and William of Malmsbury suggests he was actively hostile to the English king, the treaty may have helped to keep him neutral over the next few years. Eustace of Boulogne, however, chose to ignore his obligations, and remained loyal to the Norman duke.[12]

While Curthose continued to prepare his fleet, Henry faced a new problem. Although Anselm had returned quickly to England when summoned, he was adamant that the papal prohibition of lay investiture of prelates (their installation into their lands and dignities by lay rulers rather than ecclesiastical authority), as agreed at the council he had attended during his exile, must be strictly followed. Henry, for his part, demanded the right to continue the practices of his father, which Lanfranc had accepted. But Henry needed Anselm on his side, not least to support the validity of his kingship, so they agreed to write to Pope Paschal, both effectively asking him to relent. Anselm seems to have been very eager to work with Henry at this time: the evidence of the new appointments and corrections to the worst excesses of Rufus's reign may have convinced him that a working relationship could be forged. Both letters were taken to Rome by the king's trusted chaplain, William Warelwast, in spring 1101.[13] But Warelwast seems to have deliberately withheld Anselm's letter, unless the pope was unwilling to reply to it. A reply to Henry was brought back, almost certainly in June 1101, firmly against royal investitures and with no mention of Anselm, who wrote repeatedly to the pope over the next months, asking for clarification.[14] The pope's reply was a grave disappointment for both Henry and Anselm, since the archbishop was eager to make concessions where possible. He had originally been strongly opposed to the marriage with Matilda, because there was a suspicion that she had once taken vows as a nun, but he had changed his mind. Henry, too, was heavily reliant on Anselm. Henry of Huntingdon describes the king as utterly terrified at the threat from Normandy. Eadmer, an eyewitness, stresses the air of suspicion at court, with the king repeatedly bringing to Anselm those whom he suspected of disloyalty, so that they might be talked round. In exchange, Henry freely made promises of good government and security for the Church. Anselm managed to persuade the barons at court to renew their recently taken oath of allegiance, and Eadmer believed that, without the archbishop, Henry would quickly have lost his throne.

By early June 1101 Curthose's invasion fleet was assembled and ready at Tréport. Of the 200 ships, some would have been horse transports, and the army could not have been larger than a few thousand men, but they knew they could rely on large numbers of reinforcements once they reached England, as well as generous supplies from the lands of their co-conspirators.[15] But, although the fleet was relatively small, it was still much too large to be kept secret. Henry certainly had agents in Flanders, and probably in Normandy too, and his envoy William Warelwast had crossed this part of the Channel very recently.

Just after Whitsun, therefore, Henry called out his levies from the shires, demanding an oath of obedience against all men 'and especially against the King's brother, Robert Duke of Normandy, until Christmas Day'.[16] With the loyalty of his magnates remaining doubtful, these levies were vitally important to supplement the modest number of household knights on whom the king could rely.[17] His problem was exacerbated since he knew that Curthose's fleet was assembled towards the eastern end of the Channel, but unlike King Harold in 1066, he could not trust the defenders of his coast. In fact, of the whole vulnerable stretch of coastline, there were only two reliable royal servants, and together they owed fewer than fifty knights. These were set against more than 150 Sussex knights of Curthose's supporters.

A further problem for Henry was that he did not know where the landing would take place. This coastline has changed dramatically in the past nine centuries, and many harbours and navigable rivers have been lost. In 1101 Curthose's allies controlled a series of safe landing places. Henry therefore took his small army south, without waiting for the levies, and by 24 June he was camped at a road junction at Wartling, guarding the roads to Pevensey and Hastings. There he waited for signs of the invasion, while he tried to restrict the power of the local magnates (Henry of Eû and William of Mortain) by granting a charter for Battle Abbey, giving its court increased powers with control over the supply of information in the area. Significantly, neither count ever witnessed this charter, despite being most nearly concerned with it. Instead, Bishop Robert of Lincoln, William Warelwast (just back from Rome) and the reliable Urse d'Abitot, who had been sheriff of Worcester since the Conquest, were the only witnesses.[18]

On 20 July 1101, with a favourable wind, Curthose's fleet set sail.[19] It met an English flotilla sent out by Henry to patrol the Channel, but, unlike in 1088, the crew and soldiers on board quickly transferred their allegiance. It seemed that all England was eager to welcome Robert this time. These first reinforcements could have given some information about Henry's dispositions, and probably confirmed Curthose's and Flambard's natural instincts to aim for Winchester. The treasury was there, and the city held a special significance within the kingdom, although Westminster was quickly taking its place. The fleet therefore continued west, outflanking Henry and sailing into Portsmouth

Harbour with its ancient fort of Porchester, where they landed on about the first of August.[20] According to Orderic, the duke was received as king, by a nobility who were already homage-bound to him.[21]

By the time Curthose was approaching Winchester, an easy march from Porchester, he was accompanied by many of the leading conspirators. Ranulf Flambard, however, having helped guide him to the shore, had apparently decided that discretion was the better part of valour, since he was still *persona non grata* in Henry's England: he is next heard of in Normandy. But then Curthose seems to have heard that Queen Matilda herself was at Winchester. Much later, the story became current that she was in childbed, but in fact she was about four months pregnant with the future 'Empress Maud'. Nevertheless, this may have been enough to make Curthose rethink his strategy. He had met Matilda when she was an infant, on his mission to the Scottish court in 1080, and he was her godfather. He now made one of his characteristically chivalrous gestures, with potentially disastrous consequences. Rather than seize the initiative and gain possession of Winchester and the treasury, he chose instead to camp outside, at a place that probably corresponds to Warnford on the River Meon.[22] There, inexplicably, he waited for Henry to move up against him.

The two armies met near Alton. With Curthose were the nobility of Normandy, Eustace of Boulogne, and many returned crusaders, together with all the leading lay magnates of England, with the sole exception of Henry Beaumont. King Henry was supported by the Beaumont brothers and his loyal inner circle, together with many of the bishops and senior abbots with their quotas of knights. Above all, there was Archbishop Anselm, well into his sixties and in poor health, but determinedly camping with his sixty knights in the field.[23]

The contest should have been settled by armed conflict, either by representatives from the two sides or in pitched battle. But Curthose, who was in by far the stronger position, was persuaded to negotiate. After nine months of preparation, he had brought an army safely across the Channel, landed successfully, and brought Henry to bay. His informants must have assured him that his brother was terribly afraid. What could possibly have made him discuss peace terms?

Three reasons are commonly given by contemporaries. First, an internecine war was to be avoided at all costs. This is a poor explanation, since the

Anglo-Norman aristocracy were inter-related to a quite remarkable degree, and this seldom stopped them from engaging in bloody feuds. In 1101 the lines were drawn more clearly between families than was often the case, with the glaring exception of the chief protagonists, where brother faced brother.

Secondly, Curthose was called on to set a good example as a crusader. This argument cut both ways, as the crusade had demonstrated that he had sterling qualities of military leadership, and non-crusaders were now expected to protect the possessions of crusaders: it could have been argued that the English succession was a 'possession' that Henry had manifestly not protected for his brother. In what sense was Curthose to set a good example?

At a distance of over 900 years, it is notoriously difficult to understand the world view of these men, and still harder to enter into the complex emotions of a returned crusader. But some light can be shed on Curthose's decision by considering the actions of other crusaders. Rotrou, Count of Perche and Mortagne, for example, went to the East with the Norman contingent. He returned home to find that his father had just died and he had inherited the county. Rotrou responded by going to the family abbey and becoming a confrater – a lay member of the community – and donating the palm fronds that he had brought back with him. Later, he fought against the Muslims in northern Spain with his cousin King Alfonso. Thus, although he was also drawn into Anglo-Norman politics by his brothers-in-law the Beaumonts, Rotrou's life continued to be coloured by his experiences as a crusader.[24] Another returned crusader, Eustace of Boulogne, remained actively involved in his county for many years, but in about 1125 his daughter and heiress was married to King Henry's favourite nephew, the future King Stephen. Eustace then withdrew to a monastery, and Stephen inherited Boulogne.[25]

At the other extreme, Odo Arpin pledged his viscounty of Bourges to King Philip by *vifgage* in 1100, and went east with Stephen of Blois in 1101. Odo was captured by the Egyptians in May 1102, but the Emperor Alexius quickly arranged for his release. He returned home via Constantinople and Rome, where the pope encouraged him to renounce the world entirely and become a monk, even though his wife was still living. Odo entered La Charité-sur-Loire near Bourges, and by 1107 was prior. He remained there until at least 1121.[26] Odo Arpin's actions after his brief experience on crusade may give an indication of the mindset of many former crusaders. Curthose returned to take up the reins of secular power in the duchy, with all the labour that entailed, and did not hesitate to embark on the invasion of 1101; but he may in some sense have found himself caught by conflicting ambitions. It may be significant in this context that Eadmer considered that Curthose's later difficulties were the result of 'piety and an almost total absence of any desire for worldly wealth'.[27]

A third argument, which almost certainly weighed especially heavily on Curthose as he pondered his options at Alton, was that Anselm appeared to be firmly behind Henry's claim to the throne. This must have been a considerable surprise, since he had neither agreed to it nor crowned him. Anselm was supporting a younger brother, against a crusader to whom all the magnates and Henry himself had been homage-bound. But canon law was clear that a king once anointed should not be toppled. Treasonable speech, conspiracy and attempted usurpation were all condemned and all merited excommunication. Lanfranc had used these arguments in 1088, and there was no reason to suppose that Anselm would not use them too.[28] Unlike his brothers, Curthose seems to have stood in awe of excommunication, not least perhaps because of his experiences in the East. Here, too, he was at a disadvantage. It was perhaps this more than anything that decided him to seek a negotiated settlement and thereby abandon all the advantages of his military position.

For the magnates, too, negotiation might be preferable. Neither of the princes had any other obvious heir, since all their closest family members were either descended through the female line or illegitimate. Should Curthose or Henry be killed or fatally wounded in the battle, chaos could well have ensued. The failed attempt to put Stephen of Aumâle on the throne six years earlier showed how hard it was to rally support behind less obvious claimants.

Orderic hints at an additional reason for Curthose's surprising acquiescence. He suggests that there was a major element of dissimulation on Henry's part throughout the encounter, with Robert Beaumont encouraging the king to make lavish promises to secure a negotiated solution: if men should demand 'London or York', he should pretend to grant their requests.[29] Here, although it is not spelled out in the chronicles, we may see the root of Curthose's inability to compete with his youngest brother.

While the two armies waited at Alton, envoys from the two camps met, and then the brothers spoke face to face. Orderic suggests that this was a deliberate ploy by Henry, knowing that Curthose would lack the tenacity to insist on his rights. An agreement was negotiated, and then ratified at Winchester. As with the treaty with Rufus in 1091, no copy survives, which is probably not surprising in view of Henry's subsequent approach to keeping it, but its terms can be reconstructed from contemporary sources. It differed from the earlier treaty in several important respects, yet its fundamental conditions were the same. The one great concession that Curthose made was that he renounced his absolute claim to the English throne, accepting the fait accompli of Henry's coronation and releasing him from his oath of homage. But each brother was to recognise the other as his heir in the absence of a legitimate son. Both already had sons: Curthose had one surviving bastard, William, brother of the Richard who had recently died in the New Forest, and Henry had about five, the eldest of whom was Robert 'of Caen', aged about 10.[30] This clause was apparently weighted in Henry's favour, since Queen Matilda was already pregnant, but in the event her first child was a girl.

Henry's biggest concession was that he agreed to renounce his claim to all the lands he currently held in Normandy. This is clearly stated in the Anglo-Saxon Chronicle, and Henry's obligation to yield Domfront and his Cotentin lands is stressed in Wace, a late but surprisingly reliable source. Only Orderic adds a story that Henry insisted on keeping Domfront, saying that he had promised the people of the town that he would never forsake them. Henry may well have made a promise to defend Domfront 'for ever' when he first captured it, and Orderic may have known this, but its unique appearance here makes this look like wish-fulfilment.[31] At Alton, Henry was in no position to drive a hard bargain, and neither Curthose nor his advisers would have tolerated an impregnable castle loyal to Henry in the heart of western Normandy.

Henry also agreed to pay Robert the huge sum of 3,000 silver marks annually. This has been described as an annuity, or a pension, implying that Henry was the dominant party in the negotiations, buying out the weaker. It might be better compared to the danegeld – a tribute to buy peace and avert future invasions. While the danegeld was heavier (the Anglo-Saxon Chronicle mentions £16,000 in 994 AD, equivalent to 24,000 marks, rising to an improbable £82,000 for Cnut in 1018), the payments to Curthose were equal in value to the total estates given by William the Conqueror to his half-brother Robert of Mortain, his most trusted lay lieutenant. This perhaps indicates the status of Curthose at Alton. Moreover, this was to be money taken from Henry's own royal resources, since he had no new lands to parcel out as the Conqueror had done. Few figures survive for Henry's cash income, but in 1130 it was about £23,000, so this tribute for Curthose was about one-tenth of the total royal budget.[32]

In addition, there was a clause stipulating that each brother would restore the lands of those who had been disseised as a result of the conflict. For Curthose, the chief beneficiaries were Eustace of Boulogne, whose father has lost his considerable English fief in a previous rebellion, and Ranulf Flambard, but there were no doubt others whom Henry had suspected of treachery and had accordingly disseised. For his part, Curthose is not known to have acted against any of Henry's supporters, but he may well have done so, particularly those such as Richard Redvers whose Norman lands were centred in the Cotentin.

Lastly, a clause stated that Duke Robert and King Henry would both come to the other's aid if summoned.[33]

Apparently satisfied at the outcome, Henry and Curthose now went to London, from where a safe conduct was sent to Ranulf Flambard in Normandy, urging him to return to England. As with all the surviving charters concerned with the aftermath of the 1101 crisis, it is witnessed by some men from each side: in this case by Duke Robert himself. The process for reinstating Ranulf into his bishopric and lands was also put in train, and then Curthose briefly went down to Sussex with Henry and William Warenne.[34] After the military build-up and the uneasy stand-off at Alton, it was a remarkable anti-climax. Yet magnates from both sides seemed willing to accept the compromise, and to work within the new status quo.

The court moved to Windsor at the end of August, and Ranulf Flambard joined Curthose and his leading supporters there.[35] Duke and king remained together until Michaelmas, and then, with every appearance of brotherly love and mutual understanding, they parted, Curthose returning to Normandy with several of his magnates including William Warenne. He had forfeited immediate possession of the kingdom, but seemed guaranteed the freedom to rule the duchy in peace and raise a family to continue the ducal line.

Chapter 9

BROTHERLY LOVE

The Treaty of Winchester acknowledged that both Curthose and Henry had legitimate claims to the English throne. What it did not do was to solve the underlying problem created by the division of the Conqueror's realms in 1087: too many of the Anglo-Norman aristocrats were still bound to two lords.[1] Superficially, the 1101 settlement allowed this problem to be shelved, but it was unlikely to go away for ever.

In 1102–3 Duchess Sibyl and Queen Matilda both gave birth to male heirs. The young Norman count was born in the ducal castle at Rouen, on 25 October 1102, and his royal cousin was born about ten months later. Neither prince was ever to have a brother. Both children were named William, after the Conqueror, and both later acquired nicknames that meant 'prince': Curthose's son was known as William Clito, his cousin as William Adelin, a corruption of the Anglo-Saxon *Ætheling*.[2] Naming their sons was almost the last thing that Curthose and Henry agreed about.

No sooner had Robert returned to Normandy and his duchess than Henry began breaking his promises. First he reneged on his verbal undertaking, made with Anselm in the crisis, that he would leave the Church free, and instead began insisting on his right to invest bishops. A letter from Pope Paschal in late spring 1102 merely reiterated the pope's position, so king and archbishop agreed to send further envoys to Rome, asking for a dispensation. Henry's three envoys were Archbishop Gerard, Bishop Robert of Chester and Bishop Herbert of Thetford, while Anselm sent two trusted monks.

The group returned in late summer, with a letter from Paschal making it clear that his position was unchanged. But astonishingly, the three bishops brought a verbal message that, the letter notwithstanding, the pope would be happy to allow lay investiture. Anselm's monks vehemently denied that any such concession had been mentioned, to which the bishops retorted that it had been deliberately kept from the ears of mere monks. Moreover, they said, 'ink on sheepskins' was worthless compared with the word of a bishop. The Canterbury party not unreasonably pointed out the fallacy in their argument, since the whole of Christianity depended on the written word! When Paschal eventually learnt the details a year later, he demonstrated where the truth lay by excommunicating the three royal ambassadors forthwith, quoting Psalm 12: 'The Lord shall cut off deceitful lips.'³ But in the meantime there was a stalemate, which dragged on into the spring of 1103 until Anselm agreed to travel to Rome himself, accompanied by Henry's chaplain William Warelwast. Unknown to Anselm, Henry had laid his plans with care, and when Paschal refused to be moved, Warelwast delivered a personal message from the king banning Anselm from England. Henry confiscated the Canterbury revenues, while Anselm began his second exile.

Of Curthose's chief supporters in 1101, only Eustace of Boulogne was fully accepted back into the English fold. The following year, he was married to Queen Matilda's sister Mary, and Henry thereby gained an important influence in this strategic county.⁴ Henry of Eû, too, made peace with the king, but he was no longer trusted with control of Hastings, and he probably spent most of his time in his Norman fief.⁵ Ivo of Grandmesnil, one of the 'rope dancers' of Antioch, was at first reconciled to Henry, but soon fell foul of him and decided to return to the East rather than face his wrath. He pledged his Leicestershire estates to the already powerful Robert Beaumont, who thereby became Earl of Leicester.⁶

The Beaumonts were the hereditary and implacable enemies of the Montgomery family, and both Robert and Henry Beaumont were now closely associated with King Henry. The Montgomerys, on the other hand, were not only Curthose's most powerful allies, but were also important English magnates. This no doubt encouraged the king's decision to take action against the three surviving Montgomery brothers. Robert Bellême was by far the most important, but his younger brothers Roger the Poitevin and Arnulf (now lord of Pembroke) also held English lands. Henry's campaign against the Montgomerys was probably planned almost as soon as the Treaty of Winchester was signed. In the spring of 1102 Robert

Bellême was confronted with a list of forty-five offences he was alleged to have committed, some certainly spurious, others legitimate, not least his construction of Bridgenorth Castle without royal consent. In doing so, Henry could claim he was not in breach of the letter of the Treaty of Winchester, since it related to the 1101 invasion and not to subsequent acts of treason. But might was in any case right, and over the next five months the royal armies captured the Montgomery castles one by one. Henry then confiscated all their vast estates: the earldom of Shrewsbury, Robert's lands in Yorkshire and Sussex, Roger the Poitevin's holdings in Lancashire and the east of England, and Arnulf's earldom of Pembroke. They were shared out among Henry's supporters, or returned to their former occupiers to encourage renewed loyalty. Arundel was administered by a steward on behalf of the king. Roger left for his wife's lands in Poitou, while Arnulf and Robert, granted safe conduct across the Channel, retreated to Normandy seething with hatred for the Beaumonts.[7]

In a fine gesture of hypocrisy, Henry sent a message to Curthose reminding him of his treaty obligations to take action against English traitors. The duke obliged to the extent of bringing an army up against a Bellême castle, but his heart cannot have been in the campaign. Part of the ducal force withdrew, and the attack collapsed. Orderic accuses Curthose of incompetence, but there can have been little incentive for him to fall out with his most powerful ally, especially in view of their mutual interest in containing the Beaumonts.

Henry now entered on the next phase of what seems with hindsight to have been a concerted plan, exacerbating and manipulating the difficult situation in Normandy from the safety of England. He gave one of his young illegitimate daughters (called Matilda) and some English lands to Rotrou, the new count of Perche and Mortagne, who was also a hereditary enemy of the Bellême.[8] Next he seized an opportunity when Ralph of Tosny and Conches travelled to England to claim his father's English lands, and gave him a wealthy heiress, encouraging him to shift his allegiance.[9] Thirdly, Henry was able to intervene in the Breteuil lordship. William of Breteuil, who had been the only baron to take Curthose's part when Rufus was killed, returned to Normandy and died there in January 1103. He left no legitimate heir, and his bastard Eustace and two more distant relations disputed the succession. Henry married off another of his bastards, Juliana the daughter of his long-term mistress Ansfride, to Eustace. Although they later rebelled in spectacular fashion, the young couple were initially loyal to Henry, and successfully defended their Breteuil inheritance in a short but bloody war, helped by Robert Beaumont. By mid-1103, they were triumphant, and Henry had consolidated a significant body of support in central Normandy, consisting of the lordships of Beaumont, Breteuil, Perche and Mortagne.[10]

With hindsight one can see that Curthose should have intervened sooner in the Breteuil succession dispute. Why did he not do so? Breteuil was one of the seven great Norman honours, and Eustace was a dangerous candidate, with pre-existing links to Henry, having taken part in the 1102 campaign against Robert of Bellême. But of the other two candidates, one was a Breton nephew, the son of Ralph of Gaël the crusader, and the other was a more distant Burgundian relation. Both were viewed as foreigners and neither was a popular candidate. Eustace, by contrast, was a son and had local support. Also, Robert Beaumont was actively backing his claim, and to oppose him would inflame the Beaumonts' antipathy. Robert was hugely powerful in Normandy as well as in England, controlling the county of Meulan as well as his Beaumont patrimony. Curthose must by now have suspected that Henry would not deal straightforwardly with him, and Robert Beaumont was his chief adviser: Henry was demanding that Robert Bellême be punished for his treason in England, yet at the same time he was himself intervening more blatantly in Norman affairs.

Another reason may be that just at this time Curthose's personal life was in turmoil. His duchess Sibyl, widely admired for her intelligence and beauty, fell ill soon after the birth of their son William Clito, and died on 18 March 1103. Orderic has a story that she was poisoned by Agnes, the sister of the crusader Anselm of Ribemont, who had died at the siege of Akkar; Orderic says that Curthose was bewitched by the widowed Agnes and agreed to his wife's murder, but after waiting so many years to find a suitable bride and having only one vulnerable infant heir (and in an age when keeping a mistress was a commonplace), who would consider such a drastic course? Moreover, Agnes's husband Walter II Giffard died only in July 1102, in England.[11] The simple tragedy of a puerperal infection is a more likely explanation. Sibyl was buried in Rouen cathedral, beneath a white marble slab, on which was carved her epitaph:

> Nor power of birth, nor beauty, wealth nor fame
> Can grant eternal life to mortal man.
> And so the Duchess Sibyl, noble, great and rich,
> Lies buried here at rest, as ashes now.
> Her largess, prudence, virtue, all are gifts
> Her country loses by her early death;
> Normandy bewails her duchess, Apulia mourns her child –
> In her death great glory is brought low.
> The sun in the Golden Fleece destroyed her here,
> May God now be her source of life.

The original slab is lost, but a beautiful cream stone now covers her grave, bearing more homely words:

Sibyl of Conversano, born in Apulia, married to Robert known as Curthose, Duke of Normandy, the son of the invincible William the Conqueror. She was snatched away too soon by bitter death, in the year 1102[12] after two years of marriage. She who was once the delight of her people is now their grief, and has submitted to the dust.

In choosing Rouen as his wife's burial place, Curthose returned to the traditions of his earliest Christian ancestors. His parents lay in their twin foundations at Caen, and his grandfather Robert I had his grave in Nicaea. Richard I and II were both buried at Fécamp, their favoured residence, where their often-altered tombs can be seen today. But the earliest dukes, Rollo and William Longsword, both lay at Rouen, and their remains had been carefully moved during the rededication of the cathedral in 1073. Rouen was not merely the administrative heart of the duchy, with the principal mint, archiepiscopal cathedral and the ducal palace with its stone keep; it was also the largest port.

William Warenne also found himself in a difficult position after 1101. His family was typical of several great Anglo-Norman dynasties enriched after the Conquest. Although they held significant lands in Normandy, their major wealth was in England, notably in Sussex, Norfolk and Yorkshire. His father, William I Warenne, fought at Hastings and was thereafter based in England; he had taken an active part in suppressing the 'earl's rebellion' of

1075, and then supported Rufus in the rising of 1088, in the course of which he had been fatally wounded. William II Warenne had inherited his father's English lands, making him the third wealthiest lay magnate there, while his younger brother had inherited family lands in Flanders.[13] Continuing the family tradition of supporting the English king, William had fought for Rufus against Curthose and Robert Bellême in 1090, and he subsequently tried and failed to marry the Princess Matilda who later became Henry I's queen.

It is therefore an indication of the disarray caused by Henry's usurpation in 1100 that William II Warenne took Curthose's part at all. Yet it seems clear that he did so. There is charter evidence that his men in Norfolk were causing disturbances in summer 1101, and although he appears at the English court that autumn, he soon afterwards returned to Normandy with his duke.[14] The extent of William's commitment to one or other of the brothers at this stage is not clear. Orderic suggests that he forfeited his English estates, but Wace does not name him as one of Curthose's supporters. Nor is it certain exactly how he later came to be drawn into Henry's camp.

Curthose is known to have visited England in late 1103, but what for is not clear. One chronicle speaks of the king giving him 'small gifts';[15] others suggest that he became caught in a trap. The story goes that Warenne complained to Curthose that he had lost his estates on his behalf, and the duke agreed to go to England to discuss the matter with Henry. But Robert Beaumont met him and warned that he was liable to be imprisoned for entering the kingdom with armed retainers without Henry's permission. Presumably realising that his brother was quite capable of carrying out this threat, and lacking the means to escape, Curthose agreed to a meeting, but more as suppliant than as an equal.

By now Curthose must have known that Henry had designs on Normandy and did not intend to abide by the Treaty of Winchester. His own options were becoming ever more limited, and he knew from past experiences contending with Rufus just how hard it was to defend Normandy from opportunistic English kings. Aid was unlikely to be forthcoming from France, as Henry seemed to be in close diplomatic contact with the young Prince Louis, who was taking an increasingly responsible role there.[16] Moreover, half the Norman magnates were also now Henry's supporters or bound to him by other ties. Hugh, Earl of Chester, who also controlled the southern Cotentin, had recently died, leaving a young boy as his heir and his lands in royal wardship. Despite his promise at Winchester, Henry had never relinquished control of any of his castles in Normandy, extending his arc of influence far across the west of the duchy. Curthose lacked the resources to contain the threat, and there was no viable external arbiter to whom he could turn. Letters to Rome took weeks, and in any case Henry had scant respect for the authority of the papacy. Anselm was once more in exile, so his restraining hand was absent at just this time when Henry began actively undermining the duchy.

There is indeed some evidence that Henry's stance during Curthose's visit to England in late 1103 was a carefully staged ploy. Both Orderic and William of Malmesbury stress Henry's anger to such an extent that they almost seem to agree with Wace that it was play-acting. Henry of Huntingdon is even clearer: 'For various reasons and because of the king's deceitfulness . . . the king and his brother were at odds . . .'.[17] The king also took care to inform the pope that he was fighting against 'enemies of the kingdom'.[18] Henry agreed to restore William II Warenne, and in exchange Curthose was obliged to forgo his annual tribute. There is no evidence that it had ever been paid to him, but since it was worth almost double William's lands, Henry was in any case the clear winner.[19] Various reasons are given for Curthose's apparent generosity, mostly involving the intervention of his god-daughter Queen Matilda; this is most unlikely to have been her own idea. Matilda does not seem to have been particularly devoted to Henry by this stage: their early affection may have worn thin, and certainly they had no more children, while Henry's continued liaison with his current favourite, Sibyl Corbett, produced at least five children. To judge by her reaction when Anselm asked for her help in preventing Henry from extorting money, Matilda was terrified of offending her husband.[20]

The following year Henry moved against Curthose's one remaining magnate in England – his young cousin William Count of Mortain, who was variously described as 'excellent in mind, passionate in action, a most honourable man' and 'troublesome, impudent and notoriously presumptuous'.[21] This time Henry moved cautiously, 'by legal means so that nothing he did gave the impression of being unjust or unfair', disputing the ownership of some manors in the south-east of England.[22] Count William took offence and departed for Normandy, allowing Henry to accuse him of treachery. The vast earldom of Cornwall thus fell into Henry's pocket, while he used the strategic castle of Pevensey to reward the Norman baron Gilbert of L'Aigle and draw him further into his net.

In Normandy, William of Mortain and his uncle Robert Bellême began a series of revenge attacks on castles and estates loyal to Henry, while Henry paid troops to stir up trouble and attack the duchy.[23] Orderic ties this period of unrest to Curthose's unwilling campaign against Robert in 1103, but the precise sequence of events is far from clear. The presence of Rotrou of Perche and Gilbert of L'Aigle in the mix supports the idea of Henry's involvement. In one armed encounter, William of Conversano, Curthose's brother in law, was captured and held to ransom by Robert Bellême.[24] But Robert was a pragmatist. It was necessary for him to find a *modus vivendi* in the new situation, and he and Curthose soon made peace. As well as taking the duke's part against Henry's partisans, he began a rapprochement with Hélias of Maine and Count Fulk of Anjou, his overlords for the southern part of his lands.[25]

In August 1104 Henry threw a calculated insult at Curthose, making an uninvited visit to Normandy. The contrast with Curthose's own visit to England the previous year could not have been greater. Henry made a point of visiting the Norman castles of his English magnates, with complete impunity. He stayed at Domfront and the other castles he held, and let it be known that he was entertained lavishly wherever he went. In a further snub, he demanded a meeting with Curthose, and accused him of failing to deprive Robert Bellême of his Norman lands; according to Orderic, he even threatened to convene a court to see if his brother was fit to continue as duke. The price Henry exacted on this occasion was the transfer of the allegiance of the hitherto faithful William Count of Evreux, who was reluctantly persuaded to abandon the duke because of the impossibility of serving two masters.[26] This was Henry's trump card, and as the more ruthless brother and by far the richer, he was willing and eager to exploit it to the uttermost.

The major obstacle in Henry's way was his dispute with Anselm. The king was not renowned for his piety, but the backing of the Church was crucial in order to give a cloak of respectability to his actions. His oft-repeated excuse for intervention in Normandy was to 'restore order' to the Church there. While increasing taxation in England to pay for the coming military campaign, Henry therefore initiated his plans to restore Anselm to Canterbury. This was all the more urgent since early in the New Year of 1104 he had received a letter from Pope Paschal, written in late November 1103, which contained a veiled threat of excommunication and a clear warning that in future the king's envoys must be honest men.[27] In December the pope sent a more explicit letter, followed by a second in early 1105, requesting an explanation for his conduct to be made available at the forthcoming Lent Synod, without which excommunication would follow. These Henry chose to ignore, but when the pope wrote to Anselm at the end of March, authorising him to excommunicate Robert Beaumont and the king's other advisers, and promising to deal with the king's own case at Easter, with copies of the letter to be publicised in England, things suddenly began to move. Anselm probably received Paschal's letter at his temporary home in Lyons soon after Easter, and he set off at once, with the intention of implementing the anathemas immediately.[28] The news of his coming must have travelled ahead, as he was met at La Charité-sur-Loire by a messenger from Countess Adela, Stephen of Blois's widow and Henry's favourite sister. She was said to be dangerously ill, and begged Anselm to visit her. The detour took several weeks, although by the time Anselm reached Blois the countess was much recovered from her 'diplomatic illness'.

Meanwhile events had not been standing still in Normandy. Over the winter Robert fitzHaimo, one of Henry's closest advisers in England, who also held the lordship of Torigni and Creully in the Bessin, had been harrying the surrounding countryside, until he was attacked and taken prisoner by the castellan of Bayeux, and William Warenne's younger brother Reginald, both staunch supporters of Curthose. They held fitzHaimo in Bayeux, and King Henry used this as his excuse to invade Normandy in earnest. He assembled the fleet and army, for which he had been preparing all the previous year with crippling taxation, and landed at Barfleur. The Treaty of Winchester was now a dead letter. Henry marched confidently down through the Cotentin, through the lands of his ward the youthful Richard, Earl of Chester and viscount of Avranches.

In desperation, Curthose met King Philip, grown fat and nearing death, but Henry's ambassadors and gold had done their work and the French king declined to intervene. He turned also to Robert of Flanders, but the treaty with Henry, perhaps strengthened in Lent 1103, prevented him from siding openly with Curthose. But the densely populated county remained conspicuously neutral and failed to supply any of the expected knights for Henry's campaign.[29]

Henry reached Carentan in time for Easter, where Bishop Serlo of Séez, who was no friend of Robert Bellême, took the service. Orderic, who used this occasion for a great set piece of Henrican propaganda against the impotence of Curthose's rule, also took the opportunity to portray Serlo chastising the English court for its lax moral standards, no better than in the days of Rufus, particularly singling out Robert Beaumont for criticism.[30]

After this initiation of his personal crusade in Normandy, Henry moved on to Bayeux, where he appeared before the city and forced the release of fitzHaimo. But once his favourite was free, Henry went further and demanded the surrender of the city, which was quite properly refused, since it was held for Duke Robert. Henry responded by torching Bayeux. Some of the inhabitants escaped, including the castellan, who was taken prisoner in his turn, but most were burnt to death, including an unknown number who had sought refuge in Bishop Odo's cathedral. Castle, town, cathedral and churches were all destroyed in the conflagration, as a high wind fanned the flames. The poet monk Serlo of Bayeux wrote an impassioned lament, which ensured that the death and destruction were remembered for many years.[31]

Leaving the smouldering ruins behind him, Henry moved on towards Caen, which, according to Orderic, surrendered because the burgesses feared that their town would suffer the same fate as Bayeux. The merchants, always more pragmatic than soldiers, handed over Curthose's loyal castellan and submitted to Henry, who rewarded them with a valuable manor in England. Orderic notes that it was known henceforth as 'Traitor's Manor'.[32]

Henry's next goal was Falaise, the birthplace of the Conqueror and one of Curthose's strongholds. But here, suddenly, his luck ran out. First, one of his ablest knights was killed: in a joust according to Orderic, or shot by a crossbow bolt from the castle defenders.[33] Robert fitzHaimo, the ostensible reason for the invasion, was also struck down, by a lance blow to his forehead that left him so disabled as to be deprived of reason. He was carried back to England, where he lingered on for two years, living on the Gloucestershire estates of Queen Matilda I, which had been granted him by Rufus, until finally he was buried in his foundation of Tewkesbury Abbey. (At his death, his daughter and heiress was married to Robert of Caen, 'The King's Son', who was then only about 17, and Queen Matilda I's lands were thereby returned to the royal orbit.)

A third blow to Henry's campaign, and probably the most decisive, was that a message reached him from his sister Adela with details of Anselm's plans, which she had carefully extracted from the ageing prelate. Eadmer believed that it was common knowledge at this time that Anselm proposed to excommunicate Henry in person when they met. Certainly something prompted Hélias of Maine to withdraw his troops from the siege of Falaise, where he had been supporting Henry. A pious man, he may well not have wished to be tainted by association with a prince threatened with anathema.[34]

Thus it was that Henry suddenly called off his campaign in late May 1105, and agreed to meet Curthose midway between Falaise and Caen. After two days of talks they failed to reach any agreement, and parted acrimoniously. Their supporters spent the remainder of the year in small-scale feuding, while Henry tried to reconcile himself to Anselm. They both wished for an agreement. Henry could not achieve his political aims with the threat of excommunication hanging over him. Anselm for his part was now aged 70, and was increasingly ill and longing to return to Canterbury. He also desired a good relationship with Henry, so that together they could work for the good of the realm. Anselm held the ultimate sanction, but he was as eager for peace as Henry was, although he does not seem to have been hostile towards Curthose; indeed he had urged William Giffard not to betray a Norman castle to Henry.[35]

Henry went straight from his meeting with Curthose to Gilbert of L'Aigle's principal residence in Normandy, where he met Anselm on 21 July. Eadmer found Henry's manner towards Anselm much improved, quite conciliatory in fact. A compromise was quickly reached, whereby the king would abandon his claim to investiture, but prelates would make a formal act of homage to him. Henry tried to persuade Anselm to leave at once for England, but the archbishop was insistent that their agreement must first be accepted by the pope. So Anselm went to Bec, where he received a stream of letters telling him of the terrible situation in England, an interesting reflection on Henry's stance as the liberator of the oppressed Norman church.

Henry's game was not finished yet. It seems that his chief, if not his only, concern in reaching an agreement with Anselm was to stave off the threat of excommunication so that he might pose as the saviour of Normandy. It is not at all clear whether Anselm was concerned with this aspect of Henry's policy; for all his scholarship, he lacked much of Lanfranc's political acumen. Having reached an accommodation with the elderly and ailing archbishop, the king was in no hurry to get the agreement ratified by the pope, and for months the process was stalled. Perhaps he feared that Anselm had been more conciliatory than Paschal wished, and that their agreement would be blocked. Certainly, with Anselm at Bec or visiting his friend Archbishop Manasses at Rheims, Henry was freer to raise funds from church property in England. Perhaps he hoped that, if he delayed long enough, Anselm would die, leaving him with a clean slate, the revenues of Canterbury and all the other vacancies, and a free hand to do as he pleased. Anselm wrote what by his usual standards was a strongly worded letter to Robert Beaumont in the autumn, expressing concern that 'people are thinking and saying that the king is not very anxious to hasten my return to England'. In January 1106 Henry devised a new delaying tactic; having heard, he said, that there was an anti-pope newly elected in Rome, did Anselm not think it would be better to wait until the situation was clarified? But the envoys were at last on their way, and Anselm would not recall them.[36]

Curthose made another visit to England, in late January 1106. This time there was no attempt to threaten him, but despite his peaceable journey, seeking restoration of his rights under the treaty, Henry was implacable. It was known in England that Curthose returned empty handed to Normandy in disgust, but Henry wrote in honeyed words to Anselm: 'you should know, reverend father, that my brother Duke Robert, came to me in England and departed in a friendly manner. You should also be aware that I am prepared to cross the sea on Ascension Day . . . and I shall do everything through your advice.'[37] Robert Bellême also visited the English court, with no more success, although he too was not arrested, as he might well have been. Henry, it seems, preferred to wait a little longer. While Henry bided his time in England, raising extra revenue by fining priests for their misdemeanours in a way that earned him a stern rebuke from Anselm (which he brushed off with a characteristic show of injured innocence[38]), Curthose spent Easter in Normandy, aware no doubt that the storm would soon break. Diplomacy had failed, and was clearly of no further use with a man as unprincipled as Henry. Perhaps after all the best hope was open war and the chances of battle, in which at least he had the advantage of experience.

The pope wrote back on 23 March, giving Anselm authority to deal as leniently with the king as he saw fit, now that progress had been made on the all-important question of investitures. The royal chaplain William Warelwast and Anselm's monk Baldwin returned to Normandy together and gave the news to Anselm at Bec, and then they crossed to England in May.[39] William Warelwast was swiftly sent back by Henry, who had decided he would prefer Anselm to do the travelling. Despite his ill health, Anselm left Bec in response to Henry's entreaties and promises of future good behaviour, but could not travel far. Orderic mentions that the spring and early summer that year were unusually hot, with frequent outbreaks of fever, catarrh and rheumy eyes afflicting many people.[40] When he was able, Anselm returned to Bec, where he suffered a relapse so severe that the clergy of Normandy gathered for his funeral. But once again he recovered, and at last Henry joined him at Bec on the Feast of the Assumption (15 August) for a formal agreement with his archbishop. Anselm then crossed to England in early September, to be met at Dover by a delighted Queen Matilda, leaving Henry secure from the threat of excommunication and free to do as he pleased in Normandy.[41]

It is easy to get the impression that Curthose sat idly back through most of 1106, while Henry finalised his plans. In fact, until the agreement at Bec in mid-August, Henry was still under threat of excommunication and unable to make a move, and Curthose had little option but to await developments. He did take up residence at Falaise, where he was better placed to confront Henry's aggression than he would have been at Rouen, but beyond that he was forced to respond to events as they occurred. If he had possessed Henry's unscrupulous determination, he might have arrested him on some trumped-up charge when he was in Normandy, but the king was exploiting the grey areas of dual lordship, and Bec was in Beaumont territory. And the difference between the brothers was that, as William of Malmesbury observed, while Henry made promises with no intention of keeping them, playing with men's credulity, Curthose always erred on the side of forgiving those who wronged him.[42]

Once Anselm was back in England, Henry moved to Caen, which he seems to have made his temporary headquarters. There a message reached him that the Abbot of Saint-Pierre-sur-Dives, a small abbey not far from Curthose's castle at Falaise, was willing to betray his recently fortified abbey to the king. But Abbot Robert, a Saint-Denis monk who had been appointed only a few months previously after making a donation to the ducal treasury, was luring Henry into a trap. Unsuspecting, Henry set off with a small company of knights and by riding all night reached Saint-Pierre as dawn broke. Curthose had sent reinforcements to spring the trap, but before they could arrive, the garrison within betrayed themselves by hurling insults over the walls. Henry's men launched an attack, stormed the abbey and set fire to it, incinerating most of the occupants who had fled into the church. Three notable prisoners were, however, taken: Abbot Robert was brought to the king, who banished him to France; Reginald Warenne was captured, but released soon after, perhaps to encourage his brother's loyalty; Robert Stuteville, the young heir to wide lands in both England and Normandy, was less fortunate and seems to have been held for several years.[43]

Now Henry sent part of his army south from Falaise and besieged a small castle belonging to William of Mortain, at a place called Tinchebray.[44] A siege castle was built, but it was unable to prevent Count William revictualling, so in frustration Henry himself came to Tinchebray, in early September. Count William appealed to Curthose and Robert Bellême for assistance, and when he arrived Curthose ordered Henry to lift the siege, since William was his vassal, in legitimate possession of Tinchebray, and had nothing to do with the English king. When Henry refused, a battle became inevitable.

Henry had not come to Tinchebray unprepared. With him were Hélias of Maine and Duke Alan of Brittany, as well as the Beaumonts and many other Norman magnates. Both Hélias and Alan would be happy to see the power of the Norman duke curtailed, and the Normans in Henry's camp had already decided that their future prosperity was centred in England. Curthose's much smaller army consisted chiefly of Count William and all his vassals, and the Bellêmes, with a small group of his close councillors, who may all have come with him from Falaise. Such is the power of Henry's propaganda that almost nothing is known of Curthose's dispositions or the composition of his force. But it seems certain that Henry was supported by a large army, which included seasoned fighters, while Curthose was obliged to manage with a much smaller force, pulled together in haste.

Henry is reputed to have begun by offering his elder brother what amounted to a retirement package, with a generous pension in exchange for relinquishing the government of Normandy. Unsurprisingly, Curthose rejected this ignominious and insulting offer out of hand. He had already experienced the value of Henry's promises. And where would he be housed? And in what conditions? The arbitration of battle was the only option, and this time, five years after Alton, there would be no drawing back. Robert of Mortain's chaplain Vitalis, who had become a hermit in the decade since his master's death, briefly interposed and tried to make peace, but to no avail.

Tinchebray, like Hastings before it, was chiefly fought on foot. Whether because a large number of Henry's knights were from England and accustomed to working with Saxon foot soldiers, or because this was becoming the norm, both sides apparently adopted this strategy, the knights dismounting before battle was joined. Henry had sufficient men to form three separate ranks, led by Ralph of Bayeux, Robert Beaumont and William II Warenne, while a mounted reserve of Breton and Manceaux knights were commanded by Count Hélias. Curthose's reserves were led by Robert Bellême. Thus it was that, on 28 September 1106, forty years to the day after the Norman invasion of England, Robert Beaumont again found himself engaged in a pivotal battle. But this time, Saxons and Normans were fighting side by side against the Duke of Normandy, on Norman soil.

As the front lines clashed, the ducal forces held their ground against heavy odds. But then Hélias led a cavalry charge, smashing through their flank and turning the tide decisively. The battle was over in barely an hour, as Robert Bellême opted for flight and abandoned the field. Waldric, Henry's chancellor, who despite his holy orders had joined in the battle, personally took Curthose prisoner, while the Bretons captured William of Mortain, whose lands ran along the Breton border; it was only with the greatest difficulty that the royal troops persuaded them to release him into their custody. Among the other prisoners were Robert Stuteville the elder, father of the young man captured at Saint-Pierre, William Ferrers, William Crispin and the unfortunate Edgar Ætheling, who had only recently returned to Normandy.

This brief encounter was an utter disaster. Curthose had gambled his future on a pitched battle, and, instead of his vastly superior experience of warfare being decisive, it was Henry's greater numerical strength and the ignominious flight of Robert Bellême that had decided the outcome. Few would have predicted that Henry, so much more skilled in chicanery and deceit, would also beat his brother in armed combat. Moreover, in the normal course of events it would be expected that noble prisoners would soon be released in exchange for a ransom, but a life of exile might well then be their only future. But there loomed the terrible precedent of Count Geoffrey of Anjou, defeated in battle and imprisoned for nearly three decades by his brother Fulk Le Rechin, who still ruled in his place.

A few days after the battle, Henry claimed in a letter to Anselm that 400 knights and 10,000 foot soldiers had been taken prisoner, with an 'unknown number' killed. This was rampant hyperbole, and moreover he omitted to mention that Count Hélias had had any part in the victory. A later Norman source speaks of the battle as almost bloodless, with no casualties on the king's side and only about sixty for Curthose. More significantly, Henry told Anselm that by this battle he had captured 'Normandy itself'. For Henry, then, this was no mere skirmish between brothers, to be smoothed over and forgotten, but it had become the moment when Normandy became his. In his letter he refers to his brother merely as count, not duke, underscoring the difference in their status. Curthose was now entirely at Henry's mercy, as were many of his supporters.

Henry's first move after the battle was to arrange for the surrender of the great ducal stronghold of Falaise. Curthose warned him that the garrison would not surrender unless explicitly ordered to do so by their duke, or by William Ferrers, who was empowered to act on his behalf. So Ferrers was sent ahead to Falaise, while Henry followed with Curthose under guard. When they arrived, Henry took possession of the castle and town, and the duke released his men there from their fealty to him. Now in truth he was defeated. But one good thing came of this visit. His young son Clito, just short of his fourth birthday, had been living with him at Falaise, and he managed to avoid his father's fate. Orderic describes an interview with Henry, who displayed unwonted tender-heartedness and allowed the boy to go free in the care of his stepsister and her husband Hélias of Saint-Saëns, supposedly for fear that, if the child should die, he would be held responsible.[45] But if Henry were so careful of his near relations' comfort, why did he not hold father and son captive together? Or why not place his infant nephew, who was the heir to Normandy and in some eyes the heir to England as well, under independent house arrest in safe hands in England? Of all the Norman barons, Clito's brother-in-law was surely the least likely to toe Henry's line. This tale of the arrangements made for Clito's upbringing seems more like an excuse for a major slip-up in Henry's otherwise slick campaign. One could more easily imagine William Ferrers arriving at Falaise a few hours or even a day ahead of Henry, alerting the garrison to the catastrophe that had befallen and making swift arrangements to spirit the heir away to safety. Indeed the Hyde Chronicle supports this, saying that Hélias took Clito under his wing because of his old oath to Curthose.[46]

From Falaise, Henry probably travelled to Caen, where he was approached by a priest of Fécamp, seeking restoration of land he had appropriated. Once his appeal had been successful, the priest wrote a letter that supplies much of our detailed information about Tinchebray. The priest was a close associate of Robert Stuteville the elder, one of Henry's prisoners, and may have been his chaplain, the Robert whom Orderic Vitalis also knew.[47] Although he was thus associated with one of Curthose's partisans, the letter describes the battle's outcome as 'good news' and mentions the involvement of both Duke Alan and Count Hélias.

Henry next took Curthose to Rouen, where he obliged him to make the castellan surrender and transfer his fealty. In some sort of general action, this was extended to all the ducal castles, officially recognising the change of regime. While he was near Rouen, Henry wrote his letter to Anselm, carefully stressing that the victory had been achieved by divine providence, and that he trusted it would mark the beginning of an age of peace for the Church. Henry had by now had time to think through the consequences of his unexpected and immense stroke of good fortune; he had conquered Normandy, God had judged between him and his older brother, and he had in his hands not only the duke but also their cousin, Count William. His grasp on England was now much more secure, and, although he refrained from using the ducal title, he assumed all the ducal prerogatives and income. Anselm responded enthusiastically to Henry's letter, but he took care to spend the greater part of his reply urging him to remember that the victory belonged to God and to carry out his promises. Eadmer, repeating his sentiments of five years earlier, commented that many people said openly that Henry's victory came about because he had made peace with Anselm.[48]

By 15 October Henry was in Lisieux, where he held a council of the Norman magnates, presumably with Curthose present to demonstrate that power had been transferred. The laws of the duchy were formally reaffirmed, and Henry assumed control of the ducal demesne, with the interesting proviso that he reneged on all the gifts that Curthose had made from it: the partisans of the erstwhile duke were thereby shorn of part of their wealth. The only conspicuous absentee from Lisieux was Robert Bellême. He had been in a difficult position at Tinchebray: on one side in the battle was his overlord for the greater part of his continental lands, but on the other was Count Hélias, his overlord for much of the rest. He also had to consider his county of Ponthieu, in France. Moreover, King Henry had it in his gift to restore his English lands, if he was so minded. This does not excuse his flight, since with his additional strength the outcome might well have been different, but it does go some way towards explaining his dilemma. He was, also, noted for acting independently in a very complex and dangerous world, and if his past record is a guide, the plight of his duke and his nephew would not have been the final arbiter when his own survival was threatened. Soon after Tinchebray, he may have approached Count Hélias to sound him out about combined action against Henry. But Maine was temporarily at peace with Normandy, and the suggestion fell on deaf ears. So Robert approached Henry himself, and was restored to favour sufficiently to witness a charter for the king in November 1106.[49] His brother Arnulf was reconciled to Henry a few months later. But Robert never really gave up his support for Curthose and Clito, and Henry for his part took care that the lands he restored to Robert were ringed by his own adherents, including two whom he had married to still more of his bastard daughters.[50]

*   *   *   *   *

Henry had now finished with Curthose. Although he remained in Normandy until early spring 1107, tidying up loose ends and binding the duchy more closely to his rule, it was becoming important to get his captives transferred to England and into secure custody. So, soon after the council at Lisieux, perhaps at the end of October, the duke and his unfortunate companions were shipped across the Channel. For now, there was nothing that could be done for his cause. Once in England, several of the prisoners were set free. Either Edgar Ætheling, the queen's uncle, was considered to be no threat, or his near relationship to Henry made it important that he was seen to receive mild treatment. In the 1120s he was still alive, living quietly on his modest English estates, perhaps grateful that after all the changes and chances of his extraordinary career things had turned out as well as they had.[51] William Ferrers, Curthose's close companion, was also soon released, perhaps in deference to his father, whose barony of Tutbury in Derbyshire made him one of the wealthier magnates in England.[52] A more surprising pardon was given to William Crispin, whose brother Gilbert was the reliable and excellent abbot of Westminster. He was set free and allowed to return to his family lands on the Vexin border, lands that meant he had divided loyalties, as future events revealed.[53] King Henry also eventually released Robert Stuteville the younger, perhaps because he held no land, and he married and had a son, also Robert (III). But his father, who was a major landholder in Yorkshire, Lincolnshire and Hampshire, as well as one of Curthose's ablest lieutenants, remained in prison for the rest of his life. By about 1135 both father and son were dead, and the grandson, Robert III, regained some of the English estates at the beginning of Stephen's reign.[54]

Henry's other young prisoner, William Count of Mortain, fared much worse. He was not only, in Henry's eyes, a traitor with regard to his forfeited English lands, but as a first cousin he was a candidate for the throne. All the sources agree that he was guarded closely, lodged in the Tower of London until Henry's death. In the only year for which there are records, 1130, he and his servants together were given an allowance of £30 1s 4d for their food and clothing.[55] This was enough to live adequately, but hardly a generous sum for a man whose English estates alone had been worth over £2,000. Much worse, during King Stephen's reign Henry of Huntingdon revealed that William had been blinded on Henry's orders.[56] There is unfortunately no reason to doubt the truth of this story. Henry considered blinding a suitable punishment for rebels, and Orderic was moved to complain against it by means of a speech he put into the mouth of Count Charles of Flanders, which was also written after Henry's death.[57] William alone of the Tinchebray captives seems to have been blinded; it was not, therefore, that he was a traitor, since other traitors were spared. More likely it was because of his close blood relationship, and because as a young and apparently popular man he represented a real threat. Nobody would rise in rebellion for a blind Pretender. In 1140 King Stephen (who had been granted Mortain by Henry) allowed William to move from the Tower to Bermondsey Abbey, where he spent his last days as a monk.[58]

As for Robert Curthose, he was at first taken to the royal castle at Wareham, at the top of Poole Harbour.[59] Soon afterwards, he was transferred to the custody of the newly consecrated Bishop Roger of Salisbury. Roger had started life as a humble priest of Avranches, who joined Henry's household in the 1090s (a later story has it that Henry was impressed by Roger's ability to say mass more quickly than any other priest he knew). Just before his consecration in summer 1107, Roger was granted Kidwelly as part of the distribution of the Montgomery family lands in the Marches. By the end of Henry's reign, Roger was not only the chief administrator of England and a leading member of the vice-regency council, but was also one of Henry's wealthiest magnates. Roger held several castles and invested his growing wealth in building works, especially at Salisbury and Devizes. Here the deposed duke probably spent most of his time, moving occasionally with the bishop's household.

Curthose's confinement was not too severe, more a house arrest than imprisonment, but he was closely guarded and escape was impossible. While Henry stopped short of killing or blinding his oldest brother, he would not countenance him ever being free again. John of Salisbury reports speaking to many men who had seen Curthose at this phase of his life, held in 'honourable captivity'.[60] Despite their widely different backgrounds, Curthose seems to have developed a good relationship with Bishop Roger. It may be no coincidence that the English history that contains most insights into his life was written by Henry of Huntingdon, whose bishop was Roger of Salisbury's protégé and nephew. Alone among the English accounts of the crusade, for example, it mentions Curthose's vital role at Dorylaeum.[61]

The 1130 royal accounts show that Curthose was still alive, aged 80, with an annual allowance paid to his warders of £35 10s. As with his young cousin William, this is hardly a lavish sum for a man who might have been king. But Henry persisted with the propaganda about his imprisonment. In 1119 he told the pope: 'I have not kept my brother in fetters like a captured enemy, but have placed him as a noble pilgrim, worn out with many hardships, in a royal castle, and have kept him well supplied with abundance of food and other comforts and furnishings of all kinds.'[62]

Chapter 10

THE EXILED HEIR

If Henry imagined that his victory at Tinchebray would complete his conquest of Normandy, he was mistaken. He was destined to rule for a further twenty-nine years, and eighteen of these would be spent in the duchy, as his power there repeatedly ebbed and flowed. Even with the vast wealth of England at his disposal, controlling Normandy was not easy. Louis VI succeeded his father King Philip in 1108 and was eager to restrict Henry's activities; the alliance with Maine ended with the death of Hélias of La Flèche in 1110; Flanders became more hostile on the death of Count Robert in 1111. Above all, any disaffected Norman baron had a rallying point in the form of Curthose's young son William Clito. Curthose's surviving bastard son had left Normandy for the crusader principalities of the East, and after a brief and successful career there he vanishes from the pages of history in about 1110.[1] Clito, the legitimate heir, represented the future for Curthose's partisans, the hope that their duke might again be free.

Henry seems to have seen himself as ruling Normandy by right of conquest. He said so in his first letter to Anselm announcing the victory, and Anselm replied in kind, styling him 'King of England and Duke of Normandy'. But Henry himself used the title very sparingly, and it came into official use only with his fourth seal, in the 1120s.[2] Perhaps this was in deference to his own propaganda, or to avoid having to pay homage to Louis. Or perhaps it was because, although he had captured and deposed Curthose, the duke's heir was still at liberty.

Until about 1112 Henry's grip on the duchy remained secure. In 1110 he renewed his treaty with Flanders, and the following year he encouraged and subsidised Count Theobald of Blois in a short campaign against King Louis. But even while Clito was a child, Henry seems to have been aware of the challenge he might pose.[3] An attempt was made to capture the boy from Hélias of Saint-Saëns's castle of Arques, but the household smuggled him out, and kept him safe until he could be reunited with his guardian. They were forced into a wandering exile, while Henry gave Saint-Saëns's castle to William Warenne as a further inducement to remain loyal.[4]

Meanwhile, Robert Bellême's wife had died in about 1105, leaving him as Count of Ponthieu in France. For now, this was all that remained of his once-vast estates. Their only son, William Talvas, began administering Ponthieu shortly before 1112, when he was in his late teens, and Robert probably then began plotting a rebellion in favour of Clito. Henry seems to have become suspicious of Robert's intentions, and, as in 1102, he issued a list of charges against him. When Robert went to the Norman court in November 1112, apparently under the impression that he would be safe because he was Louis's ambassador, Henry arrested him and had him imprisoned at Wareham. In 1130 he was still there.[5] With Robert thus immobilised and William Talvas fully occupied in Ponthieu, Henry besieged and captured the key Bellême border fortress of Alençon, which he burnt to the ground.[6]

But just as Robert Bellême was finally vanquished, the wider prospects for Henry's control of Normandy deteriorated. After the death of Hélias of Maine, he acquired an aggressive new neighbour in Fulk V, the new Count of Anjou, who was also Count of Maine through his marriage to Hélias's heiress Eremburga. In Flanders, too, the situation changed after Robert II died while campaigning with Louis against Theobald of Blois.[7] His heir Baldwin was still a youth, and for a while was fully occupied quelling disturbances in ever-restive Flanders. But once he had regained control, he welcomed his two cousins Clito and Charles of Denmark to his court. Now, to Henry's alarm, Clito and Hélias of Saint-Saëns had a permanent base, dangerously close to Normandy.

Henry reacted vigorously to these potential threats, encouraging Robert Beaumont to retaliate for the pillaging of his lands by French troops, with a raid almost to Paris. Henry and his sister Adela also persuaded Count Theobald (still under her influence although he was well into his twenties) to throw off his allegiance to Louis. He began forging an alliance with Anjou by betrothing William Adelin (aged 9) to Fulk's daughter Matilda in 1113.

He married yet another of his illegitimate daughters (another Matilda) to Conan III, Duke of Brittany. And finally, his only legitimate daughter, Matilda (or Maud, as she is often known), was married to the Emperor Henry V in January 1114, thus securing a valuable alliance with Louis's greatest enemy.

Henry had ringed Normandy with alliances, but he could not prevent Baldwin from taking Clito's part. The two young men had much in common, besides their similar ages; both were wary of Henry's intentions and it was in Flanders' interests to keep England and Normandy separate. During 1114, therefore, when Clito was still only 11, Baldwin mounted the first of a series of raids into Normandy, and two years later he knighted his guest as soon as he turned 14.[8]

In response to Baldwin's raids, and presumably to pre-empt Clito's claim to the duchy, Henry made the Norman barons take an oath of homage to William Adelin. He then returned to England, and, at a council at Salisbury on 19 March 1116, the English magnates likewise rendered homage to Adelin as heir to the kingdom, by implication reaffirming the legitimacy of Henry's own rule.[9] But Henry's spies would have been telling him that, despite his best efforts, a threefold alliance was building against him, between Louis, Baldwin and Fulk, while the allegiance of Theobald of Blois remained uncertain.

The king therefore crossed the Channel again in April 1116, to find Normandy seething with discontent. Both Baldwin and Louis organised raids almost to the walls of Rouen, while Theobald had captured Count William of Nevers, a French vassal but also the brother of Countess Helwise of Evreux. The Count and Countess of Evreux had quickly reaffirmed their loyalty to Curthose's line after Tinchebray and had been exiled by Henry. The barons whose lands lay close to Flanders, especially Henry of Eû, Hugh of Gournay and Stephen of Aumâle, were all considering transferring their allegiance to Clito, while Amaury de Montfort, William of Evreux's nearest heir and Fulk's uncle, was overtly hostile to the king.

The balance of power shifted quite suddenly in mid-1118. On 18 April William of Evreux died, and Amaury de Montfort laid claim to his title and lands. Then Queen Matilda died on 1 May, followed on 5 June by Robert Beaumont, Henry's elder statesman. The Beaumont lands in Normandy were inherited by Robert's son Waleran, while those in England passed to his younger twin, creating the novel situation of a Beaumont in Normandy who had few ties of loyalty to the English king. Robert Beaumont's young widow, Isabel of France, married William II Warenne with suspicious speed after her elderly husband's death.[10]

Count Fulk now invaded Normandy from the south, watched by the Grandmesnils and supported by many Norman barons.[11] King Louis attacked from the east, and burnt L'Aigle, while Stephen of Aumâle provided a staging post for Baldwin's invasion on behalf of Clito from the north-east. Henry captured Hugh of Gournay and Henry of Eû, whom he imprisoned in chains,[12] but for several months his regime was in danger, and he relied on extortionate English taxes to keep his army supplied. Along the southern border, he entrusted Theobald's younger brother Stephen with Alençon and other strategic castles, but Stephen was an inept ruler, and the burghers of Alençon, perhaps encouraged by Robert Bellême's brother Arnulf Montgomery, who reappears at just this time, invited Fulk in to take over their city.[13] Then at the end of 1118 Baldwin sustained an injury that obliged him to return to Flanders.

In February 1119 Henry's daughter Juliana and her husband Eustace joined the rebellion. Hostages had been exchanged during a dispute: the young son of a castellan for the two daughters of Eustace and Juliana. For some reason, perhaps at the prompting of Amaury de Montfort, Eustace had his child hostage blinded and sent back. When the grief-stricken father confronted Henry, the king ordered that his own little granddaughters should be mutilated in retaliation. It was one of his most implacable, callous actions, which Orderic, writing after Henry's death, found hard to comprehend.[14] Juliana and Eustace now prepared for war. Juliana herself took charge of the defence of Breteuil, and pretended to offer to parley with her father, only to attempt to shoot him with a crossbow. But Henry's good luck held, and she missed. Eventually Juliana was forced to flee, and Henry gave the lordship of Breteuil to Ralph of Gaël, the Breton claimant, whose daughter he married off to his bastard son Richard.[15]

In Flanders, Baldwin's wound refused to heal, and, although Henry is reputed to have offered him a physician, the young count died in spring 1119, to be succeeded by his cousin Charles of Denmark.[16] Despite the fortuitous removal of one of his chief adversaries, Henry was forced to negotiate. He came to terms with Fulk in May 1119. In exchange for a large sum of money extracted from an England already groaning under punitive taxation, and the restoration of

Alençon and many of the other ancestral Bellême lands to William Talvas, Fulk's daughter Matilda and William Adelin were married, giving Adelin the nominal overlordship of Maine and control of several border castles. Adelin was still only 16, and his bride about three years younger. It was a heavy price for Henry to pay, but it succeeded in detaching Fulk from Clito and Louis. It is also further evidence of how anxious Henry was to establish his own line and cut Clito out of the succession. It may well be that Henry narrowly avoided paying a far greater price and having to release Robert Bellême, by putting out a false story that he had died in the previous year.[17]

Henry now turned his attention to his eastern borders. Accompanied by his son Richard and by Stephen of Blois, he burnt the city of Evreux, but Amaury's garrison continued to hold out in the citadel. In mid-August, Louis advanced through the Norman Vexin to relieve Evreux, accompanied for the first time by William Clito in person, now aged 16 and eager to avenge his father's defeat at Tinchebray and secure his release. Also with him were William Crispin, Stephen of Aumâle and many high-ranking French barons. As they pressed on into Normandy, they stumbled upon Henry's army, including William Adelin, at a place called Brémule. Henry's scouts gave him enough warning to deploy carefully, dismounting his knights as he had done at Tinchebray. The two armies, neither of them larger than 500 knights, clashed, but the French, who were slightly outnumbered, attempted a mounted attack, and, when they failed to penetrate Henry's defensive line, they retreated in disorder. William Crispin, however, caught sight of Henry and charged at him, striking him repeatedly on his helmet. But yet again Henry's luck held, and the blows were deflected by his armour, while Crispin was surrounded, struck down and taken prisoner. Louis, who fled with his knights, lost his standard, and Clito lost his palfrey in the confusion, but had it returned to him the following day by his cousin Adelin. They withdrew to Les Andelys castle, recently captured from Henry, where Amaury de Montfort joined them. He urged Louis to make a second attempt, so they re-entered Normandy with a much larger army, and marched to Breteuil in mid-September to try and recapture it for Eustace and Juliana. But Henry had warning of their coming, and his army, commanded by his talented son Richard, drove them off.[18]

After the failed attempt on Breteuil, Louis withdrew from Normandy, but he had by no means abandoned his campaign. The new pope, Calixtus II, was his wife's uncle, and, when a papal council met at Rheims in October 1119, Louis laid charges against Henry. First, he said, Henry had invaded Normandy in 1105 and 1106, although it was a part of France. He had imprisoned the Norman duke, who was a French vassal. He had disinherited William Clito, the rightful heir to Normandy, who was beside Louis at the council as he spoke. He had then imprisoned Robert Bellême, Count of Ponthieu, also a French vassal, when he was serving as a French emissary. He had incited Theobald of Blois to rebellion and encouraged him to imprison William of Nevers, yet another French vassal. When Louis had finished speaking, the many French members of the council supported him noisily, but the pope deferred a judgement, merely asking all those concerned to keep the peace henceforth, with a vague promise that he would consider the case against Henry later. Of course this was what Henry most wished, since he was beginning to regain control.[19]

Deprived of external military support, the rebellions faltered. Amaury de Montfort surrendered the citadel of Evreux to Henry's troops in exchange for recognition of his right to the comital title. Juliana and Eustace, encouraged by her brother Richard, came to Henry and sued for peace. Hugh of Gournay was also pardoned, and, when Stephen of Aumâle heard that a royal army was being prepared against him, he surrendered, perhaps with some further outlay of English coin.

Now Clito's options were at an end. King Louis was no longer willing to give him help, Fulk was bound to Henry with the marriage alliance, and Count Charles of Flanders remained resolutely neutral. Within Normandy itself all his allies had come to terms. Near Aumâle, at about the time Stephen surrendered, a meeting took place between Clito and his uncle. Henry purportedly offered to take him to the English court if he would submit, but Clito refused, and instead asked for the release of his father from prison, where he had now been held for thirteen years. Henry later claimed that he promised to treat Clito as a son and train him for government, but the veracity of this must be doubted. Not only was he older than William Adelin, but questions would inevitably then be raised about the status of Curthose and his continuing captivity. The Hyde Chronicle has a much more plausible story, that Clito begged Henry to release Curthose, assuring him that they would then go together to Jerusalem and the crusader states, and trouble him no more. Henry flatly refused, and attempted to buy the young man off, but 'in anger and distress' he refused to take the king's money and returned to his exile with Hélias.[20]

In late November 1119 Pope Calixtus met Henry near Gisors. The Emperor Henry V, Henry's son-in-law, had recently appointed a new anti-pope, and Calixtus was anxious to keep Henry's support. The king loaded him with presents and smoothly answered all the charges made at Rheims. First, Curthose had not been ruling Normandy properly, so had not truly possessed it. William of Evreux, Robert Beaumont and many other prominent magnates had begged him to come and rescue the duchy. His brother had been using as councillors men whom he, Henry, had exiled for treason. Despite repeated offers of help, Curthose had refused to be guided by him. God had decided between them at Tinchebray. Curthose had always been kept in honourable captivity, not in a prison. His nephew had been given to Hélias of Saint-Saëns to be brought up like Henry's own son, but Hélias had betrayed his trust and stirred up the enemies of the duchy. Henry had repeatedly begged Clito to come and live at his court, but he had refused. King Louis was the one who had broken the peace first. He would personally order Theobald to release William of Nevers, and would once again urge Clito to make peace. According to Orderic, the pope was willing to accept this version of events, and so the Council of Rheims achieved nothing for Clito.[21]

It is a measure of the confidence that Henry and those closest to him felt that his sister the Dowager Countess Adela, still active in the government of Blois almost twenty years after her husband Stephen had returned to the East to die, now decided to retire. She was escorted by a coterie of ecclesiastics to the convent of Marcigny and, commented an eyewitness with feeling: 'There has never been a more astute, inexorable or virile female in the entire history of France!'[22]

Henry concluded a new peace with Louis in the summer of 1120, as part of which Adelin paid homage to him for Normandy. As designated heir to England, he was now also recognised as duke elect of Normandy, without his father having to pay homage for it in person. The swing between Henry's and Clito's fortunes in just one year was complete.

But just as Henry's triumph seemed assured, the pendulum swung abruptly back again. Adelin and a group of boisterous young nobles, including his half-brother Richard, the hero of the recent campaign, and their half-sister

Matilda, Countess of Perche, were the last of the Anglo-Norman court to leave Barfleur that November, aboard the *White Ship*. It was already dark before the rowers began to manœuvre the boat out of the harbour. The rest of the royal fleet was far out to sea, barely visible, and much of the wine on board had already been consumed. Stephen of Blois, alarmed at the dangerously high spirits of crew and passengers alike and feeling unwell, decided at the last minute to defer his crossing. As the *White Ship* neared open water, she struck a submerged reef and sank. Few bodies were recovered, and only one man survived, clinging to a spar before being rescued at dawn. He said afterwards that the ship's master had called out to know where the prince was, and on being told he had already drowned, sank to the bottom rather than face the king's wrath.

Henry was prostrated with grief for days. Quite apart from the personal trauma of losing three children at a stroke, all his careful plans were undone. His only legitimate son was dead, and with him had foundered the alliance with Anjou and his control of Maine, together with the peace with Louis that had depended on Adelin's homage for Normandy. William Clito had abruptly emerged as a key player again. Indeed, in many people's eyes he was now the only possible heir to both the duchy and the kingdom.

Once his distress had abated, however, Henry moved with characteristic speed and determination. On 6 January he announced that he was to marry the youthful and nubile Adeliza of Louvain, who had the additional advantage that her father ruled a small but strategic duchy close to Flanders. The bride was dispatched to England, and the marriage took place at the end of January.[23]

Meanwhile, Clito's old allies stirred. First, Fulk demanded the return of his daughter Matilda, so Henry sent her home but retained control of her dowry castles. Amaury de Montfort encouraged Fulk to side with Clito again, and this time the alliance was formalised with a marriage. Adelin's widow had already become a nun, so Clito was married to her younger sister Sibyl, and granted Maine as his marriage portion.[24] Amaury also orchestrated a renewed rebellion in favour of Clito, involving William Crispin and Waleran Beaumont.

Henry met this new challenge by sending his son Robert to Normandy in March 1123 and following himself in June. For the rest of that year, a series of indecisive military actions laid waste large areas of the duchy.

Clito attacked from Anjou, supported by Fulk, while Amaury and Waleran spearheaded the attack from the east. But with little support from Flanders and with King Louis unwilling to become openly involved, progress was limited. Henry took an aggressive line, burning Waleran's towns of Pont-Audemer and Brionne, and as an unusually harsh winter set in, conditions deteriorated. Grain was scarce, and there was widespread suffering.

In March 1124 Amaury and Waleran were returning from a raid when they were ambushed. Amaury urged flight, but the youthful Waleran plunged into the fray and was captured when his horse was shot from under him. Amaury fled to France. This brief skirmish, known as the Battle of Bourgthéroulde, had far-reaching consequences. Several of Waleran's castles still held out, but once Henry had razed one and captured a second by assault, blinding its castellan, resistance crumbled. The rebellion had been broken before it could gather momentum. Yet again Henry's luck had held, and he was in no mood to be lenient, as he soon demonstrated. Waleran, loaded with chains, was sentenced to imprisonment, while three of his vassals were blinded. Count Charles of Flanders was said to have been moved to protest at the severity of these sentences, but Henry justified them, saying the men had been his own vassals before they were Waleran's and were not bound to follow him in treachery.[25]

So, once again, Clito was abandoned by his Norman backers, as Amaury returned from France and made peace with Henry. Worse still, the alliance with Fulk was threatened as Henry now took the extraordinarily hypocritical step of demanding that Clito's marriage to Sibyl be annulled on the grounds of consanguinity, despite the fact that an identical relationship had existed between Adelin and Sibyl's sister Matilda. The marriage was technically within the prohibited degrees, since Clito and Adelin's great-great-grandfather Richard II was the brother of Sibyl and Matilda's great-great-great-grandfather through Bertrade, but the church authorities would not have objected had it not been forcibly brought to their attention. This Henry did, making no attempt to keep his efforts secret, pouring money into the papal coffers to strengthen his case. King Louis was determined that the marriage should survive, and legates shuttled between the three courts, before Henry's 'threats, entreaties, gold, silver and other weighty things' finally won the day.[26] From Henry's point of view, as long as there was still a chance that he might have an heir, it was imperative that Clito was prevented from doing so. The principal advocate for Henry's case was a colourful character called Henry of Poitou, a professional pluralist who had at various times been Abbot of Saint-Jean-d'Angéley, Bishop of Soissons, Prior of Cluny and Souvigny, Bishop of Saintes (for a week) and even Archbishop of Besançon, whence he had been expelled after only three days. According to the admittedly biased Peterborough chronicles, he came to England claiming poverty during the annulment negotiations, and was rewarded with the Abbacy of Peterborough when that rich plum fell vacant soon afterwards.[27]

With Clito thus excised from his Angevin alliance, the international situation changed further in May 1125, when the Emperor Henry V died, leaving the Empress Maud a childless widow of 23. King Henry returned to England in 1126, accompanied by his reluctant daughter. After a decade as an empress, happy in her adopted country, she did not relish becoming a pawn in her father's political schemes. But by the Christmas Court, Henry had made up his mind, and on 1 January his barons took an oath of allegiance to Maud and her putative sons as his heirs. It was a huge gamble, since there was a real risk that she was infertile, but his own second marriage had failed to produce the necessary heir. Once again, Henry had designated a successor and tried to close the door on Clito.

There were real difficulties with this oath to Maud. Although there had been queens regnant in Spain, it was highly unusual and problematic. Also, Henry had three nephews who had some claim to the throne, and who as men might be better candidates: his sister Adela's sons Theobald and Stephen, and above all William Clito. Henry's bastard Robert had no aspirations; his grandfather William the Conqueror's illegitimacy had not stood in his way, but opinions had moved on, and for all his abilities Robert was not a serious candidate. But Clito was the Conqueror's only grandson in the male line, an increasingly successful warrior, capable of attracting strong loyalty. Yet for Henry to recognise Curthose's son would be to reverse the policy of twenty years. And if Clito were acknowledged as heir, could Henry justify his own occupation of the throne?

Henry's deliberations that Christmas were assisted by Bishop John of Lisieux, no friend of Robert Curthose. One outcome of their discussions was that some of the chief political prisoners were moved into more secure hands: Waleran was brought down from Bridgenorth and imprisoned at Wallingford under the control of Brian fitzCount, a bastard of Duke Alan of Brittany, and

Curthose, clearly still regarded as a potential threat, was taken from Roger of Salisbury and handed over to the king's son Robert, who held him for a while at Bristol and then transferred him far out of the limelight to his castle at Cardiff. The Anglo-Saxon Chronicle notes that the Empress Maud was closely involved in this decision, as if she doubted Bishop Roger's loyalty.[28]

The news of Maud's proclamation as heiress flew to the French court, and Louis was galvanised into activity. Presumably he had underestimated Henry's implacable opposition to Clito, assuming that he would be the eventual heir. Now Henry had revealed his hand, Louis responded: within weeks he had married Clito to his wife's half-sister Jeanne and invested him with the lordship of the French Vexin. Clito led an armed contingent down through his new lordship and appeared before Gisors in early February and laid formal claim to Normandy, receiving the allegiance of several local Norman lords.

Then, on 2 March, Count Charles of Flanders was murdered as he prayed in Bruges. Charles had been a good ally for Henry, refusing to take Clito's part as Count Baldwin had done. But despite growing up in Flanders, he had failed to appreciate the complexities of Flemish society, and had antagonised a powerful family who were technically serfs. They had planned to follow the assassination with a coup, but other 'servile magnates' failed to join them, and the citizens of Bruges, another influential group, were deeply divided. The citizens of Ghent then took sides, and civil war threatened. Charles had no heir, and none of the possible candidates commanded much support. Nor was there an agreed procedure for deciding between them. Normally, the nobility ratified the late count's choice, and the French king then invested him. Louis took the initiative and went to Arras, taking Clito with him and summoning the barons to meet him there. After a week-long assembly, he advised the Flemish nobility to elect Clito as their new count. On 28 March, less than three months after Maud had been proclaimed Henry's heir, Clito became Count of Flanders, with the full support of King Louis, and with the agreement of the assemblies of the leading towns.

King and count spent the next six weeks rounding up the assassins and executing them, and issuing charters of liberties to the main towns. They also quelled the unrest, and defeated Clito's rivals for the comital title. On 6 May, Louis returned to France, leaving Clito to establish himself in Flanders.[29]

Word of Clito's election was brought to Henry in England, within a week.[30] This was the most serious threat to his regime yet. Although Flanders was a notoriously violent state, with tensions always close to the surface between the old aristocracy, the newly influential families in the count's service, and the wealthy manufacturing towns and cities that were rapidly acquiring a political voice, Clito had spent much of his childhood there and was as well placed as anyone to understand the delicacy of the situation. He was a tried and tested warrior, and Flanders gave him great economic and military resources, and the springboard he had hitherto lacked for a concerted assault on Normandy on his own account.

Henry had to begin outmanœuvring and sidelining his nephew all over again. In this he still had two potent weapons, his money and his newly widowed daughter. Henry poured money into Flanders, and Ghent was encouraged to break from Clito over the city's charter of liberties; in August Lille also rebelled, over the terms of the Count's Peace during the all-important city fair. The Empress Maud was a tool of equal value. With consummate hypocrisy, Henry ignored the arguments for annulling Clito's first marriage, and offered Fulk a wedding between Maud and the 14-year-old heir to Anjou, Geoffrey 'Le Bel' Plantaganet. Maud did not wish to marry him, a boy ten years her junior, heir to a mere county, but Fulk took the bait, and the mismatched couple were betrothed in late summer 1127. Roger of Salisbury later complained that the only men who had been consulted were Robert the king's son, Brian fitzCount and Bishop John of Lisieux. It was a desperate measure, but it drew Fulk away from a new alliance with Clito.

In Flanders, Clito took the initiative, attacking Stephen of Blois in his new county of Boulogne and imposing a three-year truce.[31] But Henry continued to give financial support to all the rival candidates, stirring up unrest until he saw which one might prevail. By early 1128 Thierry of Alsace was emerging as the strongest, so Henry threw his weight behind him, causing Clito to appeal to King Louis for help 'against my mighty and ancient enemy the King of England, who is disturbing the peace of Flanders with his gifts . . . sending both soldiers and boundless financial help'.[32] Louis came to Flanders in person with a French army, but after only a few weeks he was forced to return home, leaving some of his troops in Flanders, because Henry had advanced deep into French territory to draw him off.

Henry's father-in-law the Duke of Louvain caused further difficulties for Clito, blockading the passage of Flemish cloth to the Rhineland markets and causing great hardship and unrest. The towns with their mercantile interests tended to support Thierry, but Clito still had the support of the majority of the nobility, and, with Henry strangely unwilling to enter Flanders himself and try his luck against Clito in person, he more than held his own.

Normans came flocking to Clito's side, and when Henry argued with the Duke of Louvain over the control of Thierry's campaign, the duke began to cooperate with Clito instead. In June, Clito won a major victory, crushing Thierry's much larger army and causing him to flee to Bruges. In early July he orchestrated a successful siege, which caused Thierry further heavy losses, and the citizens of Bruges began to rethink their allegiance to him.

Then disaster struck. On 12 July the comital army moved on Alost, where Clito met his new ally the Duke of Louvain and began a siege. After two weeks, their combined forces were on the verge of victory, when Clito suffered a minor injury on the palm of his hand. As so often, the wound quickly became infected and Clito fell ill. He died a few days later, on 28 July 1128, aged 26, just six weeks after the marriage of the Empress Maud and Geoffrey of Anjou. The faithful Hélias of Saint-Saëns was with him to the end, and the body was carried to Saint-Omer, where he was enrolled posthumously as a monk and buried in Saint-Bertin Abbey, next to his ally and friend Count Baldwin.

Before he died, Clito wrote to his uncle King Henry, asking him to pardon him and all his supporters. The letter was carried by John, son of Bishop Odo of Bayeux. Henry is believed to have offered his forgiveness unreservedly, and the following year he released Waleran from captivity and allowed him to return to his Norman lands. There may have been a price to pay, however, since Waleran's young sister had at least one child by the king.[33] Many of Clito's supporters chose not to remain in Europe, but went to Jerusalem and the crusader states.

If anything demonstrates the great importance that Henry attached to his nephew Clito, it is that as soon as he was dead, Henry obtained the Norman regalia from Caen. Now, and only now, did he feel able to claim unequivocally to be Duke of Normandy.[34] But for many, the true heir after Robert Curthose had always been Clito, a model knight, as the poet Walo said:

Mars has died on earth, a star has fallen down,
The gods lament a god, honour mourns honour's demise.
A new thing this, that gods can die,
And immortals know they are mortal.
The hero of heroes is fallen, he who never fled,
Turned not from the fray, from arrow or danger,
First to the foe, in battle the foremost,
Thundering as the thunder.
Flanders cradles his tomb, Normandy rocked his cradle;
The bright star rose in one, in the other it has set.[35]

With the death of William Clito, Curthose's hopes were finally at an end. As long as his son lived, there was hope that one day he too might be free, to regain his duchy or at least to see his heir claim it. Orderic says that Curthose woke from a dream on the night of 28 July 1128, knowing that Clito was dead. Only later was the terrible news confirmed. But still the old duke could not die. He lived on into his eighties, forgotten by the world, imprisoned at Cardiff castle.

At last, in the twenty-eighth year of his imprisonment, Curthose died, on 3 February 1134, in his eighty-fourth year. His body was taken to Gloucester Abbey for burial, in the faded dignity of a once-royal city no longer used for courts or crown-wearings. It was an important enough place to cause no offence, but a backwater far removed from any influence or prestige. In his offering for his brother's soul, too, Henry did just enough, but nothing more. He gave one small manor, Rodley, part of the estate at Westbury-on-Severn, 'with its fishing and firewood rights, to provide one light to burn before the High Altar as a perpetual flame for the soul of his brother Robert Curthose'.[36]

THE CONQUEROR'S SONS

Among all the changes and chances of Robert Curthose's life, one thing is certain: his father's ambitions for the succession were not achieved. After the premature death of his second son, Richard, either William the Conqueror envisaged two parallel dynasties, founded by Rufus and Curthose, ruling England and Normandy; or, as has been argued here, he intended his undivided realms to pass to his eldest son. Neither occurred.

William Rufus was undoubtedly a better king than he is usually given credit for, but the true picture is irrevocably clouded, not least because it was in Henry's interests to let his reputation be tarnished. Curthose meanwhile faced hostile and unscrupulous brothers, and his realm was a convenient repository for their disaffected exiles. He also endured a siege sustained by the wealth of England, throughout his entire reign.

Curthose survived the worst that Rufus could do, and returned from the crusade battle-hardened and triumphant, but in Henry he met his nemesis. Henry was the only brother who grasped the essential need to reunite the Anglo-Norman regnum as a precondition for stability. The compromise of 1101 demonstrated that Curthose was swayed by other influences.

Henry's genius, if it can be called that, was that he had the driving ambition and relentless determination to achieve his political aims. Robert Curthose's failing, if such it was, was that he lacked the ruthlessness to subordinate solemn agreements to the pursuit of worldly goals.

NOTES

Chapter 1

1. *GR* IV.389.5: i. 703.
2. *OV* i. 88.
3. A. Cooper, '"The Feet of Those that Bark Shall Be Cut Off"': Timorous Historians and the Personality of Henry I', *Anglo-Norman Studies*, 23 (2001), 47–67.
4. *GND* i, p. lxxi.
5. The B2 manuscript of the *GND*: London, British Library, MS Harley 491; *GND* VII. Epilogue: ii. 184–91.
6. A. Sapir and B.M.J. Speet, *De Obitu Willelmi: Kritische beschouwing van een verhalende bron over Willem de Veroveraar uit de tijd van zijn zonen* (Amsterdam: Historisch Seminarium van de Universiteit van Amsterdam, 10; 1976), pp. 3–4; thanks are due to Dr A. Sapir Abulafia for this text, and to Eric Idema for translating it; M. Gullick, 'The Hand of Symeon of Durham: Further Observations on the Durham Martyrology Scribe', in D. Rollason (ed.), *Symeon of Durham: Historian of Durham and the North* (Stamford: Shaun Tyas, 1998), pp. 14–31.
7. *GND* i, pp. lxiv–lxv.
8. F. Barlow, *William I and the Norman Conquest* (London: English Universities Press, 1965), pp. 43, 177 ff.; H.R. Loyn, *The Norman Conquest* (London: Hutchinson, 1965), p. 193; O. Holder-Egger, 'Einhardi Vita Karoli Magni', *MGH, Scriptores rerum Germanorum*, 25 (1911).
9. L.J. Engels, 'De obitu Willelmi ducis Normannorum regisque Anglorum: Texte, modèles, valeur et origine', in Anon., *Mélanges Christine Mohrmann* (Utrecht/ Anvers: Spectrum Éditeurs, 1973), 209–55.

10. M.M. Tischler, 'Einharts Vita Karoli; Studien zur Entstehung, überlieferung und Rezeption', *MGH, Schriften*, 48 (2001), 20–44. Similar comparisons are made, for example, in the *Carmen de Hastingae*: F. Barlow (ed.), *Carmen de Hastingae Proelio of Guy Bishop of Amiens* (Oxford: Clarendon Press, 1999), pp. 44–5, line 736, 'promptior est Magno largior et Carolo', and by William of Malmesbury, who quotes the Life of Charlemagne several times: *GR* III.279: i. 508 and ii. 256–8.

11. E. von Tremp, 'Theganus Gesta Hludowici imp. et Astronomus Vita Hludowici', *MGH, Scriptores rerum Germanicarum*, 64 (1995), 33–4, 123–33.

12. E. von Tremp, 'Die Uberlieferung der Vita Hludowici imperatoris des Astronomus', *MGH, Studien und Texte*, 1 (1991), 17–19, 58–60; thanks are due to Charles West for his help translating this text. The exemplar for *de obitu Willelmi* is the early to mid-eleventh-century Chartres 'P1' manuscript, Paris BN lat. 5354, fos 50r–61v and *Vita Hludowici* on fos 61v–85v; *GND* i, pp. lxiii–lxiv.

Chapter 2

1. C.W. David, *Robert Curthose, Duke of Normandy* (Cambridge, Mass.: Harvard University Press, 1920), p. 4.

2. The ducal family were, however, all capable of making their own marks on documents. A grant for William's foundation of St Stephen's Caen, for example (B 46), was witnessed in autograph in 1077 by William and Mathilda, their sons Robert and William and half a dozen magnates.

3. *GND* VII.26: ii. 146–9.

4. All the chronicles agree about Henry's birth, soon after his mother went to England in 1068. See, e.g., *OV* v. 292; *GND* ii. 217.

5. F 227 and F 231 are both witnessed by all three brothers and date to early 1066. F 232 is of the same date and is witnessed by Robert and William. Four others can be dated only to 1059–66 and are witnessed by Robert and one of his brothers.

6. B 279 and B 205b.

7. The earliest surviving original charter to use the title 'dux Normannorum' is F 23, dated 1013–20.

8. *Regesta Regum Anglo-Normannorum: The Acta of William I (1066–1087)*, ed. D. Bates (Oxford: Clarendon Press, 1998), pp. 85–92.

9. F 224, F 226 and F 158. See also F 74. For a discussion of the term *regnum*, see R.H.C. Davis, 'William of Jumièges, Robert Curthose and the Anglo-Norman

Succession', *English Historical Review*, 95 (1980), 597–606, and C.W. Hollister, 'Normandy, France and the Anglo-Norman Regnum', *Speculum*, 51 (1976), 202–42.

10. From the Norman-French *rechiner*, to gnash one's teeth. *GR* III.235: i. 438–9. It is doubtful if he was called this openly in his lifetime.

11. *OV* IV: ii. 304–5.

12. 'comes Cenommanis': F 224.

13. Two post-Conquest charters use the title for Robert, and another six do so for William.

14. *GND* VII.13(31): ii. 160–1.

15. J.S. Beckerman, 'Succession in Normandy, 1087, and in England, 1066: The Role of Testamentary Custom', *Speculum*, 47 (1972), 258–60; G. Garnett, 'Coronation and Propaganda: Some Implications of the Norman Claim to the Throne of England in 1066', *Transactions of the Royal Historical Society*, 36 (1986), 91–116; I.W. Walker, *Harold: The Last Anglo-Saxon King* (Stroud: Sutton Publishing, 1997), pp. 74–119; A. Williams, 'Some Notes and Considerations on Problems Connected with the English Royal Succession, 860–1066', *Anglo-Norman Studies*, 1 (1979), 144–67.

16. F 228.

17. *OV* VII.15: iv. 92–3.

18. *GND* VI.11(12): ii. 80–1; F 60 and F 89.

19. *GR* III.235.1–2: i. 436–7. Fulk died in Metz on his return journey, and his body was carried to Anjou for burial.

20. B 251.

21. *OV* IV: ii. 196–7.

22. *GND* VII.19 and Epilogue: ii. 178–9, 184–5.

23. *The Gesta Guillelmi of William of Poitiers*, ed. R.H.C. Davis and M. Chibnall (Oxford: Clarendon Press, 1998), pp. 178–9.

24. R.H.C. Davis, 'William of Poitiers and his History of William the Conqueror', in R.H.C. Davis and J.M. Wallace-Hadrille (eds), *The Writing of History in the Middle Ages* (Oxford: Clarendon Press, 1981), pp. 71–100.

25. *OV* IV: ii. 208–9.

26. D. Bates, 'The Conqueror's Adolescence', *Anglo-Norman Studies*, 25 (2003), 1–18.

27. *OV* IV: ii. 356–7.

28. *OV* V.10: iii. 112–13.

29. *GND* VIII.2: ii. 202–3; *JW* for 1077; *GR* III.274: i. 502–3.

30. The earliest certain use of the title for William is September 1077 (B 46), and for Henry the only use in his father's reign is in a charter written between 1080 and 1083 (B 266 III).

31. B 282, B 283 and B 284; cf. F 55; the description of Robert occurs in the text of B 164 (1079 x 1087).

32. B 173 and B 229; B 175 I and II.

33. These charters are summarised, with their dating clauses published in full, in C.H. Haskins, *Norman Institutions* (Oxford: Oxford University Press; Cambridge, Mass.: Harvard University Press, 1918), p. 67.

34. *OV* V.10: iii. 98–9.

35. L.L. Gathagan, 'The Trappings of Power: The Coronation of Mathilda of Flanders', *Haskins Society Journal*, 13 (1999), 21–39; BL MS Cotton Vitellius E. xii, fo. 160v; H.E.J. Cowdrey, 'The Anglo-Norman Laudes Regiae', *Viator*, 12 (1981), 37–78; B 63.

36. *GR* IV.389: i. 700–1.

37. F. Barlow, *William Rufus* (London: Methuen, 1983), p. 38.

38. See, e.g., *OV* V.10 and *OV* IV: iii. 96–109, ii. 222–3, 356–7.

39. B 46, B 235 and B 175: two original manuscripts and an eleventh-century cartulary copy.

40. B 217: *Regesta*, ed. Bates, pp. 691–2.

41. *JW* for 1079.

42. *HA* VI.34: pp. 398–9.

43. *ASC* D for 1079.

44. B 28; Prou, no. 94.

45. B 235 and B 175; H.E. Cowdrey, *The Register of Pope Gregory VII 1073–1085: An English Translation* (Oxford: Oxford University Press, 2002), nos 7.25–7.27, pp. 356–9.

46. B 266 and B 267: see especially *Regesta*, ed. Bates, p. 802.

47. B 236, B 246 and B 257.

48. *OV* V.10: iii. 110–11.

49. Prou, no. 126.

50. 'Vita Beati Simonis Comitis Crespeiensis . . .', PL 156 (1880), 1211–24.

51. *OV* V.10: iii. 102–3.

52. W.E. Kapelle, *The Norman Conquest of the North: The Region and its Transformation, 1000–1135* (London: Croom Helm, 1979).

53. B 154.

54. *Cartularium Monasterii de Ramesia*, ed. W.H. Hart and P.A. Lyons (RS 79; 1884), i. 128–9; R. Mortimer, 'Anglo-Norman Lay Charters, 1066–*c*.1100. A Diplomatic Approach', *Anglo-Norman Studies*, 25 (2003), 153–75.

55. B 39, B 255, B 204, B 205, B 60 and B 230. All these are securely dated and located.

56. B 63. The epitaph on the tomb slab is very worn, but still quite legible; *OV* VII.10: iv. 44–7.

57. B 252; *Chronicon Monasterii de Abingdon*, ed. J. Stevenson (RS 2; 1858), ii. 12.

58. *OV* V.10 and VII.14: iii. 112–13, iv. 80–1.

59. B 156: *Regesta*, ed. Bates, pp. 513–14.

60. W.M. Aird, 'Frustrated Masculinity: The Relationship between William the Conqueror and his Eldest Son', in D.M. Hadley (ed.), *Masculinity in Medieval Europe* (London: Longman, 1999), pp. 39–55.

Chapter 3

1. *ASC* E for 1085.

2. B 326. This writ is in the style of contemporary Durham charters, and it is known that the Bishop of Durham, William Saint-Calais, was heavily involved in the administration of the Domesday survey, indicating that the writ was produced in England. Marginal notes on the corresponding Domesday folios (*DB* Surrey, i. 32r) strongly suggest that the writ post-dates these folios. See *Regesta*, ed. Bates, p. 958 and references therein.

3. B 146.

4. Three other writs, which appear to be English in origin and which date to after Bishop Maurice's consecration in 1086 (B 189, 190 and 191), mention none of the king's sons.

5. *DB* Hants, fo. 52r.

6. *GR* II.274: i. 502–3.

7. B 242.

8. *ASC* E for 1087.

9. *OV* VII.14: iv. 80–1; *GR* III.281–2: i. 510–11; *GND* VII.4(7) and VIII.1–2: ii. 104–5, 202–3.

10. The date of Robert of Bellême's marriage to Agnes of Ponthieu is not known, but in *Regesta*, i. 342 (probably 1093), he witnesses as Count Guy's son-in-law.

11. *Wace*, lines 9117–32, pp. 193–4.

12. Robert the Pious (d. 1031) designated and had crowned two sons in turn (one predeceased him). The tradition continued almost unbroken until the late twelfth century. In Anjou, Count Fulk Nerra (985) and Geoffrey IV Martel (1104) were both appointed co-ruler in their father's lifetime; A.W. Lewis, 'Anticipatory Association of the Heir in Early Capetian France', *American Historical Review*, 83 (1978), 906–27.

13. Garnett, 'Coronation and Propaganda'.

14. See, e.g., D. Bates, 'Normandy and England after 1066', *English Historical Review*, 104 (1989), 851–80; G. Garnett, 'Ducal Succession in Early Normandy', in G. Garnett and J. Hudson (eds), *Law and Government in Medieval England* (Cambridge: Cambridge University Press, 1994), pp. 80–110; J.C. Holt, 'Politics and Property in Early Medieval England', *Past and Present*, 57 (1972), 3–52; J. Le Patourel, *Feudal Empires, Norman and Plantagenet* (London: Hambledon Press, 1984); E.Z. Tabuteau, 'The Role of Law in the Succession to Normandy and England, 1087', *Haskins Society Journal*, 3 (1991), 141–69.

15. *GR* IV.305: i. 542–3.

16. Rufus is styled *comes* in B 54 (1081 x 1087), B 167 (1081 x 1086) and B 144 (1085); he attests B 146 (after April 1086) and B 242 (late 1086 or 1087) with no title.

17. *HN* 3, 5, 25: pp. 3–5, 26.

18. Gerard witnessed B 278 and B 352 between 1086 and 1088; V.H. Galbraith, 'Girard the Chancellor', *English Historical Review*, 46 (1931), 77–9; *Hugh the Chantor: The History of the Church of York, 1066–1127*, trans. C. Johnson (London: Nelson and Sons, 1961), p. 11.

19. *HA* VI.40: pp. 406–7.

20. *OV* V.10: iii. 112–13; *GND* VIII.2: ii. 202–5.

21. *OV* VIII.22: iv. 268–71.

22. Copy in the cartulary of Vains, MS Caen 104, fo. 150. Printed by Haskins, *Norman Institutions*, p. 285.

23. *OV* VII.8: iv. 42–3.

24. *Antiquus Cartularius Ecclesiae Baiocensis*, ed. V. Bourrienne (Société de l'histoire de Normandie 62; 1902), i.

25. *JW* for 1087.

26. *ASC* E for 1087.

27. *OV* X.8: v. 238–9 specifically comments on this aspect of Rufus's character.

28. *JW* for 1087; *OV* III: ii. 138–9; see also *GR* III.240 and III.200: i. 452–3, 362–3, where William of Malmesbury suggests that Wulfnoth ended his days at Salisbury.

29. Odo and Geoffrey are among the list of bishops at William the Conqueror's funeral in *OV* VII.16: iv. 104–5.

30. Acta Lanfranci, in *ASC* A: *The Anglo-Saxon Chronicle: A Collaborative Edition. Manuscript A*, ed. J.M. Bately (Cambridge: D.S. Brewer, 1986), p. 87.

31. L'abbé Sauvage, 'Des miracles advenus en l'église de Fécamp', in C. Beaurépaire, l'abbé Blanquart, *et al.* (eds), *Société de l'histoire de Normandie, mélanges 2ième serie* (Rouen, 1893), pp. 29–32.

32. Haskins, *Norman Institutions*, pp. 290–1.

33. *OV* VIII.1: iv. 120–1; *GR* V.392: i. 710–13.

34. E.C. Norton, 'The Buildings of St Mary's Abbey, York and their Destruction', *Antiquaries Journal*, 74 (1994), 254–88.

35. Cf. B 223, B 286, B 300 and B 226. A rare example of a slip in the propaganda is in Domesday for Soberton, Hants, which notes: 'Harold took it while he was reigning' (*DB* Hants, i. 38b).

36. *The Letters of Lanfranc, Archbishop of Canterbury*, ed. H. Clover and M. Gibson (Oxford: Clarendon Press, 1979), letter 41, pp. 136–7.

37. T.A.M. Bishop and P. Chaplais, *Facsimiles of English Royal Writs to AD 1100* (Oxford: Clarendon Press, 1957); T.A. Heslop, 'English Seals from the Mid Ninth Century to 1100', *Journal of the British Archaeological Association*, 133 (1980), 1–16.

38. J. Hunter (ed.), *A Brief History of the Bishoprick of Somerset from its Foundation to the Year 1174* (London: Camden Society volume 8, 1840), pp. 21–2; W. Hunt (ed.), 'Two Chartularies of the Priory of St Peter at Bath', *Somerset Record Society*, 7 (1893), 40–2.

39. See *ASC*, *JW*, *OV* VIII.2, *GR* IV.306 and *HR*.

40. 'in inicio estatis': *OV* VIII.2: iv. 134–5.

41. F 228, F 229 and F 231; Curthose's charters in favour of Fécamp are printed (with a very misleading explanation) in Haskins, *Norman Institutions*, pp. 288–9. See R. Sharpe, '1088: William II and the Rebels', *Anglo-Norman Studies*, 26 (2004), 139–57.

42. *OV* VIII.2: iv. 132–5.

Chapter 4

1. *GR* IV.312–13, 321: i. 554–9, 566–7; *OV* IX.3 and X.4 : v. 22–3, 208–9; Guibert of Nogent seems to have been the first to record Rufus's nickname; Gaimar, writing in the vernacular in about 1140, calls him 'Le Rus Rei'.

2. *ASC* for 1088; *Regesta*, ii. 556.

3. *Regesta*, i. 302; see also *Regesta*, i. 301, 320, 325.

4. *Regesta*, i. 378 relates to an inquest into crown holdings in the West Country in Lent 1096, suggesting that William of Mortain was then still a minor.

5. W.M. Aird, 'An Absent Friend: The Career of Bishop William of St Calais', in D. Rollason, M. Harvey and M. Prestwich (eds), *Anglo-Norman Durham 1093–1193* (Woodbridge: Boydell, 1994), pp. 283–97; the trial is described by Eadmer in *HN*, and in a Durham tract: 'De iniusta vexacione Willelmi episcopi primi per Willelmum regem filium Willelmi magni regis', ed. H.S. Offler, A.J. Piper and A.I. Doyle, *Camden Miscellany 34*, 5th ser., 10 (1997), 49–104; M. Philpott, in Rollason *et al.* (eds), *Anglo-Norman Durham*, pp. 125–37.

6. VCH Lancashire, i. 291–8.

7. J.F.A. Mason, 'Roger de Montgomery and his Sons (1067–1102)', *Transactions of the Royal Historical Society*, 5th ser., 13 (1963), 1–29; VCH Lancashire, i. 291–8; cf. *OV* VIII.4 with VIII.15: iv. 148–9, 220–1.

8. Cf. *GR* V.392: i. 712–13 with *OV* VIII.4: iv. 148–9.

9. This is implied by *GND* VIII.2: ii. 204–5. William Werlenc, Count of Mortain, a grandson of Duke Richard I, was removed by William the Conqueror in the late 1050s; C. Potts, 'The Earliest Norman Counts Revisited: The Lords of Mortain', *Haskins Society Journal*, 4 (1992), 23–35.

10. *OV* VIII.4: iv. 146–7.

11. *OV* VIII.5: iv. 150–7. The story of fitzGiroie's mutilation in the 1040s is dwelt on at length, with varying details, by Orderic in *GND* VII.10–11: ii. 110–11, and *OV* III: ii. 14–15. fitzGiroie survived his ordeal, made a pilgrimage to Jerusalem, entered Bec as a monk and became one of the re-founders of the monastery of Saint-Evroul.

12. *OV* VIII.10: iv. 184–5.

13. J. Green, 'William Rufus, Henry I and the Royal Demesne', *History*, 64 (1979), 337–52.

14. Barlow, *William Rufus*, p. 242.

15. *OV* VIII.23: iv. 284–5. Orderic spent his childhood in Shropshire and had connections with the Montgomery family both there and in Normandy.

16. *PR 31 HI*, pp. 64 (Kent) and 110 (Lincolnshire).

17. S. Harvey, 'Domesday Book and Anglo-Norman Governance', *Transactions of the Royal Historical Society*, 5th ser., 25 (1975), 175–93; M. Howell, *Regalian Right in Medieval England* (London: Athlone Press, 1962), app. A, p. 214.

18. *ASC* for 1100; *HN* 26, 27: pp. 27–9; Barlow, *William Rufus*, p. 239.

19. Anselm to Hugh, Archbishop of Lyon. *Anselm's Letters*, ii, no. 176, pp. 86–7; see also *HN* 43–4: pp. 44–5.

20. *GR* II.207: i. 384–7.

21. *OV* VIII.9: iv. 180–3, where some of the detail is demonstrably unreliable.

22. *Regesta*, i. 308: witnesses include Richard de Redvers, lord of Vernon and lands in the Cotentin, Aigellus of the Cotentin, and William of Saint-Calais, Bishop of Durham; *Regesta*, i. 310 concerns the restoration of the monastery of Saint-Vigor, after the depredations of the Conqueror during Bishop Odo's imprisonment. Recently rediscovered charters of Robert Curthose that relate to Cotentin lands are discussed in J.A. Green, 'Robert Curthose Reassessed', *Anglo-Norman Studies*, 22 (2000), 95–116; J.-M. Bouvris, 'La Confirmation par le duc Robert Courte-Heuse de la donation du manoir de Vains', *Annales de Normandie*, 35 (1985), 35–48.

23. La Ferté-en-Bray is named only in RHGF xiv. 68; the *Anglo-Saxon Chronicle* says King Philip refrained from further conflict with Rufus 'either for love of him or for his great treasure'.

24. *OV* VIII.15: iv. 220–1; *GR* V.392: i. 712–13; C.W. Hollister, *Henry I* (New Haven and London: Yale University Press, 2001), pp. 73–5; *The Murder of Charles the Good, Count of Flanders. By Galbert of Bruges*, ed. J.B. Ross (New York and London: Harper and Row, 1967), pp. 250–2.

25. *OV* VIII.14: iv. 212–13.

26. The *ASC* and *JW* give a detailed account, perhaps working from a written text, under 1091; Orderic gives a brief summary, focusing on what Curthose ceded: *OV* VIII.16: iv. 236–7; *Symeon of Durham, Libellus de exordio . . .*, ed. D. Rollason (Oxford: Clarendon Press, 2000), pp. 242–3.

27. *GR* IV.308–10: i. 550–3; *Wace*, lines 9531–618, p. 199.

28. The two surviving charters that they witnessed at this time are calendared in Haskins, *Norman Institutions*, p. 69, nos 14 and 15. Four manuscripts of the inquest survive: a twelfth-century copy in the Vatican, MS 596, fos 4–5; another Vatican copy, MS 2964, fos 133v–134v; a thirteenth-century copy at Avranches, MS 149, fo. 3; and a fifteenth-century copy in the French National Archives, BN Paris MS Lat. 1597 B., fos 140–1. See C.H. Haskins, 'The Norman

Consuetudines et Iusticie of William the Conqueror', *English Historical Review*, 23 (1908), 502–8.

29. See *OV* ii. 284–5, n. 5.

30. Bishop Hoel witnessed *Regesta*, i. 315 for Rufus at Dover in January 1091; *OV* VIII.11–12: iv. 192–9; the Le Mans cartulary supports Orderic here: *Cartulaire de l'abbaye de Saint-Vincent du Mans*, ed. R. Charles and S. Menjot d'Elbenne (Le Mans, 1886), i, no. 117; R. Latouche, *Histoire du comté de Maine pendant le Xe et le XIe siècle* (Paris: Bibliothèque des hautes études, 1910), pp. 149–57.

31. *OV* VIII.18: iv. 252–5; *Regesta*, i. 318 has been used in the past to show that Henry was swiftly reconciled to his older brothers and accompanied them on this expedition, but this charter is now thought to be a forgery: see *Durham Episcopal Charters 1071–1152*, ed. H.S. Offler (Gateshead: Surtees Society 179, 1968), pp. 48–53.

32. Both *HR* and the *De iniustia vexacione* (lines 645–9: Offler *et al.*, 'De iniusta vexacione Willelmi episcopi primi', p. 99) say this was three years to the day after his deprivation, i.e. 11 September.

33. *HR* for 1093; *De iniusta vexatione*, lines 653–6 ('De iniusta vexacione Willelmi episcopi primi', ed. Offler *et al.*, p. 100); V. Wall, 'Malcolm III and the Foundation of Durham Cathedral', in Rollason *et al.* (eds), *Anglo-Norman Durham*, pp. 325–37.

34. *ASC* and *JW* for 1091; *Regesta*, i. 327.

35. Hoel appears in the Charters of Saint-Julien de Tours after November 1091: 'Chartes de Saint-Julien de Tours (1002–1227)', ed. L.-J. Denis, *Archives Historiques du Maine*, 12/1 (1912), nos 43, 44; Helias begins witnessing as count from winter 1091–2: Latouche, *Histoire du comté du Maine*, pp. 149–57.

36. *Regesta*, ii. 1134; *OV* iv. 258, n. 1; P. Bouet, 'Le Domfrontais de 1050 à 1150 d'après les historiens normandes contemporains', in J.C. Payen (ed.), *La Légende arthurienne et la Normandie* (Condé-sur-Noireau: Charles Corlet, 1983), pp. 73–94; *Cartulaire de l'abbaye de Saint-Vincent*, ed. Charles and Menjot d'Elbenne, i, no. 765; *PR 31 HI*, p. 42, has a Henry of Domfront, nephew of Achard, in receipt of a small sum under the honour of Arundel.

37. *Regesta*, i. 348.

38. *Charters and Custumals of the Abbey of Holy Trinity Caen. Two Volumes. Part 2. The French Estates*, ed. J. Walmsley (Oxford: Oxford University Press for the British Academy, 1994), p. 125.

39. *OV* VIII.20: iv. 260–1 and n. 3.

40. *HN* 30–42: pp. 31–43.

41. *JW* for 1093.

42. *ASC* for 1094.

43. *ASC* and *JW* for 1094.

44. *ASC* for 1096; *HR* for 1095.

45. *ASC* for 1096.

46. *Symeon of Durham, Libellus de exordio*, ed. Rollason, iv.10: pp. 254–5; Aird, 'An Absent Friend'.

47. Haskins, *Norman Institutions*, p. 70, no. 31.

48. A. Nissen-Jaubert, 'Fouilles archéologiques du prieuré Saint-Symphorien', *Le Domfrontais médiéval*, 8 (1991), 5–13; G. Louise, 'Châteaux et pouvoirs dans le Domfrontais médiéval (XIe–XIIIe siècles)', *Le Domfrontais médiéval*, 9 (1993), 11–28.

Chapter 5

1. Rodulf Glaber 3.vii.25: *Rodolfi Glabri Historiarum Libri Quinque . . .*, ed. J. France (Oxford: Clarendon Press, 1989), pp. 136–7.

2. *OV* IX: v. 10–15.

3. *OV* IX.2: v. 10–11.

4. *OV* III and IV: ii. 68–75, 254–5; Guibert of Nogent: *Guibert de Nogent: Autobiographie*, ed. E.R. Labande (Paris: Société d'édition Les Belles Lettres, 1981), pp. 246–9.

5. *Actes des Comtes de Flandre, 1071–1128*, ed. F. Vercauteren (Brussels: Commission Royale d'Histoire, 1938), no. 20, p. 63.

6. *GND* VI.2: ii. 46–7.

7. J. Riley-Smith, *The First Crusaders 1095–1131* (Cambridge: Cambridge University Press, 1997); G. Constable, 'Medieval Charters as a Source for the History of the Crusades', in P. Edbury (ed.), *Crusade and Settlement* (Cardiff: University College Cardiff Press, 1985), pp. 73–89.

8. Rodulf Glaber 1.v.21 and 4.vi.20: *Rodolfi Glabri Historiarum*, ed. France, pp. 36–7, 202–5; *GND* VI.11–12: ii. 80–5; F 90, pp. 231–9; *OV* VIII.25: iv. 306–9.

9. J. Riley-Smith, *The First Crusade and the Idea of Crusading* (London and New York: Continuum Press, 2003), p. 43; R. Allen-Brown, 'The Status of the Norman Knight', in J. Gillingham and J.C. Holt (eds), *War and Government in the Middle Ages* (Woodbridge: Boydell, 1984), pp. 18–32; A. Hyland, *The Medieval Warhorse from Byzantium to the Crusades* (Stroud: Sutton Publishing, 1994).

10. *Cartulaire de l'abbaye de Saint-Vincent*, ed. Charles and Menjot d'Elbenne, no. 460, cols 266–7.

11. *Cartulaire de St-Jean-d'Angéley*, ed. M.G. Musset (Saintes: Archives Historique de la Saintogne et de l'Aunis, 1901), i, no. 319, p. 384.

12. 'Hugh of Flavigny's Chronicle', ed. G.H. Pertz, *MGH, Scriptores*, 8 (1925), 474–5.

13. *Gesta Pontificum Anglorum*, ed. N.E. Hamilton (RS 52; 1870), V.271: p. 432; *HN* 75: pp 78–9.

14. Riley-Smith, *The First Crusaders*, pp. 125–6; Prou, no. 146, p. 368.

15. Riley-Smith, *The First Crusaders*, p. 120; C. Tyerman, *The Invention of the Crusades* (London: Macmillan, 1998), pp. 22–4.

16. Haskins, *Norman Institutions*, pp. 66–70, nos 3, 4, 5, 9, 32; *Actes des Comtes de Flandre*, ed. Vercauteren, no. 22, p. 67; Riley-Smith, *The First Crusaders*, p. 118.

17. *OV* X.8: v. 230–3 and p. 231, n. 1.

18. L. Delisle, *Littérature latine et histoire du moyen âge* (Paris: Leroux, 1890), pp. 28–9.

19. FC I.c.vi: RHC Oc. 3.i, pp. 327–8, which may, however, refer to the Blois contingent.

20. HC, pp. 301–2.

21. *GND* VIII.8: ii. 214–15; *OV* XII.3: vi. 190–3.

22. E. Jamison, 'Some Notes on the Anonymi Gesta Francorum, with Special Reference to the Norman Contingent from South Italy and Sicily in the First Crusade', in O. Rhys (ed.), *Studies in French Language and Medieval Literature* (Manchester: Manchester University Press, 1939), pp. 183–208; BD RHC Oc. 4, p. 333; *OV* VIII.16 and IX.8: iv. 230–1, v. 58–9. Ilger may already have been in Italy: Orderic describes him fighting under Tancred in Palestine (*OV* IX.15: v. 170–1); William Grandmesnil was temporarily in exile in Byzantium with his wife, after an unsuccessful rebellion against Robert Guiscard.

23. *OV* IV, X.4 and XI.42: ii. 286–7, v. 210–11, vi. 172–5; S. Edgington, 'Pagan Peverel: An Anglo-Norman Crusader', in Edbury (ed.), *Crusade and Settlement*, pp. 90–3.

24. *AA* III.xlviii, V.xxx: RHC Oc. 4, pp. 372, 451; *Cartulary of Whitby Abbey*, ed. J.C. Atkinson (London: Surtees Society 69; 1879), i. 1–2; *Regesta*, i. 427; *OV* III and IX.4: ii. 82–5, v. 34–5.

25. 'Chartes de Saint-Julien de Tours', ed. Denis, i, no. 51, pp. 72–3; *Calendar of Documents Preserved in France, Illustrative of the History of Great Britain and Ireland*, ed. J.H. Round (London: HMSO, 1899), i, no. 471, p. 168.

26. RHC Oc. 3, p. 604; *GF* X.39: p. 93; *OV* V: iii. 10–11.

27. *OV* IV: ii. 352–3; *Cartulaire de l'abbaye de Ste-Croix de Quimperlé*, ed. L. Maitre and P. de Berthou (Rennes: Bibliothèque Bretonne Armoricaine, 1904), no. 82,

pp. 234–5; BD I.xxiv and II.i: RHC Oc. 4, pp. 28, 33; *OV* IX.7, 8: v. 54–5, 58–9; L.-R. Ménager, *Hommes et institutions de l'Italie normande* (London: Variorum Reprints, 1981), p. 374; *Cartulaire de l'abbaye de Redon*, ed. A. de Courson (Paris: Imprimerie Impériale, 1863), nos 366 and 367, pp. 318–21; *ASC* D and E for 1075.

28. *Cartulaire de l'abbaye de Saint-Vincent*, ed. Charles and Menjot d'Elbenne, nos 101, 317, 522, 666, 738, 745, cols 69, 190–1, 301, 384, 419–20, 423.

29. FC: RHC Oc. 3.i, pp. 317–485, and in English translation in E. Peters, *The First Crusade: The Chronicle of Fulcher of Chartres and Other Source Materials* (Philadelphia: University of Pennsylvania Press, 1998), where, however, the chronology is unreliable.

30 *Odo of Deuil: De Profectione Ludovici VII in Orientem*, ed. V.G. Berry (New York: Columbia University Press, 1948), pp. 24–5.

31. J.W. Nesbitt, 'The Rate of March of Crusading Armies in Europe: A Study and Computation', *Traditio*, 19 (1963), 167–81.

32. V. Ortenberg, 'Archbishop Sigeric's Journey to Rome in 990', *Anglo-Saxon England*, 19 (1990), 197–246; F.P. Magoun, 'The Pilgrim-Diary of Nikulas of Munkathvera: The Road to Rome', *Medieval Studies*, 6 (1944), 314–54.

33. e.g. *HN* 39, 101: pp. 40, 104; C. Wickham, *Community and Clientele in Twelfth-Century Tuscany: The Origins of the Rural Commune in the Plain of Lucca* (Oxford: Clarendon Press, 1998).

34. D.J. Osheim, *An Italian Lordship: The Bishopric of Lucca in the Late Middle Ages* (Berkeley and Los Angeles: University of California Press, 1977).

35. P. Jaffé, *Regesta Pontificum Romanorum* (Graz: Akademische Druck-u. verlagsanstalt, 1956), i. 689–90.

36. P. Hetherington, *Medieval Rome: A Portrait of the City and its Life* (London: Rubicon Press, 1994); R. Krautheimer, *Early Christian and Byzantine Architecture* (London: Penguin, 1975).

37. FC II.v and vii: RHC Oc. 3.i, pp. 325–9.

38. G.A. Loud, *The Age of Robert Guiscard: Southern Italy and the Norman Conquest* (London: Longman, 2000).

39. *Die Kreuzzugsbriefe aus den Jahren 1088–1100*, ed. H. Hagenmeyer (Innsbruck: Verlag der Wagner'schen Universitäts-Buchhandlung, 1901), pp. 142–3, before 25 March 1098.

40. *Anna Comnena*, X.vii: pp. 313–15.

41. *Anna Comnena*, X.viii and XIII.x: pp. 315, 422–3; *GF* VIII.19: pp. 43–4.

42. J.M. Pryor, *Geography, Technology and War: Studies in the Maritime History of the Mediterranean, 649–1571* (Cambridge: Cambridge University Press, 1988), pp. 87–9; R. Macrides (ed.), *Travel in the Byzantine World* (Aldershot: Ashgate Variorum, 2002), p. 27.

43. The charter is a thirteenth-century copy. G.A. Loud, pers. comm.

44. Ménager, *Hommes et institutions*, pp. 260–390.

45. *OV* VIII.1 and X.4: iv. 118–19, v. 210–11; D. Bates, 'The Character and Career of Odo, Bishop of Bayeux (1049/50–1097)', *Speculum*, 50 (1975), 1–20.

46. *OV* XII.45: vi. 378–9.

Chapter 6

1. Ménager, *Hommes et institutions*, pp. 353–4.

2. J. Hill and L. Hill, *Raymond IV de Saint-Gilles, 1041/2–1105* (Toulouse: Privat, 1959).

3. *Anna Comnena*, X.vii–xi: pp. 313–31; *GF* II.5–6: pp. 10–14; *RA* II: RHC Oc. 3.i, pp. 237–8; FC I.viii and ix: RHC Oc. 3.i, pp. 329–32; K. Belke, 'Roads and Travel in Macedonia and Thrace in the Middle and Late Byzantine Period', in Macrides (ed.), *Travel*, pp. 73–90.

4. FC I.ix: RHC Oc. 3.i, p. 332; Stephen of Blois, to Adela, from Nicaea, RHC Oc. 3.ii, pp. 885–6.

5. S. Runciman, *A History of the Crusades* (3 vols; London: Penguin, 1951), i. pp. 336–41, estimated between 60,000 and 100,000; a more conservative recent estimate of between 50,000 and 60,000 is discussed in J. France, *Victory in the East: A Military History of the First Crusade* (Cambridge: Cambridge University Press, 1994), pp. 122–42. Contemporary estimates seem wildly overstated at the start of the crusade, but towards the end of the campaign they become more credible.

6. *Anna Comnena*, V.v: p. 167.

7. *RA* III: RHC Oc. 3.i, p. 239; FC I.x: RHC Oc. 3.i, p. 332; *GF* II.8: pp. 15–16.

8. Stephen of Blois to Adela, from Nicaea, RHC Oc. 3.ii, pp. 886–7.

9. *Anna Comnena*, XI.iii: pp. 341–2.

10. FC I.xi: RHC Oc. 3.i, p. 335.

11. FC I.xii: RHC Oc. 3.i, pp. 335–6; *RA* IV: RHC Oc. 3.i, pp. 240–1; *Anna Comnena*, XI.iii: pp. 341–2; *GF* II.9: pp. 18–21; *RC* XXV–XXVI: RHC Oc. 3.ii, pp. 623–4.

12. *GF* IV.10: pp. 23–4; FC I.xiii: RHC Oc. 3.i, pp. 336–7; *RA* IV: RHC Oc. 3.i, p. 241; *AA* III.iv: RHC Oc. 4, pp. 341–2; *Anna Comnena*, XI.iii: pp. 341–2.

13. *GF* IV.11: pp. 25–6.

14. *GF* IV.11: p. 27.

15. The story, second hand and rather garbled, is told in Albert of Aachen III.xiv, III.lix and V.xxiv: RHC Oc. 4, pp. 348–9, 379–380, 447.

16. *RA* V: RHC Oc. 3.i, pp. 241–2.

17. *AA* III.xxxxviii and xxxxix: RHC Oc. 4, pp. 372–3.

18. Stephen of Blois to Adela, from Antioch, RHC Oc. 3.ii, p. 889.

19. Caffaro of Genoa III: RHC Oc. 5, p. 50; see J. Pryor, 'Types of Ships and their Performance Capabilities', in Macrides (ed.), *Travel*, pp. 33–55, for an analysis of contemporary sailing times.

20. *RA* XVIII: RHC Oc. 3.i, pp. 290–1; Kemal-ad-Din: The Aleppo Chronicle, RHC Or. 3, p. 578; *Kreuzzugsbriefe*, ed. Hagenmeyer, p. 142.

21. *RA* V: RHC Oc. 3.i, p. 242; *GF* V.13: p. 70; J. Koder, 'Maritime Trade and the Food Supply for Constantinople in the Middle Ages', in Macrides (ed.), *Travel*, pp. 109–24.

22. *Kreuzzugsbriefe*, ed. Hagenmeyer, pp. 165–7.

23. *RA* V: RHC Oc. 3.i, p. 243; *PT* VI.viii: RHC Oc. 3.i, p. 43.

24. *RC* LVIII: RHC Oc. 3.ii, p. 649.

25. *Kreuzzugsbriefe*, ed. Hagenmeyer, pp. 144–6; *RA* V: RHC Oc. 3.i, p. 243.

26. *GF* VI.16: p. 35.

27. R. Levine (ed.), *The Deeds of God through the Franks: A Translation of Guibert of Nogent's Gesta Dei per Francos* (Woodbridge: Boydell, 1997), pp. 132–3.

28. *GF* VI.17: pp. 35–8; *PT* VI.viii–xi: RHC Oc. 3.1, pp. 43–5; *RC* LV: RHC Oc. 3.ii, p. 647; *AA* III.lxi: RHC Oc. 4, pp. 380–2.

29. *OV* X.12: v. 270–3; Letter from the People of Lucca, *Kreuzzugsbriefe*, ed. Hagenmeyer, pp. 165–7; The Edwardsaga: see J. Shepard, 'The English and Byzantium: A Study of their Role in the Byzantine Army in the Later Eleventh Century', *Traditio*, 29 (1973), 53–92.

30. *OV* X.12 and X.20: v. 268–9, 324–5; *Kreuzzugsbriefe*, ed. Hagenmeyer, pp. 174–5 (December 1099); J. Brundage, 'An Errant Crusader: Stephen of Blois', *Traditio*, 16 (1960), 380–95.

31. Stephen of Blois to Adela, 29 March 1098, from Antioch, RHC Oc. 3.ii, p. 890.

32. *Kreuzzugsbriefe*, ed. Hagenmeyer, pp. 165–7.

33. John of Antioch: C. Cahen, *Orient et occident au temps des Croisades* (Paris: Aubier Montaigne, 1983), pp. 221–2.

34. *RA* IX: RHC Oc. 3.i, p. 252; *AA* III.xxxiii, xxxv, IV.xxvii: RHC Oc. 4, pp. 362–3, 407–8.

35. This description is based on *RA*, *PT* and *GF*, all written by eyewitnesses, supplemented by *AA*.

36. *OV* IX.10: v. 98–9.

37. *GF* IX.26, 28: pp. 62, 65.

38. *Kreuzzugsbriefe*, ed. Hagenmeyer, pp. 155–6; *GF* I.4: pp. 7–8; Riley-Smith, *The First Crusaders*, p. 101; the treaty is noted in Caffaro of Genoa VIII: RHC Oc. 5, p. 56.

39. *OV* VIII.25: iv. 302–3; Edith's second husband was a near neighbour, the French crusader Drogo of Mouchy-le-Châtel, *GND* VIII.8: ii. 214–15 and *OV* IX.4: v. 30–1.

40. *Anna Comnena* (XI.vii: p. 353) believed that the transfer was delayed until 1100; *AA* VI.lv: RHC Oc. 4, pp. 500–1.

41. *RA* XIII: RHC Oc. 3.i, p. 262.

42. *RA* XVI: RHC Oc. 3.i, p. 276; *AA* XXX: RHC Oc. 4, p. 451.

43. *RC* CVII: RHC Oc. 3.ii, p. 681.

44. France, *Victory in the East*, pp. 306, 317–24; *RA* XVI: RHC Oc. 3.i, p. 277.

45. Ekkehard, Abbot of Aura, who visited Palestine in 1101 and wrote *c*. 1115: RHC Oc. 5, pp. 171–2.

46. BD IV.ix: RHC Oc. 4, pp. 96–7.

47. Caffaro of Genoa IX: RHC Oc. 5, pp. 56–7 (in 1100 Caffaro sailed to the East with one of these captains); *RA* XX: RHC Oc. 3.i, pp. 294–5.

48. *RA* XX: RHC Oc. 3.i, pp. 297–8.

49. 'honestissimus clericus': *PT* XIV: RHC Oc. 3.i, p. 106.

50. *RC* CXXVI: RHC Oc. 3.ii, p. 693.

51. *GR* IV.389.5: i. 702–3; *HA* VII.18: p. 443.

52. *Cartulaire de l'abbaye de Redon*, ed. A. de Courson, pp. 318–21.

53. *GF* X.39: pp. 95–7; *PT* XVI: RHC Oc. 3.i, p. 116.

54. Pryor, *Geography, Technology and War*, pp. 98–9; *Cartulary of Whitby Abbey*, ed. Atkinson, p. 2; *AA* XII.xix: RHC Oc. 4, p. 701.

55. *Actes des Comtes de Flandre*, ed. Vercauteren, pp. 70–5; *ASC* for 1100.

56. J.-M. Martin, *La Pouille du VIième au XIIième siècle* (Rome: École Française de Rome, 1993), pp. 736–7.

Chapter 7

1. *Kreuzzugsbriefe*, de Hagenmeyer, pp. 165–7.

2. *Kreuzzugsbriefe*, de Hagenmeyer, pp. 167–76.

3. *OV* X.4: v. 208–9.

4. *ASC*; *OV* X: v. 232–51.

5. *OV* X.5: v. 214–15; *Regesta*, ii. 414a.

6. *ASC* for 1100; *HN* 116–17: pp. 120–1; 'The Brevis Relatio de Guillelmo Nobilissimo comite Normannorum, written by a Monk of Battle Abbey', ed. Elizabeth M.C. van Houts, *Camden Miscellany 34*, 5th ser., 10 (1997), 36–7.

7. 'Actus Pontificum Cenomannis in urbe degentium', ed. G. Busson and A. Ledru, *Archives historiques du Maine*, 2 (1901), 404.

8. *GR* IV.333: i. 574–5.

9. *JW* for 1100; there is scant evidence for such depopulation in Domesday Book: F.H.M. Parker, 'The Forest Laws and the Death of William Rufus', *English Historical Review*, 27 (1912), 26–38; H.C. Darby and E.M.J. Campbell (eds), *The Domesday Geography of South-East England* (Cambridge: Cambridge University Press, 1962), p. 324.

10. *OV* X.15: v. 290–1.

11. John of Salisbury, *Vita Sancti Anselmi Cantuariensis*: PL 199, 1031; *Suger*, ch. 2: pp. 27–8.

12. Nicholas Brooks, pers. comm.

13. *OV* X.14: v. 282–3.

14. *HR* for 1100; *OV* XI.9: vi. 50–1.

15. See especially D. Grinnell-Milne, *The Killing of William Rufus: An Investigation in the New Forest* (Newton Abbot: David and Charles, 1968).

16. *Regesta*, ii. 488 b and d; R.W. Southern, *St Anselm and his Biographer: A Study of Monastic Life and Thought 1059–c.1130* (Cambridge: Cambridge University Press, 1963), p. 168, n. 2; but see also Chibnall (*OV* v. 296, n. 2), who suggests Walter may have been granted the title by Rufus.

17. *HN* 117: p. 121.

18. Parker, 'The Forest Laws'; C.N.L. Brooke, *The Saxon and Norman Kings* (London: Collins, 1963), pp. 162–74; Grinnell-Milne, *The Killing of Rufus*; E. Mason, *William II: Rufus the Red King* (Stroud: Tempus, 2005), p. 230.

19. M. Murray, *The God of the Witches* (London: Sampson Low, Marston and Co., 1933), pp. 160–8.

20. E. Mason, 'William Rufus and the Historians', *Medieval History*, 1 (1991), 6–22; Mason, *William II*, pp. 230–1.

21. *Wace*, lines 10505–50, p. 210.

22. Brooke, *Saxon and Norman Kings*, p. 172.

23. Hollister, *Henry I*, p. 105.
24. *Anselm's Letters*, ii, no. 212; *HN* 120: p. 126.
25. *OV* X.15: v. 291; *GR* V.393: i. 715.
26. *HN* 119: pp. 124–5.
27. *GR* IV.333: i. 575.
28. *GR* V.393: i. 715.
29. *Regesta*, ii. 488–91; *HR* for 1100.
30. *Suger*, ch. 14: p. 62.

Chapter 8

1. *Anselm's Letters*, ii, no. 213.
2. *Wace*, lines 9691–8, pp. 200–1.
3. *OV* X.18: v. 302–7; 'Actus Pontificum Cenomannis in urbe degentium', ed. G. Busson and A. Ledru, *Archives historiques du Maine*, 2 (1901), 404; *Cartulaire de l'abbaye de Saint-Aubin d'Angers*, ed. B. Brousillon (Documents historiques sur l'Anjou, 1; 1896), p. 127; David, *Robert Curthose*, p. 126, n. 25.
4. B.E. Cracknell, *'Outrageous Waves': Global Warming and Coastal Change in Britain through Two Thousand Years* (Chichester: Phillimore, 2005), pp. 117–59.
5. *Wace*, lines 9397–422, p. 197.
6. *Annales Monastici*, ii. 41; Wace (*Wace*, lines 6425, 6430–4) says his father told him there were 696 ships in the Conqueror's fleet.
7. *Anselm's Letters*, ii, no. 212.
8. *HR* for 1101; *Regesta*, ii. 508.
9. *The History of the Church of Abingdon*, ed. J. Hudson (Oxford: Clarendon Press, 2002), ii. 182: pp. 186–9; *HN* 142: p. 150.
10. HC, p. 306; *JW* for 1102.
11. *HR* for 1101; *Suger*, ch. 13–14: pp. 61–4.
12. R. Nip, 'The Political Relations between England and Flanders (1066–1128)', *Anglo-Norman Studies*, 21 (1999), 145–67.
13. *Anselm's Letters*, ii, nos 214, 215; Warelwast is known to have witnessed *Regesta*, ii. 509, at Christmas 1100 and then nothing until ii. 529, on 24 June 1101.
14. *Anselm's Letters*, ii, no. 216; letters 217–20 to the pope were finally answered in letter no. 223, in April 1102.
15. C.M. Gillmor, 'Naval Logistics of the Cross-Channel Operation, 1066', *Anglo-Norman Studies*, 7 (1985), 105–31.

16. *Regesta*, ii. 531; W.H. Stevenson, 'An Inedited Charter of King Henry I. June–July 1101', *English Historical Review*, 21 (1906), 505–9.

17. J.O. Prestwich, 'The Military Household of the Norman Kings', *English Historical Review*, 96 (1981), 1–35.

18. *Regesta*, ii. 529, 530; E. Searle, *Lordship and Community: Battle Abbey and its Banlieu, 1066–1538* (Toronto: Pontifical Institute of Medieval Studies, 1974), pp. 204–14.

19. *HR*: the Caligula A.viii manuscript has an independent entry for 1101, which supplies detailed information not present in *JW* and gives the impression of being based on an eyewitness account. C.W. Hollister, 'The Anglo-Norman Civil War 1101', *English Historical Review*, 88 (1973), 315–34.

20. *HA* says before August; *JW* says about 1 August; *ASC* gives the 3rd.

21. *OV* X.19: v. 314–15.

22. Hollister, 'The Anglo-Norman Civil War'.

23. *HN* 127: p. 132.

24. *OV* XIII.1–2: vi. 394–7; Riley-Smith, *The First Crusaders*, p. 144.

25. *Calendar of Documents Preserved in France*, ed. Round, i, no. 1385.

26. *OV* X.20, 22, 23: v. 324–5, 346–7, 350–3; *Suger*, ch. 10: p. 47; *Cartulaire du prieuré de La Charité-sur-Loire*, ed. R. Lespinasse (Nevers: Morin-Boutillier, 1887), p. 119; J. Shepard, 'The "Muddy Road" of Odo Arpin from Bourges to La Charité-sur-Loire', in P. Edbury and J. Phillips (eds), *The Experience of Crusading*. ii. *Defining the Crusader Kingdom* (Cambridge: Cambridge University Press, 2003), pp. 11–28.

27. *HN* 165: p. 176.

28. The Pseudo-Isidorian Decretals from the Fourth and Seventh Councils of Toledo: Lanfranc's own copy of the Decretals, with what appear to be his marginal notes, is preserved as Trinity College Cambridge MS B. 16. 44: 328; Garnett, 'Coronation and Propaganda', pp. 108–10.

29. *OV* X.19: v. 316–19.

30. *OV* X.14: v. 282–3 and n. 6; *GND* VIII.29: ii. 248–9.

31. *OV* X.19: v. 316–19.

32. Green, 'William Rufus'.

33. *ASC*, *JW* and *HR* for 1101; cf. the *HR* Caligula MS: Hollister, 'The Anglo-Norman Civil War'; *Wace*, lines 10443–72: p. 209; *Regesta*, ii. 534, 535, 536, 538.

34. *Regesta*, ii. 539, 540, 541, 543.

35. *Regesta*, ii. 544–9.

Chapter 9

1. N. Strevett, 'The Anglo-Norman Civil War of 1101 Reconsidered', *Anglo-Norman Studies*, 26 (2004), 174–5.

2. The pope's letter of congratulations to Henry is dated 23 November 1103, but an August letter from Anselm in Normandy to Queen Matilda makes no mention of a child: *Anselm's Letters*, ii, nos 296, 305; for Clito's birth see *HR* Caligula MS, fo. 41: Hollister, 'The Anglo-Norman Civil War', p. 330, and *OV* X.12: v. 278–9; cf *OV* X.12: v. 270–1 (*Edgarus Adelingus*).

3. *Anselm's Letters*, ii, nos 216, 223, 224, 250, 280, 281, 283; *HN* 137–40: pp. 144–8.

4. *JW* for 1102.

5. Searle, *Lordship and Community*, p. 209.

6. *OV* XI.2: vi. 18–21.

7. *OV* XI.3: vi. 20–33; *JW* for 1102; *GR* V.396–7: i. 718–21; *HA* VII.24: pp. 450–1; *ASC* for 1102; Mason, 'Roger de Montgomery'.

8. *OV* XIII.3: vi. 396–9.

9. *OV* XI.10: vi. 54–5.

10. *OV* XI.4: vi. 40–1.

11. *OV* XI.4: vi. 36–9.

12. i.e. before 25 March 1103.

13. HC, p. 299; C.T. Clay, *Early Yorkshire Charters*. viii. *The Honour of Warenne* (Yorkshire Archaeological Society Record Series, 1949).

14. *Regesta*, ii. 542, 544, 548–9, 621.

15. *Annales Monasterii de Wintonia AD 519–1277*, ed. H. Luard (*Annales Monastici*, ii; RS 36 ii; 1864–9), p. 42.

16. *Suger*, ch. 16: p. 70.

17. *HA* VII.24: pp. 450–3.

18. *Anselm's Letters*, ii, no. 305.

19. Cf., e.g., the Anglo-Saxon Chronicler's comments about taxation in 1101 to 1105.

20. *HN* 173: p. 185.

21. *HA* VII.24: pp. 452–3; *GR* V.397: i. 720–1.

22. *GR* V.397: i. 720–1.

23. *ASC* for 1104.

24. *OV* XI.3: vi. 34–7.

25. K. Thompson, 'Robert of Bellême Reconsidered', *Anglo-Norman Studies*, 13 (1991), 277.

26. *OV* XI.10: vi. 58–9.

27. *Anselm's Letters*, ii, no. 305.

28. *Anselm's Letters*, iii, nos 348, 351, 353, 354, 361; *HN* 163–5: pp. 173–6.

29. *HN* 146: p. 154.

30. *OV* XI.11: vi. 62–7.

31. *The Anglo-Latin Satirical Poets*, ed. T. Wright (RS 59; London, 1872), ii. 241–1.

32. *OV* XI.17: vi. 78–9.

33. *OV* XI.17: vi. 80–1; *GR* V.398: i. 722–3.

34. *OV* X.8, XI.17: v. 232–3, vi. 78–9; *HN* 166: pp. 176–7.

35. *Anselm's Letters*, iii, no. 322.

36. *Anselm's Letters*, iii, nos 367, 369, 370, 377, 378; *HN* 166–75: pp. 176–87; S.N. Vaughn, 'St Anselm and the English Investiture Controversy Reconsidered', *Journal of Medieval History*, 6 (1980), 61–86; C.W. Hollister, 'War and Diplomacy in the Anglo-Norman World: The Reign of Henry I', *Anglo-Norman Studies*, 6 (1984), 72–87.

37. *ASC* for 1106; *HA* VII.25: pp. 452–3; *Anselm's Letters*, iii, no. 396.

38. *Anselm's Letters*, iii, nos 391, 392.

39. *HN* 177–9: pp. 189–92.

40. *OV* XI.15: vi. 74–5.

41. *HN* 181–3: pp. 194–6; *Anselm's Letters*, iii, nos 397, 399.

42. *GR* IV.389: i. 704–5.

43. *Annales Monasterii*, p. 42; *OV* XI. 14, 19: vi. 72–5, 80–3.

44. *ASC* for 1106; *Anselm's Letters*, iii, no. 401; *JW* for 1106; H.W.C. Davis, 'A Contemporary Account of the Battle of Tinchebrai', *English Historical Review*, 24 (1909), 728–32; H.W.C. Davis, 'The Battle of Tinchebrai: A Correction', *English Historical Review*, 25 (1910), 295–6; *GND* VIII.13: ii. 222–3; *HA* VII.25: pp. 452–5; *OV* XI.20: vi. 82–91.

45. *OV* XI.20: vi. 90–3.

46. HC, pp. 307–8.

47. Davis, 'A Contemporary Account'; OV XI.13: vi. 72–3.

48. *HN* 184: p. 197; *Anselm's Letters*, iii, nos 401, 402, 404.

49. *Regesta*, ii. 798; *OV* XI.22: vi. 94–9.

50. Thompson, 'Robert of Bellême', p. 278; *OV* XI.37: vi. 164–5.

51. *ASC* for 1106; *GR* II.228: i. 416–17.

52. Hollister, *Henry I*, p. 172.

53. J.A. Green, 'Lords of the Norman Vexin', in J. Gillingham and J.C. Holt (eds), *War and Government in the Middles Ages: Essays in Honour of J.O. Prestwich* (Woodbridge: Boydell and Brewer, 1984), pp. 46–63.

54. Clay, *Early Yorkshire Charters*, ix. 86–7.

55. *PR 31 HI*, p. 143.

56. *HA* X.1: pp. 698–701.

57. *OV* XII.39: vi. 352–5.

58. *Annales Monastici*, iii. 436.

59. *Annales Monastici*, ii. 42; *DB* Dorset, 78.d.

60. *Policraticus . . . by John of Salisbury*, ed. C.C. Webb (Oxford: Oxford University Press, 1909), vi. 18.

61. *HA* VII.7: pp. 426–7; cf. *GR* IV.359: i. 628–31, which has a fearful Curthose appealing for rescue.

62. *OV* XII.24: vi. 287.

Chapter 10

1. *AA* X.xlvii and XI.xl: RHC Oc. iv, pp. 653, 682.

2. Hugh Dogherty, pers. com.

3. See S.B. Hicks, 'The Impact of William Clito upon the Continental Policies of Henry I of England', *Viator*, 10 (1979) 1–21, *passim*.

4. *Regesta*, ii. 794–5; *OV* XI.37: vi. 162–5; Clay, *Early Yorkshire Charters*, viii.

5. *PR 31 HI*, p. 12; *JW* and *ASC* for 1112 and 1113; *HA* VII.28: p. 458.

6. *OV* XI.45: vi. 182.

7. *ASC* for 1111.

8. *Actes des Comtes de Flandres*, ed. Vercauteren, no. 66.

9. HC, pp. 308–9, 319.

10. *HA* VIII.3.7–8: pp. 596–9.

11. *ASC* for 1118.

12. *OV* XII.2, 6–7: vi. 190, 204; HC, p. 313; *Suger*, ch. 26: pp. 114–15.

13. *OV* XII.8: vi. 205–8.

14. *OV* XII.10: vi. 210–12.

15. *OV* XII.10, 33: vi. 214, 328–31.

16. *Suger*, ch. 26: p. 116; HC, p. 315; *GND* VIII.16: ii. 230–3.

17. *Regesta*, ii. 1204a; *ASC* for 1119 and 1120; *Annales Monastici*, i. 10; Thompson, 'Robert of Bellême', p. 279, n. 80.

18. *OV* XII.18: vi. 236–43; HC, p. 318; *Suger*, ch. 26: p. 117.

19. *OV* XII.21: vi. 256–65.

20. *OV* XII.24: vi. 288–9; HC, pp. 320–1.

21. *OV* XII.24: vi. 282–91; *Hugh the Chantor*, trans. Johnson, p. 77.

22. *Hugh the Chantor*, trans. Johnson, pp. 91–3.

23. *JW* for 1121; *Regesta*, ii. 1241–5.

24. *HR* and *ASC* for 1122–4; *GND* VIII.38: ii. 274–5; *OV* XII.33–4: vi. 330–3.

25. *OV* XII.39: vi. 346–57; *GND* VIII.21: ii. 234–7; *ASC* for 1123.

26. RHGF xv. 251; *ASC* for 1127; *OV* XI.37: vi. 164–7.

27. *The Chronicle of Hugh Candidus*, ed. W.T. Mellows (Oxford: Oxford University Press, 1949), p. 101; *ASC* for 1127; C. Clarke, 'This Ecclesiastical Adventurer: Henry of St-Jean d'Angély', *English Historical Review*, 84 (1969), 548–60.

28. *ASC* for 1126.

29. *Suger*, ch. 30: pp. 138–41; *The Murder of Charles the Good*, ed. Ross, pp. 190 ff; *OV* XII.45: vi. 368–71.

30. *HA* VII.37: pp. 476–7.

31. *OV* XII.45: vi. 370–3.

32. RHGF xv. 341.

33. *OV* XII.45: vi. 376–9; *GND* VIII.29: ii. 250–1.

34. *Regesta*, ii. 1575 (1129).

35. Latin text: *HA*, app., pp. 836–8.

36. *Historia et Cartularia Sancti Petri Gloucestriae*, ed. W.H. Hart (RS 33; 1863), i. 110–11; *DB* i. 163.

BIBLIOGRAPHY

Primary Sources

L'abbé Sauvage, 'Des miracles advenus en l'église de Fécamp', in C. Beaurépaire, l'abbé
   Blanquart, *et al.* (eds), *Société de l'histoire de Normandie, mélanges 2ième serie* (Rouen,
   1893), pp. 29–32

Actes des Comtes de Flandre, 1071–1128, ed. F. Vercauteren (Brussels: Commission
   Royale d'Histoire, 1938)

'Actus Pontificum Cenomannis in urbe degentium', ed. G. Busson and A. Ledru,
   Archives historiques du Maine, 2 (1901)

The Alexiad of Anna Comnena, trans. E.R.A. Sewter (London: Penguin, 1969)

The Anglo-Latin Satirical Poets, ed. T. Wright (RS 59; London, 1872), ii. 241–51

The Anglo-Saxon Chronicle, ed. D. Whitelock, D.C. Douglas and S.I. Tucker (London:
   Eyre and Spottiswoode, 1961)

The Anglo-Saxon Chronicle: A Collaborative Edition. Manuscript A, ed. J.M. Bately
   (Cambridge: D.S. Brewer, 1986)

Annales Monasterii de Wintonia AD 519–1277, ed. H. Luard (*Annales Monastici*, ii;
   RS 36 ii; 1864–9), pp. 1–125

Antiquus Cartularius Ecclesiae Baiocensis (Livre Noir), ed. V. Bourrienne (Société de
   l'histoire de Normandie 62; 1902), i

Baldric of Dol, *Historia Jerusalem qualiter Christiani a remotis partibus mundi . . . Domini
   Baldrici Archiepiscopi* (RHC Oc. 4)

'The Brevis Relatio de Guillelmo Nobilissimo comite Normannorum, written by a
   Monk of Battle Abbey', ed. Elizabeth M.C. van Houts, *Camden Miscellany 34*, 5th
   ser., 10 (1997), 1–48

Calendar of Documents Preserved in France, Illustrative of the History of Great Britain and Ireland, ed. J.H. Round (London: HMSO, 1899)

Carmen de Hastingae Proelio of Guy Bishop of Amiens, ed. F. Barlow (Oxford: Clarendon Press, 1999)

Cartulaire de l'abbaye de Saint-Aubin d'Angers, ed. B. Brousillon (Documents historiques sur l'Anjou, 1; 1896)

Cartulaire de l'abbaye de Ste-Croix de Quimperlé, ed. L. Maitre and P. de Berthou (Rennes: Bibliothèque Bretonne Armoricaine, 1904)

Cartulaire de St-Jean-d'Angéley, ed. M.G. Musset (2 vols; Saintes: Archives Historique de la Saintogne et de l'Aunis, 1901)

Cartulaire de l'abbaye de Saint-Vincent du Mans, ed. R. Charles and S. Menjot d'Elbenne (Le Mans, 1886)

Cartulaire de l'abbaye de Redon, ed. A. de Courson (Paris: Imprimerie Impériale, 1863)

Cartulaire du prieuré de La Charité-sur-Loire, ed. R. Lespinasse (Nevers: Morin-Boutillier, 1887)

Cartularium Monasterii de Ramesia, ed. W.H. Hart and P.A. Lyons (2 vols; RS 79; 1884)

Cartulary of Whitby Abbey, ed. J.C. Atkinson (London: Surtees Society 69; 1879)

Charters and Custumals of the Abbey of Holy Trinity Caen. Two Volumes. Part 2. The French Estates, ed. J. Walmsley (Oxford: Oxford University Press for the British Academy, 1994)

'Chartes de Saint-Julien de Tours (1002–1227)', ed. L.-J. Denis, *Archives Historiques du Maine*, 12/1 (1912)

The Chronicle of Hugh Candidus, ed. W.T. Mellows (Oxford: Oxford University Press, 1949)

The Chronicle of John of Worcester. Volume Three, ed. P. McGurk (Oxford: Clarendon Press, 1998)

Chronicon Monasterii de Abingdon, ed. J. Stevenson (2 vols; RS 2; 1858)

'De iniusta vexacione Willelmi episcopi primi per Willelmum regem filium Willelmi magni regis', ed. H.S. Offler, A.J. Piper and A.I Doyle, *Camden Miscellany 34*, 5th ser., 10 (1997), 49–104

The Deeds of Louis the Fat: Suger, trans. R. Cusimano and J. Moorhead (Washington: Catholic University of America Press, 1992)

Domesday Book: History from the Sources, ed. J. Morris (Chichester: Philimore, 1975–86)

Durham Episcopal Charters 1071–1152, ed. H.S. Offler (Gateshead: Surtees Society 179, 1968)

Eadmer's History of Recent Events in England: Historia Novorum in Anglia, trans. G. Bosanquet (London: Cresset Press, 1964)

The Ecclesiastical History of Orderic Vitalis, ed. M. Chibnall (6 vols; Oxford: Clarendon Press, 1969–80)

Episcopal Charters 1071–1152, ed. H.S. Offler (Gateshead: Surtees Society 179; 1968)

Fulcherii Carnotensis Historia Hierosolymitana (PL 155; 1880)

Gesta Francorum . . .: The Deeds of the Franks and the other Pilgrims to Jerusalem, ed. R. Hill (London: Nelson and Sons, 1962)

The Gesta Guillelmi of William of Poitiers, ed. R.H.C. Davis and M. Chibnall (Oxford: Clarendon Press, 1998)

The Gesta Normannorum Ducum of William of Jumièges, Orderic Vitalis and Robert of Torigni, ed. E. van Houts (2 vols; Oxford: Clarendon Press, 1992)

Gesta Pontificum Anglorum, ed. N.E. Hamilton (RS 52; 1870)

The Gesta Regum Anglorum. The History of the English Kings. William of Malmesbury, ed. R.A.B. Mynors, R.M. Thomson and M. Winterbottom (2 vols; Oxford: Clarendon Press, 1998)

Gesta Tancredi in Expeditione Hierosolymitana. Ralph of Caen (RHC Oc. 3.ii)

Guibert de Nogent: Autobiographie, ed. E.R. Labande (Paris: Société d'édition Les Belles Lettres, 1981)

Henry, Archdeacon of Huntingdon: Historia Anglorum. The History of the English People, ed. D. Greenway (Oxford: Clarendon Press, 1996)

Historia et Cartularia Sancti Petri Gloucestriae, ed. W.H. Hart (RS 33; 1863)

The History of the Church of Abingdon, ed. J. Hudson (Oxford: Clarendon Press, 2002)

Historia Hierosolymitana . . . Albert of Aachen (RHC Oc. 4)

The History of the Norman People: Wace's Roman de Rou, trans. G. Burgess (Woodbridge: Boydell, 2004)

Hugh the Chantor: The History of the Church of York, 1066–1127, trans. C. Johnson (London: Nelson and Sons, 1961)

'Hugh of Flavigny's Chronicle', ed. G.H. Pertz, *MGH, Scriptores* 8 (1925)

Die Kreuzzugsbriefe aus den Jahren 1088–1100, ed. H. Hagenmeyer (Innsbruck: Verlag der Wagner'schen Universitäts-Buchhandlung, 1901)

The Letters of Lanfranc, Archbishop of Canterbury, ed. H. Clover and M. Gibson (Oxford: Clarendon Press, 1979)

The Letters of Saint Anselm of Canterbury, trans. W. Fröhlich (3 vols; Kalamazoo, Mich.: Cistercian Publications, 1990–4)

Liber monasterii de Hyda, ed. E. Edwards (RS 45; 1886)

The Murder of Charles the Good, Count of Flanders. By Galbert of Bruges, ed. J.B. Ross (New York and London: Harper and Row, 1967)

Odo of Deuil: De Profectione Ludovici VII in Orientem, ed. V.G. Berry (New York: Columbia University Press, 1948)

Petri Tudebodi sacerdotis siuracensis: Historia de Hierosolymitana itinere (PL 155; 1880)

The Pipe Roll for 31 Henry I (London: HMSO, 1929)

Policraticus . . . by John of Salisbury, ed. C.C. Webb (Oxford: Oxford University Press, 1909)

Receuil des actes des ducs de Normandie de 911 à 1066, ed. M. Fauroux (Caen: Société des Antiquaires de Normandie, 1961)

Receuil des actes de Philippe I, roi de France (1059–1108), ed. M. Prou (Paris: Chartes et diplômes relatifs à l'histoire de France, 1908)

Raimundi de Agiles . . . Historia Francorum qui ceperunt Jerusalem (RHC Oc. 3.i)

Regesta Regum Anglo-Normannorum 1066–1100, ed. H. Davis (Oxford: Clarendon Press, 1913)

Regesta Regum Anglo-Normannorum 1100–1135, ed. C. Johnson, H.A. Cronne and H.W.C. Davis (Oxford: Clarendon Press, 1956)

Regesta Regum Anglo-Normannorum: The Acta of William I (1066–1087), ed. D. Bates (Oxford: Clarendon Press, 1998)

Rodolfi Glabri Historiarum Libri Quinque . . ., ed. J. France (Oxford: Clarendon Press, 1989)

Simon de Crépy, *Vita Beati Simonis Comitis Crespeiensis Auctore Synchrono: Guiberti Opera Illustranda (Additamenta)* (PL 156; 1880), cols 1211–24

Symeonis Monachi Opera Omnia. Historia Regem, ed. T. Arnold (RS 75 ii; 1885)

Symeon of Durham, Libellus de exordio . . ., ed. D. Rollason (Oxford: Clarendon Press, 2000)

Secondary Sources

Aird, W.M., 'An Absent Friend: The Career of Bishop William of St Calais', in D. Rollason, M. Harvey and M. Prestwich (eds), *Anglo-Norman Durham 1093–1193* (Woodbridge: Boydell, 1994), pp. 283–97

—— 'Frustrated Masculinity: The Relationship between William the Conqueror and his Eldest Son', in D.M. Hadley (ed.), *Masculinity in Medieval Europe* (London: Longman, 1999), pp. 39–55

Allen-Brown, R., 'The Status of the Norman Knight', in J. Gillingham and J.C. Holt (eds), *War and Government in the Middle Ages* (Woodbridge: Boydell, 1984)

Barlow, F., *William I and the Norman Conquest* (London: English Universities Press, 1965)

Barlow, F., *William Rufus* (London: Methuen, 1983)

Bates, D., 'The Character and Career of Odo, Bishop of Bayeux (1049/50–1097)', *Speculum*, 50 (1975), 1–20

—— 'Normandy and England after 1066', *English Historical Review*, 104 (1989), 851–80

—— 'The Conqueror's Adolescence', *Anglo-Norman Studies*, 25 (2003), 1–18

Beckerman, J.S., 'Succession in Normandy, 1087, and in England, 1066: The Role of Testamentary Custom', *Speculum*, 47 (1972), 258–60

Belke, K., 'Roads and Travel in Macedonia and Thrace in the Middle and Late Byzantine Period', in R. Macrides (ed.), *Travel in the Byzantine World* (Aldershot: Ashgate Variorum, 2002), pp. 73–90

Bishop, T.A.M., and Chaplais, P., *Facsimiles of English Royal Writs to AD 1100* (Oxford: Clarendon Press, 1957)

Bouet, P., 'Le Domfrontais de 1050 à 1150 d'après les historiens normandes contemporains', in J.C. Payen (ed.), *La Légende arthurienne et la Normandie* (Condé-sur-Noireau: Charles Corlet, 1983), pp. 73–94

Bouvris, J.-M., 'La Confirmation par le duc Robert Courte-Heuse de la donation du manoir de Vains', *Annales de Normandie*, 35 (1985), 35–48

Brooke, C.N.L., *The Saxon and Norman Kings* (London: Collins, 1963)

Brundage, J., 'An Errant Crusader: Stephen of Blois', *Traditio*, 16 (1960), 380–95

Cahen, C., *Orient et occident au temps des Croisades* (Paris: Aubier Montaigne, 1983)

Clarke, C., 'This Ecclesiastical Adventurer: Henry of St-Jean d'Angély', *English Historical Review*, 84 (1969), 548–60

Clay, C.T., *Early Yorkshire Charters. viii. The Honour of Warenne. ix. The Stuteville Fee* (Yorkshire Archaeological Society Record Series; 1949, 1952)

Constable, G., 'Medieval Charters as a Source for the History of the Crusades', in P. Edbury (ed.), *Crusade and Settlement* (Cardiff: University College Cardiff Press, 1985), pp. 73–89

Cooper, A., '"The Feet of Those that Bark Shall Be Cut Off": Timorous Historians and the Personality of Henry I', *Anglo-Norman Studies*, 23 (2001), 47–67

Cowdrey, H.E., 'The Anglo-Norman Laudes Regiae', *Viator*, 12 (1981), 37–78

—— *The Register of Pope Gregory VII 1073–1085: An English Translation* (Oxford: Oxford University Press, 2002)

Cracknell, B.E., *'Outrageous Waves': Global Warming and Coastal Change in Britain through Two Thousand Years* (Chichester: Phillimore, 2005)

Darby, H.C., and Campbell, E.M.J. (eds), *The Domesday Geography of South-East England* (Cambridge: Cambridge University Press, 1962)

David, C.W., *Robert Curthose, Duke of Normandy* (Cambridge, Mass.: Harvard University Press, 1920)

Davis, H.W.C., 'A Contemporary Account of the Battle of Tinchebrai', *English Historical Review*, 24 (1909), 728–32

—— 'The Battle of Tinchebrai: A Correction', *English Historical Review*, 25 (1910), 295–6

Davis, R.H.C., 'William of Jumièges, Robert Curthose and the Anglo-Norman Succession', *English Historical Review*, 95 (1980), 597–606

—— 'William of Poitiers and his History of William the Conqueror', in R.H.C. Davis and J.M. Wallace-Hadrille (eds), *The Writing of History in the Middle Ages* (Oxford: Clarendon Press, 1981), pp. 71–100

Delisle, L., *Littérature latine et histoire du moyen âge* (Paris: Leroux, 1890)

Edgington, S., 'Pagan Peverel: An Anglo-Norman Crusader', in P. Edbury (ed.), *Crusade and Settlement* (Cardiff: University College Cardiff Press, 1985), pp. 90–3

Engels, L.J., 'De obitu Willelmi ducis Normannorum regisque Anglorum: Texte, modèles, valeur et origine', in Anon., *Mélanges Christine Mohrmann: Nouveau recueil offert par ses anciens élèves* (Utrecht/Anvers: Spectrum Éditeurs, 1973), pp. 209–55

France, J., *Victory in the East: A Military History of the First Crusade* (Cambridge: Cambridge University Press, 1994)

Galbraith, V.H., 'Girard the Chancellor', *English Historical Review*, 46 (1931), 77–9

Garnett, G., 'Coronation and Propaganda: Some Implications of the Norman Claim to the Throne of England in 1066', *Transactions of the Royal Historical Society*, 36 (1986), 91–116

—— 'Ducal Succession in Early Normandy', in G. Garnett and J. Hudson (eds), *Law and Government in Medieval England* (Cambridge: Cambridge University Press, 1994), pp. 80–110

Gathagan, L.L., 'The Trappings of Power: The Coronation of Mathilda of Flanders', *Haskins Society Journal*, 13 (1999), 21–39

Gillmor, C.M., 'Naval Logistics of the Cross-Channel Operation, 1066', *Anglo-Norman Studies*, 7 (1985), 105–31

Green, J., 'William Rufus, Henry I and the Royal Demesne', *History*, 64 (1979), 337–52

Green, J.A., 'Lords of the Norman Vexin', in J. Gillingham and J.C. Holt (eds), *War and Government in the Middle Ages: Essays in Honour of J.O. Prestwich* (Woodbridge: Boydell and Brewer, 1984), pp. 46–63

—— 'Robert Curthose Reassessed', *Anglo-Norman Studies*, 22 (2000), 95–116

Grinnell-Milne, D., *The Killing of William Rufus: An Investigation in the New Forest* (Newton Abbot: David and Charles, 1968)

Gullick, M., 'The Hand of Symeon of Durham: Further Observations on the Durham Martyrology Scribe', in D. Rollason (ed.), *Symeon of Durham: Historian of Durham and the North. Studies in North-Eastern History* (Stamford: Shaun Tyas, 1998), pp. 14–31

Harvey, S., 'Domesday Book and Anglo-Norman Governance', *Transactions of the Royal Historical Society*, 5th ser., 25 (1975), 175–93

Haskins, C.H., 'The Norman Consuetudines et Iusticie of William the Conqueror', *English Historical Review*, 23 (1908), 502–8

—— *Norman Institutions* (Oxford: Oxford University Press; Cambridge, Mass.: Harvard University Press, 1918)

Heslop, T.A., 'English Seals from the Mid Ninth Century to 1100', *Journal of the British Archaeological Association*, 133 (1980), 1–16

Hetherington, P., *Medieval Rome: A Portrait of the City and its Life* (London: Rubicon Press, 1994)

Hicks, S.B., 'The Impact of William Clito upon the Continental Policies of Henry I of England', *Viator*, 10 (1979), 1–21

Hill, J., and Hill, L., *Raymond IV de Saint-Gilles, 1041/2–1105* (Toulouse: Privat, 1959)

Holder-Egger, O., 'Einhardi Vita Karoli Magni', *MGH, Scriptores rerum Germanorum*, 25 (1911)

Hollister, C.W., 'The Anglo-Norman Civil War 1101', *English Historical Review*, 88 (1973), 315–34

—— 'Normandy, France and the Anglo-Norman Regnum', *Speculum*, 51 (1976), 202–42

—— 'War and Diplomacy in the Anglo-Norman World: The Reign of Henry I', *Anglo-Norman Studies*, 6 (1984), 72–87

—— *Henry I* (New Haven and London: Yale University Press, 2001)

Holt, J.C., 'Politics and Property in Early Medieval England', *Past and Present*, 57 (1972), 3–52

Howell, M., *Regalian Right in Medieval England* (London: Athlone Press, 1962)

Hunt, W. (ed.), 'Two Chartularies of the Priory of St Peter at Bath', *Somerset Record Society*, 7 (1893)

Hunter, J. (ed.), *A Brief History of the Bishoprick of Somerset from its Foundation to the Year 1174* (London: Camden Society volume 8, 1840)

Hyland, A., *The Medieval Warhorse from Byzantium to the Crusades* (Stroud: Sutton Publishing, 1994)

Jaffé, P., *Regesta Pontificum Romanorum* (Graz: Akademische Druck-u. verlagsanstalt, 1956)

Jamison, E., 'Some Notes on the Anonymi Gesta Francorum, with Special Reference
    to the Norman Contingent from South Italy and Sicily in the First Crusade', in
    O. Rhys (ed.), *Studies in French Language and Medieval Literature* (Manchester:
    Manchester University Press, 1939), pp. 183–208

Kapelle, W.E., *The Norman Conquest of the North: The Region and its Transformation,
    1000–1135* (London: Croom Helm, 1979)

Koder, J., 'Maritime Trade and the Food Supply for Constantinople in the Middle Ages',
    in R. Macrides (ed.), *Travel in the Byzantine World* (Aldershot: Ashgate Variorum,
    2002), pp. 109–24

Krautheimer, R., *Early Christian and Byzantine Architecture* (London: Penguin, 1975)

Latouche, R., *Histoire du comté de Maine pendant le Xe et le XIe siècle* (Paris:
    Bibliothèque des hautes études, 1910)

Le Patourel, J., *Feudal Empires, Norman and Plantagenet* (London: Hambledon Press,
    1984)

Levine, R. (ed.), *The Deeds of God through the Franks: A Translation of Guibert of
    Nogent's Gesta Dei per Francos* (Woodbridge: Boydell, 1997)

Lewis, A.W., 'Anticipatory Association of the Heir in Early Capetian France', *American
    Historical Review*, 83 (1978), 906–27

Loud, G.A., *The Age of Robert Guiscard: Southern Italy and the Norman Conquest*
    (London: Longman, 2000)

Louise, G., 'Châteaux et pouvoirs dans le Domfrontais médiéval (XIe–XIIIe siècles)',
    Le Domfrontais médiéval, 9 (1993), 11–28

Loyn, H.R., *The Norman Conquest* (London: Hutchinson, 1965)

Macrides, R. (ed.), *Travel in the Byzantine World* (Aldershot: Ashgate Variorum, 2002)

Magoun, F.P., 'The Pilgrim-Diary of Nikulas of Munkathvera: The Road to Rome',
    Medieval Studies, 6 (1944), 314–54

Martin, J.-M., *La Pouille du VIIème au XIIième siècle* (Rome: École Française de Rome,
    1993)

Mason, E., 'William Rufus and the Historians', *Medieval History*, 1 (1991), 6–22

—— *William II: Rufus the Red King* (Stroud: Tempus, 2005)

Mason, J.F.A., 'Roger de Montgomery and his Sons (1067–1102)', *Transactions of the
    Royal Historical Society*, 5th ser., 13 (1963), 1–29

Ménager, L.-R., *Hommes et institutions de l'Italie normande* (London: Variorum Reprints,
    1981)

Mortimer, R., 'Anglo-Norman Lay Charters, 1066–c.1100: A Diplomatic Approach',
    Anglo-Norman Studies, 25 (2003), 153–75

Murray, M., *The God of the Witches* (London: Sampson Low, Marston and Co., 1933)

Nesbitt, J.W., 'The Rate of March of Crusading Armies in Europe: A Study and Computation', *Traditio*, 19 (1963), 167–81

Nip, R., 'The Political Relations between England and Flanders (1066–1128)', *Anglo-Norman Studies*, 21 (1999), 145–67

Nissen-Jaubert, A., 'Fouilles archéologiques du prieuré Saint-Symphorien', *Le Domfrontais médiéval*, 8 (1991), 5–13

Norton, E.C., 'The Buildings of St Mary's Abbey, York and their Destruction', *Antiquaries Journal*, 74 (1994), 254–88

Ortenberg, V., 'Archbishop Sigeric's Journey to Rome in 990', *Anglo-Saxon England*, 19 (1990), 197–246

Osheim, D.J., *An Italian Lordship: The Bishopric of Lucca in the Late Middle Ages* (Berkeley and Los Angeles: University of California Press, 1977)

Parker, F.H.M., 'The Forest Laws and the Death of William Rufus', *English Historical Review*, 27 (1912), 26–38

Peters, E., *The First Crusade: The Chronicle of Fulcher of Chartres and Other Source Materials* (Philadelphia: University of Pennsylvania Press, 1998)

Philpott, M., 'The De iniusta vexacione Willelmi episcopi primi and Canon Law in Anglo-Norman Durham', in D. Rollason, M. Harvey, and M. Prestwich (eds), *Anglo-Norman Durham 1093–1193* (Woodbridge: Boydell, 1994), pp. 125–37

Potts, C., 'The Earliest Norman Counts Revisited: The Lords of Mortain', *Haskins Society Journal*, 4 (1992), 23–35

Prestwich, J.O., 'The Military Household of the Norman Kings', *English Historical Review*, 96 (1981), 1–35

Pryor, J.M., *Geography, Technology and War: Studies in the Maritime History of the Mediterranean, 649–1571* (Cambridge: Cambridge University Press, 1988)

Pryor, J., 'Types of Ships and their Performance Capabilities', in R. Macrides (ed.), *Travel in the Byzantine World* (Aldershot: Ashgate Variorum, 2002), pp. 33–55

Riley-Smith, J., *The First Crusaders 1095–1131* (Cambridge: Cambridge University Press, 1997)

—— *The First Crusade and the Idea of Crusading* (London and New York: Continuum Press, 2003)

Rollason, D., Harvey, M., and Prestwich, M. (eds), *Anglo-Norman Durham 1093–1193* (Woodbridge: Boydell, 1994)

Runciman, S., *A History of the Crusades* (3 vols; London: Penguin, 1951)

Sapir, A., and Speet, B.M.J., *De Obitu Willelmi: Kritische beschouwing van een verhalende bron over Willem de Veroveraar uit de tijd van zijn zonen* (Amsterdam: Historisch Seminarium van de Universiteit van Amsterdam, 10; 1976)

Searle, E., *Lordship and Community: Battle Abbey and its Banlieu, 1066–1538* (Toronto: Pontifical Institute of Medieval Studies, 1974)

Sharpe, R., '1088: William II and the Rebels', *Anglo-Norman Studies*, 26 (2004), 139–57

Shepard, J., 'The English and Byzantium: A Study of their Role in the Byzantine Army in the Later Eleventh Century', *Traditio*, 29 (1973), 53–92

—— 'The "Muddy Road" of Odo Arpin from Bourges to La Charité-sur-Loire', in P. Edbury and J. Phillips (eds), *The Experience of Crusading. ii. Defining the Crusader Kingdom* (Cambridge: Cambridge University Press, 2003), pp. 11–28

Southern, R.W., *St Anselm and his Biographer: A Study of Monastic Life and Thought 1059–c.1130* (Cambridge: Cambridge University Press, 1963)

Stevenson, W.H., 'An Inedited Charter of King Henry I. June–July 1101', *English Historical Review*, 21 (1906), 505–9

Strevett, N., 'The Anglo-Norman Civil War of 1101 Reconsidered', *Anglo-Norman Studies*, 26 (2004), 174–5

Tabuteau, E.Z., 'The Role of Law in the Succession to Normandy and England, 1087', *Haskins Society Journal*, 3 (1991), 141–69

Thompson, K., 'Robert of Bellême Reconsidered', *Anglo-Norman Studies*, 13 (1991), 263–86

Tischler, M.M., 'Einharts Vita Karoli; Studien zur Entstehung, überlieferung und Rezeption', *MGH Schriften*, 48 (2001), 20–44

Tyerman, C., *The Invention of the Crusades* (London: Macmillan, 1998)

Vaughn, S.N., 'St Anselm and the English Investiture Controversy Reconsidered', *Journal of Medieval History*, 6 (1980), 61–86

von Tremp, E., 'Die Uberlieferung der Vita Hludowici imperatoris des Astronomus', *MGH, Studien und texte*, 1 (1991)

—— 'Theganus Gesta Hludowici imp. et Astronomus Vita Hludowici', *MGH, Scriptores rerum Germanicarum*, 64 (1995)

Walker, I.W., *Harold: The Last Anglo-Saxon King* (Stroud: Sutton Publishing, 1997)

Wall, V., 'Malcolm III and the Foundation of Durham Cathedral', in D. Rollason, M. Harvey and M. Prestwich (eds), *Anglo-Norman Durham 1093–1193* (Woodbridge: Boydell, 1994), pp. 325–37

Wickham, C., *Community and Clientele in Twelfth-Century Tuscany: The Origins of the Rural Commune in the Plain of Lucca* (Oxford: Clarendon Press, 1998)

Williams, A., 'Some Notes and Considerations on Problems Connected with the English Royal Succession, 860–1066', *Anglo-Norman Studies*, 1 (1979), 144–67

INDEX